7 Figure Publications Presents . . .

A Treacherous Hustle

by

Sereniti Hall

Names, characters, places, and incidents either are the product of the author's imagination or are used fictitiously, and any resemblance to actual persons, living or dead, business establishments, events, references or locales are entirely coincidental.

Copyright © 2017 by Sereniti Hall

All rights reserved.

7 Figure Publications

PO Box 9334

Augusta, GA 30916

http://7figurepublications.com

No part of this book may be reproduced in any form, stored in any retrieval system, or transmitted by any means, electronic, mechanical, photocopying, recording, or otherwise, without written permission from the author.

ISBN-10: 0-9988984-2-2

ISBN-13: 978-0-9988984-2-1

Library of Congress Cataloging-In-Publication Data:
LCCN 2017952844

Cover design by Lisa Sims of Passionate 2 Design

Published September 2017

LCCN: 2012909756

Dedication

To Falicia Rose Blakely

Acknowledgments

Falicia, I am humbled by the experience of being able to meet you, and I am even more grateful that you entrusted me with your story. Over the time that I have gotten to know you, I feel that you are a beautiful person inside and out, despite your shortcomings and your current status. No one, including myself, has the right to judge. That is solely up to God and in the end, only God knows your true heart. I pray that you will always keep God in your heart and in your spirit, for he will catch you when you fall. God Bless. Your Friend for Life.

To my family, I love you guys, always have and I always will. Man, you are now a part of our family, and we welcome you with warm hugs and unconditional love.

I would like to acknowledge the editor, L.J Wilson. She is awesome, outstanding, and wonderful. I don't know what I would do without her on my team. I wouldn't trade her for anything in this world. L.J. has worked diligently on this project, and I mean blood, sweat, and tears. She never does anything less because she always wants her best work to stand out. I'm glad I met you, and I want you to know that I absolutely love your honesty. There's no other way to be in life than upfront and honest. You are a Godsend to me.

I'd like to thank Sheila Peele-Miller and Deanna Michelle Smith for assisting with this project. Hopefully, we'll be working together for a long time.

Lisa Sims has been designing book covers for 7 Figure Publications, and I know that I get on her last nerve, but she hangs in there with me. Thank you so much, Lisa, and I wouldn't trade you for anything.

I'd like to thank all of my supporters, and on behalf of Falicia Blakely, I'd like to thank actor, Lance Gross for thinking enough of her to send her an inspiring email. She was drenched in tears of joy.

God grant me the serenity to accept the things I cannot change, courage to change the things that I can, and the wisdom to know the difference.

I pray on bended knees that all young women take heed to this book, and I pray that it saves lives. I pray that it keeps young ladies from walking down the dark road that Falicia Blakely had to travel.

Also, I pray that God keeps all three of my beautiful daughters, Rockell, Cleopatra, and Honee lifted as I pray for all women around the world.

To God be all the Glory and all the Praise.

Mom, I love you!

PROLOGUE

Bitter always came after the sweet.

"Sunshine, baby," Ike chimed in, barely above a whisper.

"Daddy!" Falicia cooed into her cell phone. Excitement always filled her at the sound of his voice. "Where are you? And whose phone are you using?" She matched his lowered tone.

"Check the move." He ignored her questions. "Take care of that lil bit over there. Then meet me in the parking lot at Body Tapp." As always, his tone was serious and direct when he gave orders. A cold silence lingered between them as Falicia tried to collect her confused thoughts. *How did he get out of jail so fast?* Ike's voice broke in, ending her curiosity.

"Just handle that, and let's go, baby. It'll be perfect. We'll leave the Honda in the parking lot. Last time anybody saw you, you left the club with a trick. And very few know that I made bond. I'm just ready, Sunshine. Ready to get away from these 'hos and start over." It was everything Falicia wanted—to get back to life when it was only the two of them, well the three of them—Ike, her son Man, and Falicia, but one thing stood in their way.

"Daddy, I can just leave now and come straight to you." She smiled, envisioning them driving away from all the drama in the ATL and into a new state and a new life.

"Naw, ma. Get that money first," he instructed.

Instead of responding, Falicia looked around the dining room of the man she intended to rob. The initial plan was to get enough money to bail Ike out of jail, who just so happened to be out already. "Well, now that you already out—"

"Just off the nigga and come on!" Ike said in a gruff voice.

The smile left her face as Falicia searched her brain for anything to change his mind. "He has a stick shift, Daddy. And I can't drive a stick."

"Then call me when you done. We'll come pick you up."

"But . . . he only got like $700. Maybe you should just try to get that and run." After Joe had purchased cocaine from her, he told her he only had $700 left for his rent. Joe hadn't lied. She had gone through his wallet and counted seven 100 dollar bills, but hadn't taken any of it. Not yet. She heard him approaching and quickly placed the wallet back on the coffee table.

"You heard what I said."

Shit! Falicia's mind raced with apprehension. Her stomach churned. "But . . . there's one more problem." She glanced down the hall for any signs of Joe.

"What!" Ike didn't seem moved in the least bit.

"Just before you called, he rolled me a joint and I was reaching inside my purse for a lighter and my pistol went off. I didn't even feel the trigger. I could've been shot, but the bullet went into the baseboard. And that shit got Joe shook. He was pacing and on edge and everything. It blowed me too. Maybe it's a sign."

"Sunshine, it's a sign to go ahead and handle your business. Crazy shit always happens right before you're about to take care of some real shit." Ike didn't understand.

"But, Daddy. He was practically walking on egg shells. He asked me what the hell I was doing with a gun. His hand was shaking when he picked up my purse to put the safety on the pistol."

"What you tell that trick?"

"That I'm a female dancer, and I sell dope. I would be stupid to be out here in these streets without one. Joe just shook his head and told me to be careful. I could tell he was spooked 'cause he was still trembling. He told me I made his nerves bad. So he just went in the other room to snort some coke to calm down. I'm just waiting for him to finish. I thought I just heard his footsteps coming back though."

"A'ight. Perfect. Go 'head and do that lil bit. Then come to daddy. If you need me to come get you, just call me. Then start walking." Ike ended the call. If it was possible, he would have heard Falicia swallow her fear.

As she waited for Joe to return, not even five minutes later, her phone rang again. "Hello?" Falicia answered, sounding flustered.

"Uh, Unique, you ready?" Joe asked, calling Falicia by the moniker he believed was her government name. His sudden presence startled her. She turned to find him standing there glassy-eyed, with his thin, hairy chest on display.

"Yeah," Falicia replied, then pressed the end button on her phone and flashed him a nervous smile. *How can I get this trick's money without any blood spill?*

Joe let her lead him down the hall to his bedroom. "Oh wait! Let me go get my purse. I'ma put my phone in it so we won't have any interruptions." She rushed back to the living room and grabbed her purse off the table, dropping her phone inside. The pressure from Ike was getting to her. Briefly, she stared at the pistol. *There's no fuckin' way I can kill this man.* Fear of death, jail, and her own safety also threatened her mentally. She returned to the room. Her phone vibrated. Joe's smile dissolved quickly when she snatched it out of her purse.

"Yes!" was all Falicia offered when she answered.

"What the fuck!" Ike screeched into the receiver. She peered over at Joe, paranoia setting in his eyes as he watched her every move.

"Now is not a good time," she replied.

"I don't give a fuck! Do you know I'm sitting out here in this parking lot waiting on you?" His voice boomed.

"I'm going to have to call you back." Falicia hung up and turned to meet Joe's cautious stare.

"Sorry about that," she said.

Joe glanced at her purse, looking more uncomfortable as he sat on the bed and removed his pants. She placed her purse on the nightstand and got in bed next to him. Again her phone vibrated.

"Don't worry, Joe. I'm not answering it. No more interruptions," she said, hoping to put his weary mind at ease.

That night was filled with several ignored calls from Ike to Falicia that even proceeded into morning. By 6:00 a.m., Ike's demand changed from "take care of the nigga" to "just bring your ass home." He didn't want to hear any explanations about why she didn't come through with the plan. Ike just wanted his bitch—Falicia—in his possession. In that instant, she knew this wouldn't turn out good.

Falicia waited while Joe showered and then got dressed for work. Soon, they were in his Volvo driving down a congested I-285 toward her apartment. The sky was cloudless. She wouldn't be studying the shape of each cloud and making them into what she wanted. No magic carpet, or her own private jet to get her the hell away from what she knew was coming when she got home. Nowhere to run and nowhere to hide. The uncomfortable rumbling in her stomach confirmed her fears.

Damn! She rubbed both arms, staring ahead. The sun beat against her skin, despite the cool air that seeped through the vents. Although Falicia wasn't trapped, she couldn't shake the suffocating feeling that her anxiety brought on. She glanced at Joe, who kept his hands on the steering wheel at ten and two, staring ahead. She couldn't read what he was thinking, but last night he clung to his wallet like desperately needed oxygen. Then again, Joe was just a coke-sniffing trick, driving her back home. So his thoughts really didn't matter. Money did. It's the only thing that ever mattered.

Joe hit brakes suddenly. She noticed the traffic jam they were in and welcomed the delay. By the time her heartbeat returned to its normal pace, they were moving again, but slowly. Once traffic moved enough for him to make his exit, he seemed to pick up speed. Blocks later, she instructed Joe to, "Make a left right here," as he entered Mechanicsville.

Her heart pounded and her palms moistened. Falicia's mind

raced with thoughts of stinging, vicious slaps and powerful, solid body shots that always landed. And blood. *He's about to beat my ass! I know it!* Once the car stopped in front of the walkway that led up to the entrance, she opened the door to Joe's silver Volvo.

"If I never see you again," she said calmly to the man whom she'd been exotic entertainment for, and to whom she'd been selling cocaine to for months, "know that God was with you."

"What?" Joe asked as he rubbed his shiny baldhead. His brows bent as his puzzled eyes met the side of her expressionless face.

"I was supposed to kill you last night, Joe, and the fact that I didn't may have cost me my life." Tears threatened to fall, but she knew crying wouldn't do any good.

His eyes widened as if a ghost sat beside him. "What! Unique, please get outta my car."

Falicia grabbed her purse, her heart pumping fiercely with the same dread she was certain Joe now felt. As she stood and slammed the car door, she winced. Feeling Ike's fist smash against her cheekbone before a single blow ever landed on her face.

CHAPTER 1

August 25, 1999 . . .

"You need to hurry up and get here!" Falicia's stepsister Mylena yelled into the phone.

"Girl, I'm coming!" Falicia retorted, rolling her eyes as she moved the phone from her ear. *I'm not tryna hear her fussing. He just gone have to wait,* she thought.

Falicia knew she was wrong, but it was her last night in Jacksonville, Florida, and this six-foot-tall Caribbean cutie had been chasing her for months. Unable to resist him any longer, she accepted his invitation to a popular Reggae joint, looking forward to her upcoming sixteenth birthday. The Caribbean Cutie was officially her first one-night stand. And Falicia was truthful with him about moving to Atlanta. But not about the promotion that her mother received. Falicia had claimed it as her own, giving Caribbean Cutie the impression that it was her reward, and she was about to celebrate it along with her *twenty-first* birthday.

Mylena's voice ruined Falicia's happy thoughts. "Well, Kevin called and said he was on the way. Falicia, your damn flight leaves at eight o'clock."

So what! That's my mama's man, not mine! Falicia glanced at the time on her cell phone. *Wish Mylena would stop actin' like she my damn mama!* Caribbean Cutie took hold of her free hand and kissed the back of it, sending tingles all over her body as he had done when they first met.

"I said I'm coming, Mylena. Damn! I didn't know I would be gone this long," she whispered.

"I don't wanna hear it," Mylena shot back. "You should've never left in the first place. Leaving here with that strange man. I don't know what your problem is, but you better get yourself—" Falicia ended the call.

Sereniti Hall

Five minutes later, her cell rang again. "We on the interstate. I'm coming!" she snapped.

"What am I supposed to tell this man?" Mylena fussed.

"I don't care what you tell him. He'll be all right until I get there!"

Falicia wasn't the least bit sympathetic toward Kevin, her mother Letty's man. In Falicia's opinion, he only served as another wedge between her and her mother. There were plenty of nights that she spent alone because Letty was with him. But that wasn't all—the missed track meets and her homecoming, in which she was announced as the short flag co-captain during her freshman year.

Kevin, with his tall, lanky frame, reminded Falicia of Eddie Kane Jr., the lead singer in the *Five Heartbeats*. He had become the model for what Falicia believed men were best for—fulfilling whatever need she had. Kevin, on the other hand, wasn't her sugar daddy, but she treated him as such because he acted nothing like a father figure. That shit went out the door the day his eyes lingered over her physique—long enough to make her extremely uncomfortable.

The instant Falicia arrived at her grandmother's house, where Mylena and her two sons and a cousin also resided, she ran inside to kiss her family and say her farewells. She grabbed her small John Casablanca modeling bag, stuffing what was left of her life in Jacksonville inside. The rest of her belongings had already been sent via UPS thanks to Kevin. *Should I change?* She toyed with the idea of changing her powder pink DKNY peek-a-boo belly top and matching silk skirt. One look at her silver heels with the clear straps, along with her expensive-looking sew-in, placed her appearance at twenty years or older.

She could hear her mother Letty's voice in her head. "Falicia, you need a bra on with that blouse." That alone encouraged her not to change clothes. *Naw, I suppose I'll just introduce Letty and Atlanta to this fly, slim beauty.*

Instead, Falicia ran to her grandmother's room one last time and sat on her lap. To everyone else Falicia always rocked a tough exterior, but she allowed a few tears to fall in her grandmother, Olivia's, presence. She had been more of a mother to her than a grandmother.

"You sure you want me to do this, Ma?" Falicia asked, holding Olivia's face, hoping she'd tell her she didn't have to go. Filled with nothing but love, Falicia stared into the eyes of the copper-skinned woman with Cherokee Indian features. Her grandmother's house had served as her refuge many times. A year ago, Olivia had taken her in. "Ma, you remember when I first moved with you?" Falicia asked.

"Of course I do. I'll never forget it." Olivia nodded. Falicia remembered that day as if it had just occurred . . .

"Good race, kid! You're one awesome runner for a freshman," the school bus driver said as Falicia exited the bus. He waved goodbye.

"Thanks," she said with a proud grin and waved back. He always watched her until she unlocked the front door and headed inside her home.

Disappointment rose in her throat as she shut the door. She cut on the lights in each room as she made her way to her bedroom and placed the medals she'd just won at a regional track meet on the dresser. There was no one to celebrate with, not even to discuss the record she'd made in the female's 100-meter race. Nor could she call anyone, because there was no landline. "I'm so sick of this," she said, sitting on the edge of the bed staring out the window. Suddenly, Falicia hopped up and ran to the pay phone planted on the opposite corner near her backyard. Calling her grandmother was her normal routine.

"Hey, baby! What's the matter?" Olivia lovingly inquired. The mere sound of her grandmother's voice brought tears to Falicia's eyes. Although she wiped away her tears, more tears fell nonstop.

Sereniti Hall

"It's just that no one is here . . . *Again*. And she didn't even show up for my track meet, Ma. I just don't understand . . ."

"Oh, baby . . ." Olivia said. "Maybe it's not meant for you to understand. But she loves you. I want you to go pray for her. Go get on your knees and tell God how you feel, okay?"

Falicia shook her head as if Olivia could see her nodding yes. Loving her mother always brought her so much pain.

"Can I come over there with you, Ma?" she asked.

"Yes, baby. Anytime."

As she walked the seventeen-block distance to her grandmother's house, Falicia's mind was made up. "I'm never going back to Letty's empty ass house. Ever!"

Olivia's voice brought Falicia back to the present, to reality, where she sat on her grandmother's lap smothered in a loving embrace, knowing she was leaving her grandmother and Jacksonville, Florida for good.

"Yeah, I still remember that day too, Falicia. But the past is the past, baby. I am so sorry that happened between you and Letty, but today is a new beginning."

Falicia didn't respond. Olivia sighed, albeit lightly.

"Baby girl, I think it's best to give your mother another chance," she advised, holding Falicia safely in her arms. "This could be really good for you. And for Letty. Kind of like y'all making up."

"Ma, I hear you, but she's been gone a year and just up and decided to send for me now. Shoot, I didn't even know she was living in Atlanta." Falicia thought it would all be a waste of time anyway. *What type of mother moves to another state and doesn't even tell her only child?*

"Now, you listen here." There were very few times that Olivia got stern, but when she did, it got Falicia's undivided attention. "That's your mother and she loves you. No two people express themselves the same. Give her a chance, do you hear me?"

"Yes, Ma." Falicia nodded up and down. "But Ma, if I leave you, who's gonna clean the house and take time to get under your bed real good?" Falicia smirked at the thought of her six-year-old cousin's many toys hidden under Olivia's bed, along with her snacks.

"You'll just have to come down and do it. Visit me from time to time." She smiled.

But who else is gonna have older guys that only want my coochie, buying you groceries and beer and putting money in your pocket? she wondered. "Ma, it's not gonna be the same without you." Falicia hugged her tighter.

"Well, sugar, you know you can call me every single day, and when things get hectic, remember what I always tell you."

"Get down on my knees and pray," they said in unison.

Falicia's life was being disrupted in a major way. It made little sense to leave her family for her mother. None of this felt right. Her stomach agreed and rumbled a warning. *Don't leave.*

CHAPTER 2

Should I just go off on her, then slap her for bringing me all the way here? . . . Then hug her? Nah, she'll kill me. Shoot! I don't even know how I'm supposed to feel once I see her. What do I even say? Falicia's heart pounded fast as she searched for her mother in the huge airport.

"Boo-Boo!" Letty, a brown-skinned, thick woman waved with much excitement. "Come here. Give me a hug."

All that inner tough talk vanished from Falicia's mind like a courtesy flush does a turd. Falicia blinked twice. Letty's open arms blew her away. She couldn't believe the joy that filled her mother's face was even real. But nevertheless, she felt it. It seeped into her like an electrical current. The two met up and hugged in the middle of the airport. Letty embraced her with such love and compassion. Falicia wasn't sure what to make of it, so she just looked into her mother's misty eyes, and it made her heart smile. She felt like an adored daughter.

Letty pulled her closer. "Oh, I missed you, Boo-Boo!" Then she took a step back and looked her over. "You've grown too."

Falicia had no words, but the love she felt from the woman she loved so deep within, broke through the fortress she had built after suffering one disappointment after the other. In that moment, she opened herself to receive and accept what her mother was offering.

"Do you have any luggage? You shouldn't since I got all your stuff last week," Letty said.

"Yes, just one bag though," Falicia responded.

"Okay, well let's go get it." Letty ushered her daughter to baggage claim.

Falicia's curiosity got the best of her as she looked around the airport in amazement at all of the restaurants, bars, and souvenir shops. Hartsville International made Jacksonville's airport seem ancient. People even moved at a different pace here. It felt as if it was a different world, but Falicia didn't realize just how different and how fast Atlanta's vibe pulsed.

"Is that yours?" Letty asked, pulling Falicia from her exploration to point out her luggage. She nodded yes. "So you still have your modeling bag, huh?" Letty made more of a statement than asked a question.

As she held the bag at arm's length, Falicia studied her mother's expression. It was as if she was seeing it for the first time. She knew Letty loved the idea of her modeling, just as much as she believed her physique was made for magazines and the runway. But all that was just a memory now. Falicia had quit modeling some time ago. It was a difficult decision to make, but in her immature mind, she wanted to hurt Letty the way Letty's absence had hurt her.

"I been stopped modeling. You're late." They began their walk to the car.

"Oh. I didn't know that." Letty looked off, but suddenly turned back toward Falicia wearing a big grin. "You're going to love it!" she said, as if she was proud of herself.

"Love what?"

"Your new place."

And how do you know that?" Falicia inquired, wearing a smile that matched her mom's excitement. They entered the shiny black vehicle, and Letty started the ignition.

"Because I already got your room situated. And we stay across the street from Greenbriar Mall."

"A mall!" Falicia had forgotten she had her seatbelt on as she attempted to sit on the edge of the seat to get a better look at Letty. "A mall, Mom?" *Oh yeah! I might be all right in the ATL!* She saw herself boosting clothes from several stores and looking fly as always.

During the rest of the ride from the airport, Falicia sat back on the new leather seats trying to imagine what her life would be like now that she was in a city full of possibilities, entertainment, and pleasure. This was Atlanta. The Atlanta that you always heard about no matter which state you resided in. The actors, the professional athletes, the singers, the rappers, the money, the mansions, and fancy cars. The strippers.

She glanced at Letty, admiring how pretty she looked with her small box braids and no make-up. Letty was slightly slimmer than Falicia last recalled, but she was still a beautiful thick woman. The two women shared little resemblance. Falicia had a darker mahogany complexion, was very slim and tall. But she did inherit some of her mother's curves that made her physically attractive. She gazed out of the window, taking in the beauty of ATL and inhaled, opening herself up to the newness of it all, opening herself up to change. The air even smelled different. Fresher. *Maybe things will be better this time*, she reasoned. Even more excitement surged through her body when Letty turned into a gated community, Continental Colony, and parked the car. Falicia hopped out and grabbed her bag as if a gun sounded during one of her track meets.

"Which one, Mama?" she asked, looking back.

"That one." Letty pointed to the townhouse just to their left. Falicia took off like lightning.

"Boo-Boo, wait for me!" Letty shouted, running until she finally caught up. She unlocked the door, and Falicia stepped inside. "I can't wait to see your reaction!" Letty rushed past Falicia as she was glancing around the living room. A black leather sectional outlined the wall that led to the stairwell. Vinyl blinds dressed the huge window that stretched across the front of the house. She spotted an entertainment center equipped with a 32-inch TV, DVD player, and music equipment. Pictures of Falicia were positioned on top. Falicia recognized a few pieces of furniture from their previous house. For some strange reason, it felt like home.

Together they mounted the stairs, Letty in the lead. At the top of the stairwell was a door to the far right.

Sereniti Hall

"That's my room," Letty indicated, then directed Falicia's attention to the left, a short distance away. She opened the door. "And this is your room, which is not decorated. But you'll have plenty of time to decorate it."

This is really nice. Could be a lil bigger though, Falicia thought as she looked it over. "Okay, we can do that. That'll be cool."

"And oh yeah, you'll be responsible for cleaning up the bathroom down the hall. I have my own bathroom in my room."

"Sounds like that should've been my room." Falicia grinned as if she was teasing, but her selfish eyes and tone were clear indications that she meant every word. She often stated that she was "a young queen in the making." But actually, she was a brat who spent the previous year away from her mother and received little guidance from her grandmother. As a result, some of her decisions put her in some risky situations. About six months ago, Falicia almost placed herself in a position that would have left her standing at the altar as a Muslim guy's concubine . . . not his wife!

On a Saturday night, Falicia checked her makeup one more time to make sure she didn't look like a fifteen-year-old high school sophomore. She exited the bathroom, ready to party. The DJ was blasting the latest by DMX when she walked by and brushed up against a photographer, who was taking pictures of patrons.

"Can I buy you a drink?" the Muslim man quickly asked with the sexiest eyes Falicia had ever seen. She loved going to little 'hole in the wall' spots like *After Eleven*. The men were older, employed, and could easily provide her wants.

All it took was one yes from Falicia, and the married man and father to a set of five-year-old triplets, who was at least thirty years older, had begun spending time with her, stopping by her grandmother's place. The Muslim man had purchased everything from beer and groceries for her grandma, to manicures and pedicures for Falicia and her stepsister Mylena, and her cousins, which ever one of them was present at the time.

His attraction to Falicia was clearly driven by lust. After a couple months of sex, soon the Muslim man began to reason with his wife why Falicia needed to become his concubine when she turned eighteen. Never mind that he'd lied to his wife about Falicia being his good friend's child out of wedlock. The man was so gone off the sex with Falicia, that he brought her home to have dinner with his family. And they indeed, did all sit down to eat together, fueling Falicia's attitude that she was the shit and hell yeah, she was entitled!

But the relationship was short-lived once he discovered her true age. Also, Falicia realized his wife had been her previous third grade teacher that she used to look up to. Falicia simply got ghost and did a disappearing act. Of course she'd miss the money, but there was a lot more of that where that came from. Men were in abundance at the club. Every club.

"So, you do like it!" Letty said, stirring Falicia from reminiscing about the crazy thing she had done in the past.

"It's beautiful, Mama!" Falicia finally stated when she placed her bag on the floor of her new room. "Thank you."

A mahogany headboard with two nightstands on each side, and a dresser with a vanity mirror gave the room a middle-class vibe. So did the tiny flowers neatly spread across the cream-colored comforter and curtains. Letty always had a way with decorating. She really felt her sentiments were on point once her feet now sunk into cream plushness, a definite step up from the thin carpet at her grandmother's house.

She allowed the happiness to replace her doubt. Falicia jumped in the center of her comfortable bed that would now hear her unexpected griefs, disappointments, and even momentary joys. Letty laughed, feeling satisfied with her daughter's reaction.

"Go ahead and get settled. We'll go shopping later to get the little what-nots you need," Letty spoke, after turning to leave and shutting the door.

Sereniti Hall

Taking another look around her new room, Falicia lay in bed and thought how drastically her life was about to change. She would definitely miss the nightclubs on the weekends and the sporadic pool parties and cookouts. Falicia wouldn't even permit herself to think about Hezron, her on-again and off-again boyfriend. She didn't even call and tell him she was leaving. Oh well. It was too late now anyway.

She swiped her hand across her skirt. Her clothes! Lord knows that was a subject she didn't want to dwell on. But it was a must that she get an entirely new wardrobe. The weather was different here; she'd definitely hit up a few stores to get herself straight. Regardless of Letty's come-up, she already knew her mother didn't have the means to maintain the lifestyle she had grown accustomed to.

As soon as she turned sixteen, which was ten days away, she planned to get a job, but even that little check would only go but so far. *Dang, I really gotta start all over. Gotta hit the clubs to find new sponsors and everything. In the meantime, I guess I better check out what type of sensors they got in the mall.* There was only Burlington and Macy's at Greenbriar. Neither store was her norm for shopping, but they would do. Falicia's mouth widened into a smile.

"Atlanta," she whispered, "I'm here, baby. I'm here . . ." Living in the burgeoning city made her feel inspired; maybe she would become a model one day. This was Atlanta, one of the fastest growing cities where she'd be sure to shine. Falicia lay there lost in her thoughts until she dozed off.

Several hours later, a ringing phone woke her up. She hopped up quickly. *Wonder if that's Grandma.* She got up and stuck her head out of the bedroom door.

"Ma!" she called out. "Is that Grandma calling?" She didn't want to walk into her mother's room for the phone if her grandma wasn't the one calling. Letty didn't answer her. "Ay, Ma! I need a calling card too so I can call back home. My phone doesn't work here since I'm out of state!" she yelled a little louder.

"Where is my Pumpkin Baby?" a male voice said. "Falicia, where are you?" Falicia dropped her smile. Hurt and anger coursed through her body. She felt balloon-ish—deflated.

"Oh my God! You have got to be kidding me." Falicia rolled her eyes in disgust as the sound of Kevin's voice drew closer. *No this nigga didn't just fly his ass here from Jacksonville. I can't even get ten minutes alone with my very own momma! Am I the only one who thinks I just might need some time alone with her?* She took a deep breath. *Damn!* It had been a year since she and Letty had been together. But who was she fooling? It was and always would be about Letty's man!

With little effort, Falicia built her wall back up and decided to rein in any line of respect she considered giving Letty. It was clear nothing had changed. Letty was either too blind to see just how much her actions rejected her only child, or she didn't care enough to notice. Falicia was over it.

Done!

CHAPTER 3

Falicia was a week and a half in as an official Atlanta resident, and it was also her sweet sixteen birthday that didn't seem all that sweet. Leaving her grandmother, best friends, and cousins was difficult enough. Now here she and Letty were, set up in a townhouse with a pool and other amenities, like Kevin and his young son Fred, and a cake that Falicia welcomed, but she had been expecting so much more. Way more.

Dressed in a two-piece swimsuit, Falicia pounced down the stairs and met her momma in the dining room. She had barely touched the cake. Letty wore a smile so big, Falicia was almost convinced she was glad she was there.

"Oh, you look so cute," Letty complimented. "I like how that little print is all over." Falicia looked down at the white leaf-print covering her top and bottoms.

"Thank you! I was a little more comfortable with these boy shorts over the bikini cut." Falicia looked past Letty and saw Kevin approaching. *Ugh! Sure don't feel like looking at his ass, and definitely don't want him looking at me.* She wrapped her towel around her body and headed out the back patio door. Seconds later, she heard footsteps running to catch up with her.

"Falicia, wait for me!" She turned to look behind her. Fred, Kevin's son, was out of breath by the time he caught up.

"Great! So now I'm babysitting on my damn birthday." She glared at the shirtless, high-yellow little boy.

"Falicia, don't say that! I just want to go with you. I don't want to stay in the house with them. I only agreed to come because Dad said you were here, but you act like you don't want me around." Falicia stared into his innocent face, knowing she shouldn't have taken her frustrations out on him. At that moment she decided to do better by him.

"Come on, Fred. Let's go then," she said.

"All right!" Fred grinned wide and followed her like an obedient puppy.

After hanging out at the pool for a while, they returned home. Falicia realized she had actually enjoyed herself. She wasn't sure if her "new face, fresh meat" had drawn a few boys to the pool, but she found it highly entertaining. She lay on a foldout chair next to the pool acting nonchalant as the boys attempted to get her attention. One boy was cute, but realistically, they were all just too young for her. A boy her age could only bring her a headache. He was in no position to contribute to her life, so Falicia preferred not to waste anyone's time. For some strange reason, she appreciated the attention of the male species. Even if she didn't wish to entertain them in return.

Fred thoroughly enjoyed himself and made the announcement the second they walked through the patio door. Falicia had no intentions of recounting the afternoon, so she walked past Letty and Kevin and headed toward the stairwell near the front room. Halfway there, her mother called after her.

"Yes, ma'am." Falicia turned on her heels, feeling a little jolly. She stood in the living room where her mother sat on the sectional sofa watching TV. Kevin was seated on the other end in the recliner.

"What are you doing?" Letty asked.

"Going to my room." Falicia's tone was polite. It was the first time she'd spoken without hostility since Kevin had arrived.

"You don't want to hang out here with us?" Letty asked, desperate to reach her sixteen-year-old daughter, whose line had suddenly become disconnected.

"Yeah!" Kevin's eyes got stuck on the way Falicia's boy shorts outlined her curves. "Why you keep staying cooped up in that room, girl?"

"What are you looking at?" Falicia's blood shot past the roof.

"What? What!" Kevin asked, realizing that she was addressing him. His thirsty eyes abandoned her physique. "What you talkin' 'bout, girl?" He grinned nervously. Falicia threw her hands on her hips.

"Nigga, you heard me! What are you looking at?" Falicia fumed as she made her way toward Kevin. Letty was stunned.

"Girl, what are you talking about?" he asked, properly.

"Kevin, don't play with me! You have no business looking at me. I don't give a care what I got on. You don't have a right to—"

"Boo-Boo, just calm down," Letty intervened. She stood between Falicia and Kevin, blocking her daughter's murder-filled eyes.

"Whatever!" Falicia shot back. "He's still a grown ass man looking at your sixteen-year-old daughter. But you can't see that, can you?" Falicia stormed away and went up to her room. She slammed the door and dropped onto her bed, making a brace for her head with the pillow. *Kevin's eyeballs were all over me, and all Momma worried about is a damn modeling career that I lost hope in when she packed up and moved to Atlanta without a word. Who did she think was supposed to take me back and forth to my classes? But then again, she was never there anyway, especially when I needed her most.* Falicia repeated the words 'especially when I needed her most.'

Images from Falicia's past rushed into her head so forcefully that she couldn't push them back.

"Hey! Stop that whining and be a big girl. Come kiss me right here." Kenzie gestured toward her vagina.

Although Falicia squeezed her eyes tight to erase the terrible scene, her brain moved forward from one traumatic event to the next.

"So I think we should play house," fourteen-year-old Sophie from next door suggested as she pulled Falicia in front of the mirror. "You want me to show you how to really play?" Falicia shrugged. "You can be the momma, and I'll be the dad."

Sereniti Hall

Ten-year-old Falicia smiled at her friend. Sophie was right there the first time Falicia stole candy from the convenience store. Saved her from the painful experience of playing Hide and Go Get It with the neighborhood boys, which should have been called Hide and If You Get Caught You Get Humped to Death! Sophie was also there the first time Falicia rolled up some trees in paper and smoked them. Was there when Falicia played with fire. Played in her mother's perfume and lipstick.

Sophie ran her fingers through Falicia's hair. "Okay, so are you going to play in my hair?" Falicia asked innocently, shying away.

"You should put on a dress," Sophie said.

"Okay." She led Falicia by the hand to the closet she shared with Letty. Their small room was across the hall from her grandmother Olivia's bedroom. Falicia picked out the beach dress her mother Letty wore to her favorite bar or pool party. Sophie helped her put it on, staring her in her eyes.

"Come here. I want to show you something," Sophie said gently. She sat Falicia on the bed and slid the drooping strap off Falicia's shoulder. Falicia's confused expression displayed the questions she wanted to ask. "Trust me, Falicia," Sophie said. "You know I won't hurt you, right?" Falicia nodded. "Do you? Say you do."

"I do. I know you won't hurt me."

Sophie laid Falicia back and slipped off the oversized dress. She climbed on top of Falicia and grinded against her. Every time Falicia stiffened, Sophie said, "Trust me." Gradually her pace increased, and she spread Falicia's legs.

Confused, Falicia's underarms grew sweaty, and her heart raced. Then her body betrayed her with a rush of pleasure. She sat up, knocking Sophie off her. Sophie eyed Falicia with a smirk of satisfaction. Every time Falicia saw her afterward, she wanted to tell Letty, but never could find the courage to do so.

Tears threatened to pour from sixteen-year-old Falicia's eyes, thinking about how nasty she felt after Sophie violated her.

Something similar had happened to Falicia with Letty's goddaughter Kenzie, after she'd left the two girls home alone. Falicia had been at their mercy, and no one would take advantage of her again. Especially not Kevin. Not like that. She picked up her pillow and stared at the door, hoping Letty would come to her and want to discuss how she really felt for a change. Those past incidents increased Falicia's sex drive and made it easier for her to hook up with guys for sex, even a guy on the chat line, which ended in an STD diagnosis. She thanked God that it was curable. Falicia flicked away the one tear that fell, wishing that for her to simply say, "Ma, I need to talk to you," didn't always result in Letty replying, "Oh my God! Don't tell me you're pregnant, Boo-Boo!"

Letty and Falicia continued to bump heads, sometimes over the smallest things. Or at least Falicia felt they were small, insignificant things that seemed to drive Letty crazy. For instance, Falicia finally showed off her tattoo so her mother could get a good look. She had it done a few days before she arrived in the ATL. Yes. It was her slick way of irking her mother. And just as she thought Letty's reaction would be, Letty's jaws dropped open in shock.

"Why on God's green earth would you mess with your beautiful skin, Boo-Boo? God said not to pollute . . . but what about modeling?" She'd really freak out if she saw the tattoo of the two cherries on her breast. One of the cherries appeared bitten and dripped juice. The word 'JUICY' was written above it. Falicia thought her mother was too dramatic and old fashioned. "You know what? I'm not even gone let you drive me crazy. And don't forget, school starts in a week, Boo-Boo," Letty said from the hallway. "And I need to take you to get your shots."

"Well, I can't start until my school records get here anyway," Falicia argued. "I should just start working until then." Falicia had already gotten hired on the spot at Taco Bell, but Letty didn't have a clue. She knew her mother didn't have the money to provide her with the things that she was used to. The men in Florida that she had been entertaining weren't exactly kingpins, but they definitely enabled Falicia to live a breath above poverty. In her opinion, she was grown! She had been taking care of herself for several years already. Also, she didn't want to place any added stress on Letty about money.

"Work is for *after* school, *Falicia*. You need an education," Letty countered.

"Therell High School is the neighborhood school. What am I gonna do there?" Falicia asked, knowing it was the school she was expected to attend.

"Learn," Letty responded.

Riverdale High or North Gwinnett were the two schools that her heart was set on. They outplayed everyone in sports. She wanted to be a part of the winners. And she hoped for a scholarship in track and field that Therell couldn't provide.

The following day, Letty and Falicia arrived at the dean's office after standing in a line that wrapped around the gym. The dean stared over his glasses at Letty, who was perched on the edge of her seat. Sweat dampened her forehead. "I'm sorry," he reiterated. "But that's our policy. We can't count Falicia's credits from Jacksonville, Florida. Therefore, she can't be promoted to the tenth grade. She is going to have to do her freshman year over."

Falicia shook her head at Letty. "No, Ma. I'm not repeating ninth grade."

"Yes you will!" Letty snapped.

"I'll do open campus," Falicia offered.

"Girl, have you lost your mind? My only child is not about to attend community college and get a GED. You're too damn smart for that." Falicia didn't have the will to start all over.

She returned home disappointed. They stood in the living room, both mother and daughter, equally frustrated.

"Momma, what you're not understanding is if I go to regular school, night school, and summer school for the next four years, when will I have time to work?"

"Falicia, work doesn't matter right now, school does. As long as you graduate with the class of 2002, then you can do all the working you want to." Falicia's eyes narrowed.

"But what you're not taking into consideration is that I need a job, *Momma!*"

"Excuse me." Letty's posture straightened.

"Winter in Florida is not like winter here, and you can't afford to give me every single thing I need."

"This shit is not up for discussion. We're done, dammit!" Letty squeezed those words out through pinched lips. Her stance was just as daring as her daughter's.

Falicia was promoted to the drive-thru cash register within a month of starting at Taco Bell, on one contingency. She had to stay in school, or Letty threatened to come there and show her behind. After spending her first check in her favorite department store on a black suede coat, some boots, and one pair of pants, she was back to broke. And because she was sixteen, she was limited to the hours she could work.

Friday nights were the most exciting. There wasn't any telling what might roll up to the drive-thru. Like a champagne-colored Lincoln with a brown complexioned male rocking diamonds in his mouth. The redbone female in the backseat sported a short blonde cut. Her eyes bore into Falicia. The redbone on the passenger side wore a wig that complimented her like she was a movie star.

"Daddy! She cute," she said. "And it looks like she got a little shape on her."

Falicia stared back. "Are y'all strippers?" she asked before she realized what she said.

Sereniti Hall

"Why? You wanna make some money?" the lady who looked like a movie star asked. "More than your entire check in one week."

Falicia glanced from the thirsty hyena in the back to the grinning diamond-toothed man. She had never seen diamonds in a man's mouth, gold or platinum. *I could think of a lot more I could do with diamonds that put 'em in my mouth.* She reached for the $50 bill he held out and spotted the fur coat he was wearing. *What do they really do for a living?* she wondered. After she handed them the food and the taco sauces, she put his change in his hand.

"Falicia," the driver said, with his eyes on her name tag. He grabbed her hand.

"Will you let me go?" she stated with an attitude. Although the driver didn't know it, the threatening tone she used really expressed her discomfort.

"I really wish I didn't have to." He slipped his business card in her hand. Falicia glanced at it with a frown. *Is he flirting with me in front of his woman?* "Call me," he added.

Falicia rolled her eyes and slammed the drive-thru window. On her break, she could barely wait to take his card out of her pocket. A smile appeared on her face once she spotted the zodiac sign Scorpio, and the words: *LA. Call 24 hours a day.*

CHAPTER 4

I can't take no more of this. It's Friday! I'm ready to get into some thangs, Falicia thought as she slammed her books in her locker. She had three classes left, but she wasn't stepping a foot into any of them. Never mind that it was only noon. *I'm outta here!* Falicia exited Therell High School through the gym doors and headed home.

She snuck in through the back door. The telephone began ringing. Normally, when she skipped her remaining classes on a Friday, she didn't dare answer the phone in the middle of the day. Letty was slick enough to call home from work just to make sure Falicia hadn't left school early. But Falicia didn't want to lie about ditching school this afternoon. Today she felt brave enough to be honest for some reason.

"Hello?" she answered, eyeing the food in the refrigerator.

"Is this Falicia?" a male voice asked.

Who is this? She tried to catch the voice as she grabbed a soda. "Who's asking?" she said, wanting to sound mature.

"This is LA."

Falicia wasn't sure what to think after his announcement. "And how may I help you?" She was on her way upstairs to her room.

"Excuse me!" He chuckled. "What do you mean?"

"You called me because . . ." Falicia dropped her backpack on the floor and sat on the bed and kicked off her shoes.

"I *been* calling you. I don't know if you're telling folks to tell me you're not there or what. But I've been reaching out." He sounded genuine.

"What folks?"

"Some woman . . . I guess it was your mom."

"What!" Shocked, she stood to her feet. "You spoke to my mother?"

"Well no. I gave the phone to Ms. LA when your mom answered. So she asked for you."

"Ahhh, you're a coward. Too scared to ask for me, huh?" Falicia put her hand on her hip, amused.

"Scared doesn't have anything to do with it."

He's so full of shit. Falicia sucked her teeth. *Just making up any excuse. If he was too afraid to ask for me, then he know good and well his old ass don't have no business talking to me.* And this was the very thing. The very reason Falicia thought the way she did about men. Men like LA were only good for sex and giving her money. Most of the dope boys in her old neighborhood usually paid for her groceries when she went to the local convenience store. She also heard how her male friends, male cousins, and even the boys in school almost always degraded and mistreated women. So she began to see the relationship with dudes in three ways: 1. They just wanted to fuck. 2. They would pass her on to their boys. 3. They would take care of her.

Falicia decided that although the sex was cool, she needed to be sponsored financially. Nothing else would do. "So why did you call me?" she finally asked.

"Because I been missing you," he replied.

"Do you seriously think I'm that gullible?" Her initial call to LA a few weeks ago was strictly to learn what he did for a living. He invited her out to lunch. That day Falicia rocked a bad ass red spandex dress that she knew would draw the attention she so desperately craved. A little teasing never hurt anybody.

"Girl, you is hell!" LA had said, looking her over like he wanted to devour her.

"Naw, I'm just honest," Falicia had responded. But that crazy day had come to an abrupt end, and today she was curious about his phone call.

"So what's up, LA?"

"Well, please allow me to apologize about Mr. Charlie and shit."

"Empty." Falicia rolled her eyes, thinking about the incident with Mr. Charlie.

"What does that mean?" he asked.

"It makes no sense in apologizing for something you did intentionally." She knew LA tried to pull a move on her. After they had lunch, he drove her to a fancy house and asked her to do him a favor and sit with Mr. Charlie. She declined several times, but LA was persistent. After being continuously pressured, she finally gave in for the sake of peace, thinking LA only meant to keep Mr. Charlie company by sitting with him and listening to his conversation.

"That's not fair."

"What's not fair is how I had to endure that bullshit. And I was late for work too. Completely inconsiderate." Falicia ended up in a room waiting with Mr. Charlie's perverted ass for several minutes too long. He was aggressive, and his sexual advances made Falicia both nervous and angry. Stroking himself in front of her and inviting her to have sex. And when she made sure he understood that she wasn't getting with him in any kind of way, he called some 'ho who seemed to 'appear' on cue to perform oral sex on him after he gave her crack. Falicia hadn't come there for all that bullshit.

"You're right. Let me make it up to you," he said.

"How you gone do that?" Falicia asked.

"Well, you can come chill with us tonight."

"Who is us? And why would I do that?"

"Me and Ms. LA. Because we're good company. And we want you to. Ms. LA said you're easy to talk to, and she doesn't come across many females like that." Falicia smiled and went to her drawer and removed a bottle of fingernail polish.

"Hello? You still there?"

"Yeah." Falicia did have a good conversation with Ms. LA during lunch. She was straightforward, and Falicia liked that.

"So what exactly do y'all do together?" She questioned him about his profession. LA was honest.

Sereniti Hall

"The life that Ms. LA and I live is simply a business, Falicia. And in this business, it's all about survival and maintaining a certain lifestyle where I'm the financial guide, and she is all about making money."

Soaking up that information, Falicia painted her big toe with a clear coat. "So why does she call you daddy?"

"Because I'm her man."

"So then why are we even having this conversation? I don't believe in sharing!"

"I'm not her man in the sense that you're thinking. I'm what some would call a pimp, Falicia. It's a uhhh . . . business arrangement. Ms. LA is my bottom bitch, my ride or die. And whatever she does, is for us."

"Get the fuck out of here! So what you're saying is that they—these 'hos just use their bodies to make money for you?"

"Exactly! Because sometimes you may need someone to guide you in how you spend your money," he replied. "And how to make it."

"Whatever! So I'll be ready to go by nine. And I wish I *would* give a nigga my money!" Falicia hung up.

Later, she tossed Letty some random place where she was going out to party. Her mother asked not a single question of her whereabouts for the evening.

Just as he promised, Ms. LA knocked on her front door at 9:00 p.m. sharp.

"Boo-Boo, somebody is at the door for you," Letty yelled.

Falicia came downstairs dressed in denim hip huggers, a colorful tube top, and Candie heels. Her mother Letty looked her over long and hard as she fastened her hoop earrings. She then slid her feet into her black leather shoes. "Me and Kevin are headed to the bowling alley. You look cute," Letty said.

"Thanks." Falicia was ecstatic that her outfit didn't get her mother's censors going off, and that was a good thing. At least she didn't have to spend ten minutes arguing with her about changing clothes.

"You ready, Letty?" Kevin asked as he headed out of the kitchen with a piece of Church's Chicken on a slice of bread. His eyes almost shot out of his head seeing how packed and stacked Ms. LA was. She rocked tight-tight jeans that gave them an entirely different meaning. Falicia grabbed her bag and headed out the door, bumping Kevin out of the way.

"See y'all!" She smiled, admiring Ms. LA wearing the hell out of her jeans. She complimented her and strutted her own soft curves as if they were equally proportioned. They headed around the corner where LA was parked, waiting in a gray Crown Victoria. Red, the other woman whom Falicia saw at Taco Bell with LA was already seated in the backseat.

"Hi. I remember you."

"What's up, Falicia?" Red replied. "Good to see you again."

LA entered the ramp, and they were on I-285 in minutes. He exited on Old National Avenue and turned into the parking lot of a building that read 'Burning Sands Sports Bar.' They exited the car, and LA drove away to find a parking space.

"Here, take this." Ms. LA handed Falicia an ID. She rolled along with it and gained entrance to the club. She wasn't prepared for the activity happening inside.

CHAPTER 5

"What's up, Ms. LA?" the bouncers greeted her as she escorted Falicia to the bar that housed only top-shelf liquor. Men of various ages, sizes, and attire were all over. Many of them were flashy like LA and wore fur coats in different colors, Kangol hats, and canes loaded with diamonds or stones. A man drinking from a huge gold chalice snatched Falicia's attention. *This nigga reminds me of medieval times,* she thought. *He's a clown. A joke.* Like the rest of the men who looked as if they were in some type of best dressed contest. But then she saw diamonds . . . Lots of them. On fingers, necks, and wrists. Everybody wasn't frontin'. She couldn't help but look down at her jeans. *Damn, did I fail to dress for the occasion?*

Slot machines filled the room and were posted in stations where black jack and other games could be played. The minute they made a right, the scent of greasy food invaded her nostrils. Her stomach growled. *Them hot wings smell good as hell!* They rounded the corner and the room got darker. A disco ball was spinning above a woman winding her body to a reggae song. *Got-damn! I would only wear that to the beach,* Falicia thought, watching the vixen sway her hips in a silver bra and matching thong. Her virgin eyes took in the scene. Mostly men filled up rows and rows of chairs. Female exotic dancers were either working their middle as they sat in the men's laps or danced beside them. It wasn't the kind of dancing that Falicia was accustomed to. Their bodies moved with sensual skill and technique. The woman on the main stage moved each ass cheek separately to the beat booming from the speakers.

Amazed, Falicia finally sat down and observed the men, mesmerized by the women that stood in front of them, using their bodies to breathe life into their sexual fantasies. Like a scene from the movie *Players Club*. She was intrigued and secretly yearned to be a part of this world. Dancing came easy to Falicia, but this was a new type of dance.

Sereniti Hall

Ms. LA tapped Falicia's shoulder. "I'll be right back."

"Huh? Oh okay." Falicia felt a bit out of place being left alone. As she glanced left, she saw Red heading toward the bar and started to join her, but changed her mind when she saw LA dapping up the man holding the gold chalice. He was much older and less attractive than LA and stood wide-legged and tall. His cane obviously was more for show than necessity. *Cocky ass nigga.* Slick ponytail. He gestured with his hand, giving orders to a few girls who jumped at his bidding. Red stared down at her three-inch heels the entire time she stood in their presence. *For her to be grown, Red act like she scared to look a nigga in the eyes. Weird ass!* Falicia thought. *I wish somebody would tell this man his hands get dirty like everyone else . . . over there acting like his manicured nails can't get a thing on them. Frontin' ass dudes.* LA spoke in her ear and Red walked up to Falicia.

"Oooh, Ms. LA, when you're done on stage, come see me," a man shouted from his seat at the end of the bar. Falicia looked his way, but turned back to watch Ms. LA's reaction. She smiled and walked toward the dance floor, hypnotizing Falicia with her thick thighs, wide hips, and plump backside. The sheer yellow two-piece was tied on each side of her waist and covered her ass like a bikini. The top tied like a halter. Her six-inch, black patent leather heels crisscrossed her ankle.

Red tapped Falicia's shoulder. "LA wants you."

"Okay. I'll be a minute though," Falicia answered, finding Ms. LA's sexy dance more fascinating than LA's cocky ass friend. Before the song hit the chorus, Falicia was blown away by the way Ms. LA moved like liquid, all of her dance moves flowing together. From every angle in the room men approached her, peeling off dollar after dollar, going ape-shit when she made each butt cheek bounce. She dropped into a split, lay on her back and spread her legs in the air, making her vagina breathe through her bottoms.

How in the . . . Oh my goodness! This bitch here . . . Falicia's jaws almost cracked. She had to know how this was done. Astonished, she carefully studied the expressions on the men's faces. The yearning in their eyes, the lust! They were beyond excited, tossing dollars and cheering and singing praises, as if Ms. LA was a queen. *Damn I want to be desired in that way. I have to have that kind of power.*

Falicia lay in the bed across from LA in a motel room he and Ms. LA called home. The clothing rack in the corner of their room was full of her seductive attire and genuine furs in various styles. A multitude of shoes were crammed into a pantry-sized closet. And next door inside the cramped bathroom, the sink was covered in female hair and body products. Based on their material items, it appeared they led a life to be envied, but the cheap motel room clearly proclaimed a different story. *What the hell? I thought we would be laid up in a luxury condo.*

Near Falicia's position, Red was naked and bent over the bed. Ms. LA wore a red G-string and matching bra and strapped on a dildo the size of an overgrown penis. Moans coming from Red made Falicia sit up. She wasn't aroused, but more irritated by the noises than anything. *Hurry up and shut the fuck up!* she thought. Ms. LA locked her hand between Red's legs, stroking her with intensity and pounding into her. Red moaned and thrashed about wildly, almost dropping to her knees when she climaxed.

"You want next?" LA asked Falicia with a laugh.

"Hell no!" she replied, appalled. *This nigga got me twisted.* Falicia had never been with a woman, let alone sexually active in front of an audience.

Ms. LA pulled Red back into position, licking down her spine. LA tossed his hand at her.

"Now come see about me."

After she removed the dildo, Ms. LA then mounted him and

began riding him slowly with LA's hands locked on her thick hips. Falicia turned her back and closed her eyes, trying to block them out with sleep. They groaned with so much pleasure. Falicia rolled over on her stomach to look at them.

"Are y'all niggas really serious right now?" she complained.

LA flipped Ms. LA over on her belly. His fingers pressed into her side as he humped her doggy style with her faced buried in a pillow. He stared into Falicia's eyes. *He's trying me again. I done already told him.* Falicia grabbed her shoes from under the bed and hurried into the bathroom. *Time for me to go home!* She took a glance in the mirror over the sink, recognizing a faint resemblance of the sweet, young girl she once was. One who was passive and innocent. She straightened her clothes and took a deep breath as she walked out.

"I'm ready," Falicia said in the now quiet room.

"Ready for what?" LA asked as he lay on his back with Ms. LA in his arms.

"To go home." He shot Ms. LA a look as if it was her duty to change Falicia's mind. She sat up beside him.

"Falicia—" Ms. LA said.

"It's no point, sweetheart. I'm ready to go. So don't waste your time." She walked to the door.

"Falicia, we're in bed," LA stated.

"That's plain to see." She shifted her weight from one leg to the other. "So, Mr. LA, you can either get up and give me a ride, or—"

"I don't have the car anymore. It's my homie's from next door."

A pimp with no car? Picture that. "Okay, as I was saying, you can take me, or ask someone to take me, or call me a cab." She unlocked the door and opened it. "Thank you for an interesting night." She closed the door behind her.

They were in the middle of the hood where anything could possibly happen to her. She turned back facing the closed door, rethinking her decision. Her pride was much too big for that, and she had a point to prove. While contemplating her next move, LA exited wearing a pair of pants and some slides.

"So this is the way you want to leave me?" he said.

Falicia wanted to laugh in his face. "LA, spare me the bullshit, okay."

"What? Why are you so upset?" Falicia shot him an 'are you serious' look. "Is it because you want me and don't want to see me with another female?"

You old as hell! What you talkin' 'bout! Falicia's back straightened. Still, curiosity lingered in his eyes. "Is it, Falicia?" he spoke, barely over a whisper. "Falicia, answer me please." He stepped closer.

This nigga's weak for me. "No, LA! It's about respect. Always ask first. You don't take people's choices away from them. I wouldn't do that to you. Now, please take me home, or get me a ride. I'm ready to go!"

"Falicia." LA made one final attempt. She cut him a glance like: What! "Can you call me and let me know you made it home okay?"

She smiled to herself. "I'll think about it."

During the ten-minute drive home, the light-skinned dude introduced himself. "I live next door to LA. I'm his homie Rob."

"Nice to meet you," Falicia said. He asked her some basic questions: her name, if she was a dancer, her age, and if she was interested in the lifestyle. Falicia wondered if he was a pimp as well, but didn't ask. "And you said your name is Rob, right?"

"Right."

"Funny. I know someone named Rob-G, and he was very . . . What's that big word? . . . Ummm impress . . . impressionable!"

"I hope it was in a good way."

Falicia shrugged. "Thanks. And good night." She exited the car.

Once she entered the empty townhouse, she took a long shower. She considered calling LA. *Nah, he needed to be left with his thoughts so he can figure out how to handle a young woman of my caliber.* After her shower, she lay across her bed and closed her eyes. Her thoughts took her back to Jacksonville.

Her six-year-old cousin Lexi and her dad, Robert, or Rob-G, as many called him, lived next door. Often Falicia got Lexi ready for school, and she would call Rob-G to come get her. At that time Falicia wasn't going to school much. Aside from getting Lexi ready in the morning, she'd help her with homework in the afternoon. Falicia would start her dinner, iron her clothes, put her to sleep, and do it all over again the following day. It was a weird arrangement. Since Rob-G lived in the house next door, he'd grab the keys out of the mailbox and lock the door so Falicia could go back to bed. Around this time, Falicia was making frequent trips to the mall boosting lingerie, thongs, and teddies—things a fifteen year old should not have or be selling.

Having slipped on a black sheer teddy that she would never let Letty catch her in, she was in the throes of a deep sleep when she woke up feeling another presence in the room. Falicia looked around the room that she shared with her mother, but didn't see anyone. She dozed back off. The powerful sensation from an orgasm woke her up. Her body shook uncontrollably as she clawed at the sheets. Once it passed, she sat up. Rob-G got off his knees near the foot of the bed. "I knew that you would taste like that." He put his pants on and left the room.

Shock and guilt kept Falicia from moving any further. Rob-G was her favorite aunt's baby daddy. She didn't know what her aunt Tasha would do if she found out. True enough they weren't together, but some lines should never be crossed. They shared a child, Lexi, who would always be Falicia's cousin for the rest of their lives. Although the event was never mentioned, Falicia often caught him looking at her while trying to calm her aunt Tasha down about something.

Consequently, Falicia had her own battle going on with her first love, Norris. Sex between them had changed because of Rob-G. The pleasure Norris once gave, was now just a build-up that made her masturbate after they parted, or toss and turn until she fell asleep.

One morning, instead of waking up to the sounds of the alarm announcing it was time to hit the mall, she felt the covers slide off her body and her legs being spread. She sat up quickly, trying to cover her exposed vagina with her satin nightgown.

"What are you doing?" Rob-G flipped Falicia's legs up, then put his tongue to work. Her body racked with pleasure, lost control. She reached a climax that penetration never fulfilled. Her heart raced, watching him take his erect penis out of his boxers. She could see his veins throbbing and pre-cum at the tip. Rob-G reached for her hand. She crawled across the bed to him. He sat down and pulled Falicia into his lap. She mounted him like a woman. Feeling all of him inside of her was nothing like sex with Norris. The deeper Rob-G was inside her, the more she thought she would lose her mind. And Norris.

His moans became louder than hers. Rob-G whispered freaky things to her; encouraged her to take control, to ride him like she had seen on the X-rated movies she had a reputation for watching. She laid him back on the bed. His arms spread out like he was being crucified. The more satisfaction she brought him, the more he moaned and his body shook. Falicia watched him the entire time. She found it unbelievable how she was making a grown man react. *I must have some good pussy*, she thought, humping Rob-G harder until he jerked her off him and cum spewed out of his penis.

Realizing what they'd just done, Falicia eased out of bed and stumbled to the shower. Tears ran down her cheeks. Although Rob-G was the father of her aunt's child, it was the best sex she'd ever encountered. So good it had her taking Lexi to visit him often, where they would slip into the bathroom while she watched cartoons. The bedroom door had no lock.

Whenever no one knew where to find her, Rob-G was taking her fifteen-year-old body beyond satisfaction and teaching her how to please him. He taught her to have his dinner ready when he got home. They bathed together. She cleaned his house and sold his drugs. The sex was so good no matter where he wanted it, or how he wanted it, she was his. Like a drug, the craving was so deeply embedded, she forgot about her loyalty.

One morning Rob-G didn't feel like driving her to school.

Bang. Bang. Bang.

The hard knocks on the door made him leap from between Falicia's legs to his feet. His bedroom window sat off the front porch. Tasha knocked on the window, peering inside. Falicia dived on the floor and pulled the covers over her head.

"Let me in, Robert!" Tasha demanded. He threw on his boxers and stormed to the door. "Give me some money," she said.

"That's why you're out here making all this noise?" he asked, sounding annoyed. "What you need money for anyway?"

"I know you not asking me about my business. You don't see me asking about what bitch laying in your bed."

He chuckled. "You jealous?"

"Boy, bye! You and I already know that you're a 'ho. Now give me some money."

Hearing her car leave, Falicia started putting on her clothes. Although she and her grandmother Olivia were the ones taking care of Lexi, Tasha had always come through for her. Like when Falicia was in the sixth grade, and Letty didn't buy her any clothes to go back to school. Tasha opened her closet to Falicia and let her wear whatever she had. The next year Falicia got suspended for fighting in seventh grade. Aunt Tasha came to her rescue.

"What the fuck is wrong with you?" Letty demanded.

"I was protecting myself. She threw the first punch," Falicia replied.

"Bitch, you ain't gon' be shit if you keep acting like this."

Tasha tore into Letty and made it a point of letting her know she needed to bring it down a notch. "Don't you ever tell my niece she ain't gon' be shit, and don't you *ever* call her out of her name again. You're the one that needs to get your pathetic ass shit together!" This was after Tasha walked in Letty's bedroom and caught her and her biker boyfriend tooting cocaine.

Falicia's next wakeup call with Rob-G came when she was stretched out in his bed after he put her to sleep with sex so intense that he almost made her cry.

"Falicia." She woke up to him standing over her, tapping her shoulder. "I need you to go home. Because I'm having company."

"What do you mean?" She sat up. Rob-G was dressed, looking and smelling delicious, like he did when she snuck out the house to hang out with him while he made his rounds.

"Ohh . . . so you plan on fucking another bitch tonight?"

"Falicia . . ." He wanted to spare her feelings.

Throwing the covers off, she stomped to the bathroom where he had taken off her silk panties and bra. Falicia snatched them up from the floor.

"Nah, fuck you, Rob!" She slammed the door in his face and vowed she would never deal with him on that level again. Four chicks later, after learning he slept with her best friend Ko-Ko, and her stepsister Mylena, the cuts were too deep for her to forgive him. And her hurt feelings made her question: "What did they do that I didn't do?"

It was her secret to deal with, just like how hostile he became whenever she brought another dude to her grandmother's house. Sometimes he would get so angry he would pull off in his car like he was going to run somebody over. Unable to admit to the turmoil he was taking her young heart through, Falicia made another promise to herself that the next man she sexed wouldn't find it that easy to shake her.

CHAPTER 6

"I was wondering if you know how to dance? You know . . . Like the women at Burning Sands?" LA asked Falicia.

Falicia giggled at the sound of LA's voice. She wouldn't admit it to him, but she missed him and didn't know why.

"I'm not even going to front. I can make my butt move. But not like that thing that Ms. LA did." It had been a week later that he finally called and offered her an apology for what went down at the hotel.

"So, have you ever given anyone a table dance?" he asked, then explained the dynamics of a lap dance by adding, "It's just like fucking."

That much was obvious, based on what she saw at the club. Falicia studied her curves in the mirror and flipped her new sew-in that she begged Letty to pay for. In exchange, she had to keep the house clean from top to bottom. She opened the closet door and grabbed the vacuum. "No, I haven't given anybody a lap dance."

"You want to learn?" LA asked.

She closed the door and looked around, as if her mother hadn't just left the house complaining about having to work on a holiday.

"Is Ms. LA going to show me?" jumped out of her mouth with more eagerness than she wanted to display.

"Uh-uh. *I'm* gonna show you."

"You?" Falicia was the one laughing now.

"I'll be there in fifteen minutes."

Before the line went dead, she raced into her bedroom just like an excited teen going on her first date, dancing in the mirror. Knowing her wife beater and Scooby Doo boxers weren't going to cut it, she pulled open her lingerie drawer and scanned through her panties and bras. Back in Jacksonville when she used to go to her favorite club where she could dance all night if she wanted, one of the older hookers told her: "Never get caught wearing mixed-matched underwear." From then on, what Falicia couldn't buy, she stole.

She held up a black satin bra and panty set trimmed in lace with the tags still on it, then darted inside the bathroom for a quick shower. Excited about her dance lesson, she carefully rubbed herself down in baby lotion, leaving her mahogany skin perfumed and glowing. Rob-G used to tell her, "That smell alone makes me want to fuck you all night."

Ready for class to begin, Falicia put on some lip gloss and hurried downstairs to answer the door. She was used to LA's fancy attire. But today there was no fur, suit, Stacy Adams, or linen socks. He was dressed in jeans, a Sean Jean T-shirt, and some Nike's. A simple but flashy watch adorned his wrist and a gold diamond-clustered pinky ring was on his right hand. He took off his Sean Jean hat when he walked in the door.

"Hey." Falicia smiled and closed the door behind him. He returned the smile and wrapped her in his embrace. He smelled good and felt even better. She didn't know she was holding her breath until he released her and she exhaled.

He took a seat on the sectional. LA's fingers folded into one another, and both hands rested on his rock-hard stomach. He didn't tap or wriggle his fingers like Falicia did when she was nervous. Nor was he smiling. She didn't know what to think. Falicia took a deep breath and looked away. Suddenly her body was yearning for him. Her focus landed on his profile. His jeans rested just right against his toned thighs. The money or his wallet bulged in his pocket. She blinked twice. *No, wait. Maybe it wasn't a wallet. Is that an erection?*

"So, what have you been up to?" It was the first thing that entered her mind. The battle of the sexes had begun. She fought to maintain eye contact and not look anywhere near his groin area.

"Same shit. Just getting this money." The heat between them grew too intense.

"Well, what are you going to do today?" The question felt stupid as hell the moment she said it. She needed to regroup so she could relax. LA being in her home was no big deal.

"Well later, I'm going to handle some business, but right now I just came to check on my baby."

Did this fool just call me baby? She rolled her eyes, but secretly she liked it. "LA, didn't I tell you not to try to play me like I'm a child."

"I hear what you're saying, but to me, you are my baby. Unfortunately for me, I live a lifestyle that you are not willing to be a part of, but that don't change how I feel about you."

"I'm thirsty. You want something?" She made the offer so she could get away from him for a moment and collect herself. *What the hell is happening?*

"Nah, thank you though."

"I'll be right back." Falicia hopped up and went into the kitchen and poured herself a glass of orange juice. Then she grabbed a chair from the dining room table and dragged it back to the front room.

"So, you ready to show me how to do this table dance thing?" She needed to get them focused on the purpose for his visit. "And don't think I'm about to do the shit Ms. LA and Red do to keep you either."

He laughed. "Girl, you're something else." LA set the chair in the middle of the floor, still amused. Falicia flipped on the stereo. "What type of music do you need?" she asked.

LA sat back down on the sectional across from her. "I need? I'm not the one dancing. You are!" He smirked. Her heart jumped a few beats. Something about him was sexy as hell today.

"Well, I didn't know I was going to be the entertainment."

He covered his mouth, muffling his laughter. "So you thought I was gonna be over here shaking my ass?"

Falicia giggled. "Now that you say it like that, it does sound kind of outrageous."

Sereniti Hall

She spent the next five minutes trying to find a song to dance to. There were plenty that made her want to move; she just didn't want to do it in front of LA. He picked up on her hesitation.

"The next song, I don't care what it is—I want you to dance to it."

"What?"

"So now you're having a hard time hearing?" He walked over to Falicia, fumbling with her CD selection. "You better pick the right one because that's the one you're dancing to." He returned to his seat as if to say, "I'm ready. So let's go."

"Big booty 'hos, hump with it!" blasted from the stereo. Her body began to move like it did when she was in the club.

LA sat up. "Wait a minute, wait a minute," he repeated over the music. Falicia looked over her shoulder and was met with a frown. "Pause that for a second."

She cut the stereo off. "Was it that bad?"

"Take that off!"

"What?"

"Woman, take off the shorts and tank top!"

"Why?" Falicia wasn't ashamed of her body. Yet, an ache settled in her stomach at the thought of being half naked in front of LA.

"Baby, if you can't do this in front of me, and it's just us. How are you going to do this in a club?" He waited for her answer. For her to sync her brain with reality and what was about to happen. Eventually she was going to dance half naked at Burning Sands.

"Who said I was going to dance at a club?" Falicia crossed her arms under her breasts. "Where you get that from, LA? You're good at assuming shit? Again!"

"Why else would we be doing this?" He looked around the room as if to emphasize his statement. "And it was you who said you wished you could do that."

"I said *I wish* I could move like them; not be in a room full of strangers half naked." Her voice escalated.

"All right, all right . . . come here." He pulled her into his lap. "If you don't want to do this, that's fine. You don't have to." He hugged her close, kissing her shoulder.

Sitting on his lap, being held gently in his arms, Falicia hadn't felt so protected in a long time.

"I do want to learn how to dance like that, LA. But I don't think I'm ready for the club scene yet."

"Okay, that's fine with me, baby." He slapped her hip. "Now, can you take that stuff off and let's take it from there?"

Falicia rose to her feet, slipped off her house shoes, and slowly wriggled out of her boxers. She stepped out of them one foot at a time and glanced at LA. His attention was on her with the same intensity as Rob-G when she got out his shower, and he waited for her to drop the towel.

"Is this better?" she questioned, dropping her wife beater at his feet.

"Girl . . ." He licked his lips. "Hell yeah!" LA shook his head. "And just think. All this time you been hiding that six pack and those pretty, long ass legs. Man, track and field is doing your body damn good. You sexy as fuck!"

They shared another laugh. Falicia cut on the music. Relaxed. Ready to entertain to rhythm of the beat. Grinding her hips like she learned to do at the reggae club. And teasing LA like she would do any man at the club. Dropping it in front of him and bouncing her butt up to his crotch. As the song ended, she paused for some feedback.

"Put on something slow," LA suggested.

Falicia switched to R. Kelly's, "It Seems Like You're Ready." Closing her eyes, she became Diamond from *The Players Club*. She rolled her body slowly, seductively. LA gripped her waist.

"Turn around," he said, pulling her into his lap. He guided her as she grinded against him. She placed her hands on top of his. Together they rubbed her firm breasts, squeezing them. "Lean back

Sereniti Hall

into me," he whispered in her ear, caressing her abs. Feeling sexy and desired, she leaned into him and arched her back.

"Follow me," he said.

Falicia placed her finger to her lips.

"Shh," she said, now taking control. Her fears were so far in the distance that she couldn't recognize them. With both hands on each of his thighs, she grinded against his erection, rolling her back and hips over and over and over. He touched her stomach, her thighs. He moaned out a curse. She turned, stroking his neck and shoulders. They locked eyes. His erection throbbed. She wasn't sure why, but when he kissed her neck, she was convinced he approved of her erotic dance moves. Again she turned with her back toward him and rocked her body against his to the melody of the song.

LA sat Falicia in the chair and got on his knees. Helping himself to a mouthful of her breast and slipping his finger inside her panties. *"I only sleep with my 'hos after they produce my quota,"* flashed through her mind. *Yeah right, nigga!* Falicia stared down at him, licking her nipple and stroking her clit. She grabbed his face.

"I don't think we should go any further," she said.

"May I have permission?" he asked, staring into her eyes. "Please."

"Permission?" She wondered what he needed permission for.

He nodded yes. The further down he kissed, the more she rubbed his head, dying to feel his tongue inside her. He slid her panties aside, his tongue trailed her hairline, and then flicked against her center. Immediate sensations of pleasure took hold of her body, surpassing what Rob-G had done. Falicia wasn't shy about the moans that escaped her mouth, or the way she convulsed when LA took her to ecstasy. Rising to his feet, he slid out of his jeans and grabbed a Magnum out of his pocket. Falicia touched herself, teasing him with her legs spread eagle, inviting him to more. Humored that this so-called pimp had just ate her out and was about to have sex with her and she hadn't given him a dime.

A Treacherous Hustle

LA pulled her to her feet, then sat in the chair. Falicia wondered who was playing who as she climbed on top of him. Guiding him where she wanted him to go. And he seemed not to care as long as she rode him like Rob-G had taught her, putting her back, ass, and pussy into her every move. Only with LA, she was in complete control. LA held on to her with all his might. Groaning out her name.

Falicia understood from the moment LA bust his last nut the type of jeopardy his reputation would be in if anybody found out how he had broken the unspoken rules concerning the conduct of a pimp. She also understood because it was the same respect she'd lost for him. He knew how to make magic with his tongue. She couldn't take that from him. But she had brought him to his knees. He left her house that day dropping her some dollars.

"So I was wondering if you had given any more thought about going to Rome with me?" LA asked. Earlier he had mentioned that he, Red, Ms. LA and a couple of other females were going to Rome, Georgia to host an after party for a local artist. "This will be the perfect opportunity for you to get your feet wet."

Falicia was still skeptical about the club scene. "So I won't have to purchase a thing, right?" She had plenty of outfits that would be appropriate for the occasion. "And you know this all depends on if I can get my mother to be okay with me leaving all weekend?"

"It's not all weekend. We'll leave Friday and be back Saturday."

With very little convincing, Letty okayed Falicia to leave on a Friday morning with a 'friend from school and her mama.' She promised to be back by Saturday afternoon. Their other line beeped while she was assuring him she could go. "Hold on for a second. Somebody else is calling," she told LA and clicked over.

"Hello?"

"Hello, this is the 9-1-1 operator. I have a Mylena Ford on the line."

"That's my sister. What's the matter?"

Sereniti Hall

Falicia headed downstairs where Letty spent most of her downtime on the living room sofa with her feet propped up. Mylena was Falicia's stepsister. Her boyfriend had beat her up and she and her children had nowhere to go. Mylena moved to Atlanta with him months after Falicia relocated with Letty.

"She can stay with us?" Falicia stated to the operator.

"Boo-Boo, what are you talking about?" Letty snatched the phone down and put it to her ear. "Does she have any money to get a room, or go back to Florida?" she asked.

"Mama, my nephews are with her. I don't want them on the street or in foster care. Mama! Those kids don't deserve that. Regardless of what Mylena does."

Letty sighed deeply. Mylena wasn't one of her favorite people, and Letty didn't have patience with the way Mylena was half-raising her children. Falicia's eyes begged her to do the right thing. She bowed her head in prayer to a God she only acknowledged when things got hectic.

"I'll tell you what," Letty said into the telephone. "Tell Mylena she can come stay here if she finds a job. She has to get up every day and seek employment until she gets it because this will only be a temporary arrangement. I'm not bullshitting, Falicia. Mylena just won't do right . . ." Letty shook her head.

"Mylena, I already told you that I'm going to a concert," Falicia stated, putting the finishing touches on her lips.

"Well, why can't I go? We used to do these type of things all the time!"

"Because these people don't have reservations for you, and there is no room in the car," Falicia responded.

"What makes you think I want to stay?" she replied.

Falicia took her overnight bag from the top shelf in her closet. "Because I've already heard you complain about being shut up in this house with my mother a thousand times. I *know* you'll want to stay."

She followed close behind while Falicia stuffed her bag. The outfit her little sister had hidden away in her closet made her stop and think. "What type of concert you going to? Who did you say was performing again?"

Falicia wasn't sure. For the sake of not getting barricaded in her room, or the possibility that she might get embarrassed in front of LA and his women, she said, "Mythical."

Mylena lit up like a Christmas tree. "What? Bitch, you just gone go see my man and not say a word? Oh, I don't give a fuck what anybody says, I'm going to Rome tonight!" Mylena had been intimate with Mythical when he came to Jacksonville to do a show the previous fall. He'd put several hundred dollars in her pocket and asked her to keep him company, but she declined for the sake of her children.

Dancing circles around the room and full of excitement, Mylena rummaged through her clothes for something to wear. She then grabbed the phone to ask her aunt Sharon to babysit her sons. Mylena was so hyped that Falicia decided not to tell her the truth and would face the consequences once she found out otherwise.

CHAPTER 7

The moment LA pulled into the Quality Inn and Suites, Falicia knew the 'big' production for featured Atlanta dancers was more talk than show! LA didn't mind that Mylena was tagging along. When they stopped for gas, Falicia didn't waste a second pulling him aside and informing him, "Mylena doesn't know the real reason we're going to Rome."

"Don't worry. I got her," LA said, confidently. What he didn't understand was, Mylena was one stubborn individual and was as sharp as a whistle.

Once they stepped inside the hotel, Falicia stepped on a piss-poor excuse for a flyer advertising Atlanta dancers printed on regular computer paper. She picked it up. *Is this nigga serious! I knew all his big talk would amount to something so wack.* LA led them past the local artists and to the end of the hall, beaming from ear to ear. Falicia glanced at the other dancers to see if anyone was as disappointed as she was. Ms. LA turned red and couldn't help but roll her eyes.

Mylena looked confused. "Who is that in there performing? You think Mythical has performed yet?" Falicia shot her an irritated mug. "What is it?" she questioned, damn near walking on Falicia's heels all the way to the door. "Don't tell me Mythical won't be here."

Falicia headed inside the suite, checking out the decent sofa, coffee table, and flat screen on the wall. The kitchenette had a small stove and refrigerator with steel pots and pans. The rest of the décor, although there was no patio, hot tub, or refrigerator full of wine, was acceptable. She sat on the bed and took a deep breath because she knew Mylena was getting ready to drill her.

"Falicia, what is going on?" she asked.

"Just chill, Mylena. You wanted to come so bad. And now, you're here."

Sereniti Hall

She put one hand on her hip and stood back on one leg. "No, little girl." She knew Falicia hated when she did that.

Falicia hopped up and grabbed the outfit she planned to wear out of her John Casablanca modeling bag.

"You're going to tell me why we're here!" She scanned the room, observing the rest of the dancers pulling out costumes and undressing.

LA walked into the room without a knock. "I'll be right back. I'm about to go holla at Buddy and make sure he let everyone know about the door fee." Everyone in the room acknowledged him in some way, whether it was an "okay" or a head nod. He turned and exited the room.

Mylena whipped back around to Falicia as if she was trying to get whiplash. "A door fee for what, Falicia?"

"For the after party!" she snapped, no longer hiding her irritation.

"So you wearing that?" Mylena pointed at the pink and black outfit Falicia placed in her bag.

"Actually, I was hoping I could wear it," Ms. LA chimed in and picked it up. "This is cute. May I?" She started emptying Falicia's bag. "Let's see, what else is in here? How about this dress?" She held up a cream suede halter dress with black sheer patches and torso high splits on both sides. "You could wear this with a black thong."

"Yeah, I think I like that one better," Falicia stated, liking the idea that she'd be covered up more. She turned to Mylena, removing her shoes. "There's some local artists performing as we speak. When their concert is over, we're having an after party here. We're dancing for them."

"Falicia!" Mylena was in such shock that she held her face. "Like taking off your clothes dancing?"

"Yeah, but *we're* not taking our clothes off." Although Falicia thought her reaction was funny, she didn't laugh.

A Treacherous Hustle

Mylena flopped down on the bed in disbelief. Falicia continued to get undressed. When she finally recovered from the shock, she looked at Falicia.

"But you're my baby sister, my little sister . . . how did you manage to get involved in this?"

Not here. Not right now. Falicia headed inside the bathroom area to shower and change into the dress she would be entertaining in. LA had returned by the time she came out and was trying to coach her sister. When the guests began to arrive, Falicia sprayed on a body spray and tried not to be nervous.

Mylena grabbed her arm. "You're not scared?" she asked.

"Just a little nervous, but Ms. LA said once I start dancing, it will go away."

The music began to play. Falicia took a deep breath and opened the bathroom door to a room packed with men sitting and standing all over the place. The instant several of them saw her, they yelled and cheered for her to come dance for them. Some were obviously intoxicated, and a few were chill, but overall these were some thirsty, overly-excited men.

She approached a man in a business suit who had his money in his hand, ready to be generous. Falicia was hesitant, but when he made it rain she closed her eyes, placed her hands on her knees and made her butt bounce. She let the man smack it and stood on the sofa with him between her legs, grinding her vagina in his face. She had no indication that she was a beautiful queen, priceless, and worth far more than gold. The prize a man sought his whole life to find! That her body was a temple created to house the spirit of God. How could she know all these things? All she could identify with was that she was sexy and beautiful for a dark-skinned girl; legs made for modeling, well-proportioned. A great fuck.

Determined to live up to whom she knew how to be, Falicia pranced around the room and encouraged her big sister to stop peeking in the doorway and join her in the degradation. Within an hour, she had so much money she couldn't keep up with it all, so she handed it to LA to hold for her.

Mylena, who had disappeared into the sleeping area with LA, emerged in a black mink vest and a black thong, looking nervous enough to pass out. Bids came in quick for her to dance. The entire room encouraged her to push past her fear. She barely opened her legs and rolled her waist before the men went wild. What she lacked in curves she made up for with her beautiful face and hair like her Caucasian mother. Mylena's high-yellow skin tone snatched the attention of men anywhere she went.

"I got a hundred for every woman that gets naked!" one man shouted.

"Me too!" another said. Several others chimed in.

Ms. LA's expression beamed as if they had hit the jackpot. She was ready! Mylena ran for her dear life. Falicia hurried behind her. With the degree of fear she displayed, she knew there was no convincing Mylena to come back out. LA even tried, but quickly recognized that she was done.

Falicia, on the other hand, had been naked amongst her peeps before and was personally impressed with her body. She collected her hundreds of dollars from the men alongside the other dancers and removed everything, only dancing to one song. When it was over, she eased out of the room, leaving Red and Ms. LA to get ready to put on a female-on-female show. She entered the room where Mylena sat down, still half dressed.

"Put your clothes on," Falicia said, opening her bag and putting her money in it along with the dress she had on top of it. Falicia dressed quickly.

"Why are you rushing?" Mylena asked as she began dressing quickly also.

"I just want to get dressed before anybody else asks me to dance."

"I still can't believe you were up there, shaking your ass like that," Mylena said. "So how much money did you make? I think I made about $300."

"I don't know. I'll count it later when we get back home."

LA hurried in and stood next to Falicia. "It's a man over there asking for you," he said.

"No thanks. I'm done for today." Falicia declined.

"Did you hear me? He said he would pay you to spend some time in private."

She shot him a look like: *how dare you.* "I said no thank you." He opened his mouth as if to say something else. Instead, he walked away.

"LA," Falicia called. "Can I get that?"

"I got you! Let me go handle this business first."

Ms. LA opened the door, wearing only her heels. "I need the room, so can y'all get out?"

"Eww . . . Ms. LA, this is where we gotta sleep!" Falicia complained.

"Don't worry. I'll do it on my bed."

"All right. Give us a minute." Falicia put her money in her pocket and threw her bag in the closet. She and Mylena went into the front room and sat on the sofa. Only a few guys were still hanging around, probably waiting to have sex.

Mylena rejected a few offers, and a few minutes later, Ms. LA came and got one of the men who was still lingering and took him into the room. Falicia and Mylena fell asleep on the sofa.

The following morning, Falicia was the first to wake up. She had little to say on the ride back to Atlanta. Not only had LA not made an effort to give her the money she handed him; she busted him more than once eyeballing Mylena the same way that he stared at her. She wasn't surprised. All he had done was make her question his intentions. Falicia asked him to drop her and Mylena off in front of Ms. Sharon's house so they could pick up the boys. They could walk the two blocks back home without a problem.

Sereniti Hall

She waited for LA to ask her how much money she made. He didn't ask. Falicia exited the car, wished them farewell, and didn't look back. Mylena shook her head. "He knew better than to ask you how much you made. Especially with your money in his pocket."

Falicia's thoughts flashed back to the day she was riding him in their living room. She smirked. "I knew he was weak when I fucked him."

Mylena gasped. Falicia focused straight ahead as she rang Ms. Sharon's bell with a fifty in her hand. She already knew Ms. Sharon probably wasn't happy that they were some hours late picking up the boys. "And there ain't no room for a weak ass nigga in my life," Falicia added.

LA was added to the list of men who pretended to be stronger than he was, as if he truly lived by the code, when he clearly contradicted his own words. That night, Falicia did her laundry and cleaned her room, preparing herself mentally for Burning Sands. She kept to herself as much as she could and had to shoo Mylena's boys out of her room to the point of locking her door. LA called. She hung up in his face after he said, "I'll be there by nine."

Mylena knocked on her door. Falicia ignored her. She knocked persistently. Falicia snatched open the door just enough to talk. Mylena worked her neck from side to side, trying to see inside her room. "You going somewhere?" she asked. Falicia let her in. She wasn't going to leave anyway.

"Yeah." Falicia nodded.

Like a kid happy with getting her way, Mylena rushed inside. "So how much money did you make last night?" Falicia smiled. The night had its benefits.

"Like over four hundred dollars?" she guessed.

Mylena gasped. "What the fuck! Are you serious?" They squealed like two little girls excited about their first kiss. She stopped and stared at Falicia. "Did LA ever give you the rest of your money? He probably tryna keep it."

Falicia waved it off. "It's all good. I got his ass! He'll pay for it. Believe that."

"What are you going to do?" she asked.

"He needs to learn who's pimping who."

Mylena shook her head. "Falicia, I want you to be careful. This is a whole different world." Falicia laced up her Reebok Classics. "So where are you going tonight?"

An overly exaggerated sigh left Falicia's mouth, like she did when she was tired of answering her questions.

"I have to ask with you?" she added, "whether you want me to ask you or not. So don't make me have to beat your ass," she joked, "to find out."

Falicia rolled her eyes with a smirk. Mylena wasn't crazy. And once again, she wasn't going to leave it alone. "I'm going to this sports bar called Burning Sands," Falicia replied.

"I can't believe I'm about to do this shit!" Mylena insisted as they followed LA and Mr. Sanders, the owner, to the back of the bar.

"And I get paid, right? For every dancer that gets paid to dance in here tonight, right?" Mr. Sanders asked, inquiring about his bar fee for allowing the girls to dance there. "Everybody dancing gotta give me a cut, right?"

Falicia eased between him and LA, tired of them going back and forth and sensing LA might've played Mr. Sanders in some kind of way and was still trying to run game. More than once he asked LA if he was sure she was old enough to be in the bar. Falicia understood Burning Sands was his life, and the bouncers at the door couldn't care less. Nevertheless, she was there to make money.

She pressed her firm breasts against his arm. He froze. She stared up at him, her smile seductive. His eyes bucked. He really did look like a deer caught in headlights.

"Right," she said. He cut his eyes at LA, still petrified. She rubbed her thigh against his leg.

Mr. Sanders led them to the back of his sports bar and flicked on the switch. Broken barstools and tables were everywhere. The mirrors on the wall were all cracked, and most of the Christmas lights hanging sloppily all over were burned out. Falicia and Mylena made a stank face at the same time. They took their time coming inside the room, air thick with stale liquor and cigarette smoke and dust.

Wasting no time, Falicia got dressed in the outfit she wore the previous night. She was strapping her last shoe when a side door opened. Falicia jumped. She hadn't noticed it. Three girls in fur coats and six-inch heels walked in carrying designer bags that definitely weren't knock-offs. Falicia could tell the real deal from a distance. Certain that her day to rock authentic labels was coming, she touched up her lip gloss and checked her teeth. A slap on her butt made her jump once again.

"What's up, New Booty?" a woman asked, exactly like the character Ronnie in *The Player's Club*. The smiling, brown-skinned woman was pretty and cocky, also like the woman in the movie. Before Falicia had the chance to respond, Mylena was in her face.

"Bitch, don't be putting your hands on my little sister!" Everybody froze, including the female who slapped Falicia's butt.

"Calm down, ma!" the woman responded.

"'Ho! Stay in your place, and I won't have to put you there!" Mylena retorted with venom.

The woman met her gaze head on, unmoved by Mylena's threat. Falicia started unstrapping her shoes. She knew Mylena was a hothead and would throw down in a heartbeat. Ms. LA stepped between Mylena and the woman about to get a beat down.

"Sis, just chill," Falicia said.

"Hell naw! Fuck her. She don't know who she fuckin' with!" Mylena spat, unwilling to let it go.

A Treacherous Hustle

Ms. LA and Falicia calmed the situation down, but Mylena was hot.

When the following weekend arrived, Falicia made Mylena swear to watch her temper, or she could no longer go out with her. With quite a lot of practice under her belt, Falicia now knew the different types of table dances. One type was when the customer didn't want physical contact. They just wanted to enjoy the presence of a woman in front of them. Then there was the kind of table dance where the guy was into the dancer and only wanted to be teased. Only a little physical contact here and there could be initiated. A sneak peek of pussy would keep him spending. The final type was the type Falicia liked the least. A full-on lap dance was the dance perverts couldn't get enough of. The dancer rode the customer's crotch the entire dance, to the point of ejaculation for some. Normally this type wore sweat pants. The thin material allowed him to receive the most sensation with the least amount of interference when he soaked his pants. This type of guy tried to sneak out the door and hide the wet spot on the front of his pants, as if nobody noticed his body jerking from pleasure. She detested these type of customers the most. She didn't *ever* want to be that desperate. Ms. LA would ride a dick until the man screamed for his mama. For Falicia, watching him empty his wallet of his rent and child support was just sad.

Late one Saturday night while she danced, LA eyed Falicia with an anxious smile. Prior to, he acted as if he was afraid to glance at her. He sat at a table with champagne bottles on ice and fat cigars with an old man dressed to what he must have thought was the nines. LA met Falicia coming off the stage.

"Somebody wants to meet you," he said. Falicia cut her eyes at the old fart he was sitting with.

"No thank you."

LA's face fell. Falicia had danced the dude's way earlier and he declined a dance and shooed her away. She dropped her booty in front of him, showing him what he missed, then danced for the next man. He could barely eat his steak for looking at the way she worked her ass. His thirsty eyes followed her to the bathroom and didn't blink until the door slammed in his face.

Falicia headed inside to freshen up. His old ass shouldn't be in a booty club if he didn't want women approaching him while they were on their grind. Everybody was trying to eat. Some just wanted the finest things life had to offer.

"Girl, do you know who you just dissed?" a dancer named Carmel asked. "Girl, that's Sir Carter!" Carmel stared at Falicia as though she was supposed to be enlightened. "*The* Sir Carter! He's one of the most respected pimps in the south!"

"Don't know and don't care," Falicia said.

"Girl, that man is as cold as they come. He has a bottom bitch named . . ." She perked up and proceeded to school Falicia on his history. Did she think Falicia would be impressed that Sir Carter had been in the game for at least twenty years and had no love for women? He was solely about his money, but so was she.

Falicia remembered seeing his bottom 'B,' an older, heavyset chick, not much to the eyes, but she was known for keeping his pockets lined. Just before closing, she collected her money from an older guy she had just danced for. LA and Sir Carter stood near the pool tables.

LA took her arm when she passed and held it firmly. "This gentleman was personally asking for you."

A young dude playing pool grinned at Falicia. She held up a finger, asking him to wait. She cut her eyes at Sir Carter. He mean-mugged her with his chest out.

"Is there a reason why you're looking at me?" she asked.

"Fantasy!" LA called Falicia by her stage name.

She spun in LA's direction. His eyes dared her. "You one disrespectful bitch," he spat with venom. She rolled her eyes at LA and turned her attention back to Sir Carter.

A Treacherous Hustle

"I don't understand how you figure I'm disrespectful when—"

"I should slap this lil bitch!" Sir Carter addressed LA. "Standing there looking me in my eyes." Falicia stepped back. "Bitch! Look at my *feet* when you're in my presence." He glared at her, his stare demanding Falicia pay him homage.

"LA, is this man serious? You must have failed to inform him that I'm not one of your 'hos." She shook her head, trying not to laugh. "And only the weak look away when they're talking to someone. Or maybe special needs people."

Mylena was at her side in no time. "Now, if the nigga don't want me to say shit to him, that's cool," she said to LA. "But I promise you I won't be looking at his feet, or your feet for that matter."

"LA, check this 'ho before I do," Sir Carter ordered.

The ice Falicia saw in LA's eyes told her he wouldn't think twice about slapping the shit out of her. "Jewel, take your sister somewhere! Get her from over here!" LA advised Mylena.

Falicia was already walking away. She demanded her respect and didn't give a damn how many names Sir Carter yelled behind her. As they headed home, LA went on and on about how it was unacceptable for a pimp to be looked directly in the eyes, and when a 'ho stepped out of line, her pimp must reconcile the situation. Sometimes even with money, on the strength of principle!

Although Falicia let him talk, but she highlighted one major fact once he finished: "I'm not one of your 'hos, LA. And you're not my pimp."

Ms. LA shot her a look that would have taken her life if possible. Falicia got out of the car, trailed by Mylena. LA opened the trunk and waited for her to get her bag. "Fantasy, how much did you make tonight?"

Falicia cut her eyes at Mylena. "I don't know? I haven't counted it yet."

"That's fine. But I'm gonna need you to hand me that."

She looked around the neighborhood to make sure he was

talking to her. They locked eyes. There was no trace of the intensity she had seen in his eyes. Or the passion.

"Well, I suppose we'll need to talk about that."

"Falicia, my 'hos are mad as hell that I'm wasting all this gas to carry you back and forth. Missing money fucking with you," he said under his breath.

"Just say what you need to say so you can go about your business."

"Falicia—"

"Daddy, can you hurry up!" Ms. LA opened the car door and got out. Falicia took her bag out the trunk and let it drop at her feet.

"So what you saying is . . . you won't be able to take me to and from work anymore?"

LA turned his gaze away.

"It's a shame . . . you can't even say it!" she spat.

"I-I-I'm saying . . ." he stuttered. "I'm saying this is it. I'm cutting all ties with you from this day forward." He glanced at Ms. LA.

"Thank you for manning up and finally saying what your bitch told you to."

"Falicia . . ." he said with his chest out. "It's because you won't break bread."

"It's cool. You ain't gotta justify yourself. Thank you for all the opportunities you did present to me though. I wish you all the best." She turned on her heels and walked away, wondering how she would get to work.

Ms. Sharon's neighbor, Mr. Fredrick, was at his door on his regular neighborhood watch. Falicia smiled. *What's a man his age doing up at two in the morning? And what is he looking for?* she wondered as she nodded. He did the same. Whatever the reason, Falicia planned to ask next time.

After missing another weekend at Burning Sands, Letty's attitude hadn't changed about Mylena pulling her weight. Falicia was even unhappier. Her pockets were low. She hadn't told Letty she quit Taco Bell, and Letty never questioned otherwise. She did, however, ask Falicia, "Why are you going to work this late at night dressed in civilian clothes and not your work uniform?"

Where there's a will, Falicia made a way. She got the bright idea to ask Mr. Fredrick to drop her and Mylena off at Burning Sands. Ms. Sharon, the usual babysitter, had plans. So Mr. Fredrick volunteered to watch the boys in exchange that they fill his gas tank.

Once they entered the club, Mr. Sanders pulled Falicia and Mylena to the side. "Fantasy, Fantasy, Fantasy," the brown-skinned, nearly six-foot-tall man in his late forties said as he shook his head. For the first time since meeting him, Falicia admired his navy-blue linen pants and cream button-down shirt. The cream and navy snake skin shoes added class to his low profile. Even amongst a club full of men with several scents, his cologne smelled the best.

"Why are you shaking your head?" she flirted, with her hand on her hip.

"I don't know what you have done, but LA don't want me to let you work here anymore."

"Or haven't done to him!" she retorted. He laughed. "I'm not stuttin' LA and neither should you. You know me and my sister bring you good money." Mylena and Falicia circled him and stole a hug.

"So what you saying is them dances you'll be giving is a main attraction in my establishment?" he asked, looking down at Falicia, resting her head against his chest.

"That's exactly what I'm saying. If you don't believe me, I can show you." She stood in front of him, letting her booty roll over his leg. He flashed a beautiful white smile. Falicia strutted away, knowing Mr. Sanders was checking her out. Older men had a thing for her as long as she could remember, and that was starting to work to her advantage. After slipping into a two-piece turquoise and white Nautica halter top and boy shorts, she sprayed on body spray and let the long braid Mylena put in her hair hang. With baby oil glistening on her tight body, she targeted her mission. He leaned against the bar with some regulars she had seen before.

Falicia approached Mr. Sanders, pressing her breasts against him, slowly rolling her body against him. His company was stunned. They stared. Mouths hanging open when she lifted his head, so he could make eye contact with her. She bit her lip, closed her eyes, and grinded against him. Head against his chest. The rhythm of her butt cheeks stroked his penis. He grabbed her waist, forgetting he was in the presence of his patrons. His erection got so hard she thought it would burst the seams of both their clothes.

She sped up the tempo, caressed his body wherever her hands could go. Keeping a steady motion, she dared to see how far he would go. His leg jerked. He grabbed her waist with both hands, then pushed her away, just enough to break contact but not so much that someone could see his erection.

"Girl, you is dangerous!" he whispered in her ear, as his hand stroked down to her hip. "You about to make me cream my pants!" They laughed as he swiped his brow. "You made your point. Now go over there somewhere." He pointed to the seating area. "I can't handle that shit."

LA couldn't either, she thought, knowing she was capable of getting money without him. Sadly, she said good-bye to the relationship with LA, but she could feel something much better was nearing her fingertips.

CHAPTER 8

Making money at Burning Sands became an addiction. So much so, that Mylena and Falicia began working weeknights too. Falicia was just finishing up a performance at Burning Sands. The club was slow for a Tuesday night. She found herself walking back and forth looking for customers for a lap dance. Even this was too much for her own liking. A brown-skinned brother with dreads stole her attention. She'd noticed him before. Always dressed nice—Gucci sweater, jeans, and boots. Not too much jewelry and his dreads were always groomed.

Should I ask him for a dance? she thought, but approaching him was too intimidating. He was too perfect, and too fine! Keeping her eyes off him presented a real challenge, so from the other side of the room, she decided to keep him within her eyesight. His pearly-white teeth beckoned her closer as he conversed with another dancer. After a few minutes, they ended the conversation. He took a seat at the end of the bar. *Forget it! I just gotta ask him if he wants a dance.* After a few deep breaths, Falicia approached him. "Excuse me," she said as she politely tapped his arm. He turned toward her, holding a glass with dark liquor over ice.

"I don't mean to interrupt." She glanced at his drink.

"Nah, nah, it's cool. What's up?" Her stomach flipped at the sound of his voice. "You want one?" He held up his glass.

"No, thank you." *He has manners. I like that.* "You look like you could use some company."

"I would actually love it if you would," he replied, holding direct eye contact. He smiled and her insides melted like slow burning wax. She danced in front of him, fluid, soft and slow, doing her best to mesmerize him with her body.

He paid her for the dance, then grabbed her hand as she turned to leave. "Hey. Hold up." He pulled her closer. "Because your skin is dark and it's also dark in here, you should wear bright colors: yellow, orange, white, and light blue. Things like that will stand out and draw attention to you."

"Really?" she said, taken aback that he even cared.

"Yeah. I've been checking you out for a second now, and it's something I've observed about you. You'll get more dances that way."

"Well, thank you." Falicia wanted to sit down and find out what else he knew. *Where is he from? Why is he in Burning Sands of all places?* But everything had its season, and she needed to get on her grind.

His advice replayed in her head as she went back into the dressing room. She looked at the outfits the house mom had on display, along with the sexy heels, and other feminine hygiene products.

"I'll take that two-piece outfit right there," Falicia said, touching the sparkly fluorescent green tube top and bottoms that tied on both sides. She changed her outfit quickly. The black lights made her glow in the dark, bringing in more dollars than she had ever made on a week night. She scanned the bar for the guy to thank him for the advice. He was gone.

Falicia purchased more outfits in bright colors and it was paying off, but there were still no signs of the guy. Her desire to talk to him intensified. She thought too hard about him daily and tried not to grin like a fool whenever she was collecting her money, thinking of how his simple advice had turned things around in her favor. Her final customer for the night had just placed money in her hand. No sooner than she thanked him and turned to make her exit, there he was. Sitting at a table as if waiting for her. Falicia smiled and joined him. The two began conversing. She learned that Cash was from Miami and had a six-year-old daughter. After talking awhile about his background, he tossed an odd question at her.

"Have you ever thought about stripping?" he asked.

"Strip? As in take off all my clothes?" she responded.

"Yeah!" he commented. "You'd make a killing because you're sexy as fuck. Plus, you're a hustler. And you know how to handle these suckers." He looked around the room to specify whom he was talking about.

"I don't know about all that." Her trip to Rome, Georgia was a nightmare that she didn't want to relive. "I don't know if I can stand being in front of a bunch of strangers naked."

"Falicia, get the fuck outta here!" He look genuinely surprised by her answer.

Chills shot up her arm. *Did you just say my name?* She ordered food that Cash insisted on putting on his tab.

"Thank you. So, how old do you have to be to work in one of the adult strip clubs?" she asked.

"Eighteen," he responded with a smirk.

"That will pose a big problem for me," Falicia said as she looked him straight in the eyes. She needed to know how that made him feel. As she waited for his response, she hoped her truth hadn't fallen on the wrong ears. Her current working environment required all dancers to be at least twenty-one years old. He didn't speak right away, and the silence was beginning to drive her crazy. She wanted to get up and walk away, but knew he was sizing her up. *What's he thinking about? Good or bad, say whatever you gotta say. Damn!*

"For a small fee, I can make that problem disappear," Cash finally spoke.

Just as Cash promised, Falicia had a new birth certificate and a social security card. She was now twenty-one-year-old Falicia Blakely. When he took her to City Hall, Falicia was scared shitless to obtain her permit to dance as Fantasia since there was already a Fantasia registered at the club. One notarized letter later, Falicia

Blakeley was also a Georgia resident. She and Mylena were hired on the spot at Dancers Elite.

Their first Friday night at Dancers Elite was on Super Bowl XXXIV weekend, January 30, 2000. Falicia and Mylena had just left the townhouse holding their bags that contained their dance outfits. Cash stepped out of a nasty blue box Chevy, which was the second vehicle she saw him driving. The first one was a tricked-out Chevy Caprice. He placed her and Mylena's bag in the trunk and opened the rear passenger door. A dark-skinned female who sat in the front seat introduced herself.

"Hey, girl. What's up? My name is Chocolate Drop, and this is my sister Reeses." She pointed to a girl who looked Falicia's age, if not younger. "And this is Chyna," she said, referring to the quiet, pretty chick sitting by the door. Chyna acknowledged them, but then went back to staring out of the window, turning her body away from everyone.

"I'm Fantasia. This is my sister Mary Jane," she replied, trying to be polite to avert her attention from Cash, who was watching her through his rearview mirror as he headed toward the freeway.

Falicia only privileged him with a few seconds of gazing back. Thanks to LA, she already knew what this setup was all about. She didn't, however, see this one coming. Falicia and Mylena glanced at each other and limited their conversation during the ride. Cash exited I-285 on Moreland Avenue. After a few minutes of driving, he pulled into a parking spot at the entrance of a store front club that screamed "hole in the wall." The neon sign on the rooftop, visible from several blocks away read: Foxy Lady. All three girls exited the car and told Falicia and Mylena good-bye.

"I'll pick y'all up after they're done," Cash said to Chocolate Drop, who was last to get out of the car.

"Okay," she replied dryly, as if she had an attitude.

Falicia snuck a quick glance at her sister. Mylena lifted an eyebrow confirming she picked up on the exchange.

"Somebody wanna sit up here?" he asked. Cash's question fell on deaf ears.

Falicia grew concerned about this entire situation. She didn't want to look at Cash, much less sit beside him. Falicia's sentiments became clear to Mylena, who got out the back and sat in the front passenger seat.

The music Cash played was the only sound in the vehicle as he drove them to Dancers Elite. As soon as he pulled in front of the club, he popped the trunk and asked Falicia to stay behind.

"I'll get your bag," Mylena informed Falicia and got out before Falicia could reply.

"What's up?" Falicia asked, still sitting behind Cash as she heard the trunk close. She watched her sister walk inside the club.

He turned to face her and admitted, "Those are my girls."

"I already know that, Cash. You could have told me this when you told me all about your daughter, or before you helped me get that ID, or even my permit. Shit, you could have told me that before you dropped me off earlier today." She couldn't conceal her attitude.

"I suppose that's why you loaned me the $350, because you have plans of pimping me too! Is that what this is about, Cash?" Falicia's feelings were hurt. Somehow, she thought he would be different than the others.

"Falicia—"

"Just answer my damn question, Cash!" She didn't want to hear any excuses.

"I don't have any ill intentions for you, but I do feel you need some guidance." She gazed up at him like: *Really?* "What have I told you that hasn't benefited you?"

"I just wish that you were straight up about your choice of survival."

"Falicia, I'm not like the rest of these cats. I'm me, and I move to my own set of drums. I did this for you."

She burst out laughing. "Now you know you went a little too far with that last remark."

He laughed too. "Nah, for real though. My situation isn't like theirs. I don't need you to provide a roof over my head. So let's just get to work so you can focus on paying me back my $350.

During the first hour, Falicia stayed at his side, awed by the different women and skills they displayed with their body. She had to nurse a few shots of tequila to relax when Cash informed her it was against the law to make body contact with the customers. Therefore, grinding in their lap was not permitted. By the time she walked on stage, she was tipsy and grateful for it.

"New booty on duty!" the DJ announced as he put the Ying Yang Twins' song in rotation.

Focused, Falicia grabbed the pole, looked in the mirror, and paid no attention to the men who approached the stage. Cash was on her mind. He had been around long enough to come across some of the most impressive dancers. Falicia's goal was to show him that although she was an amateur, she could hang with the best of them.

As the second song ended, the audience encouraged her to take it off. Falicia looked at Cash, who had camped out in front of a computerized game next to the VIP room. He barely made eye contact with her, but she knew it was her cue to handle her business. Falicia let the tequila convince her that she was a star and had the power to captivate the mind of every man in the room. She rolled and slow wound her slender body, caressed her long legs and used her outfit to tease them. Men stormed up to the stage, begging her to come dance for them. Cash even flashed her a gorgeous smile. The next night she did even better.

Falicia wasn't sure what it was about him. Maybe it was their early morning conversations as he was dropping her off. Or the way he looked at her with pride whenever he saw her on her grind. It could have been how he made her feel beautiful when they were alone. Cash's constant presence during that first week made Falicia feel supported. So she didn't think much of it when he asked how much money she made and she told him. If he asked for it, she gave it to him. She loved his swag, his conversation, and the way he looked at her. Falicia loved his smell and how he never pressured her to do anything.

The first month was blissful, but then a random discussion messed up Falicia's understanding. She happened to be sitting in the car with one of Cash's other girls while he and Mylena dropped off her sons at his aunt's house.

"Me and Chocolate Drop stay in this nice townhouse that Cash set us up in. It's not too far from you," Reeses stated. "But then again he should, 'cause we give him every penny we make."

"Really?" Falicia absorbed as much information as she could.

"Yeah, girl. We had it out this afternoon, and I had to beat her ass. Cash is *our* nigga. Like she ain't know that. And this bitch wanna fight me 'cause he spent some time with me. Shit, I can't help it if I'm fuckin' him better than she is. Bitch better wake up and smell reality."

"Mmph!" Falicia said, not wanting to hear any more. She had just learned a valuable lesson from LA about 'hos and money, but was hoping that Cash was different.

"I give him every penny I make just like she do," Reeses added, breaking Falicia's thought. "Shit, I really don't see what the problem is." She shrugged. "The only reason he be with her so much is 'cause that bitch is crazy! Sometimes he gotta put hands on her stupid ass to keep her in check. You should see the holes she done punched in the walls. She do stupid shit like that to provoke him."

Falicia frowned. "I see."

"Girl, the only reason I ain't ran away is 'cause I'm in love with his fine ass. I don't know why, but I just am."

Cash and Mylena got into the car that was now filled with

silence. Falicia sat quietly throughout the duration of their ride, wondering how the man she believed she was falling for could be the very thing he was to her, to two other women. Maybe even four.

As Cash opened the door to let her out, she didn't say good-bye with her usual smile, nor did she confess that she would miss him. Her disappointment in him made her push the tears back that threatened to fall. She sped up, eager to get inside Dancers Elite and get the night over with.

"Falicia," Cash called.

She wanted to take another step, but her feet wouldn't let her. Mylena stopped in the door. Falicia wasn't trailing behind her.

"What's up, sis?" Mylena asked.

"Nothing. I'm coming," Falicia insisted. She didn't want her to see her upset about a man who apparently had more than her on his agenda. "You can go ahead."

"Baby girl, what's the matter?" Cash asked. "You just gone leave me like that? No bye, no nothing?"

She hadn't even heard him approaching. He lifted her chin with his finger so he could see her eyes.

"What happened from the time I picked you up till now? What's goin' on wit'chu'?"

She wrestled with admitting the problem, but she didn't want to throw Reeses under the bus. "I just got something on my mind."

"Can we discuss it later?" he asked. Falicia attempted to walk away. He reached out for her arm.

"Maybe . . . maybe later."

"Well, try to have a good night, okay? I'll be back."

Mylena met her coming into the dressing room. "Falicia, you know you don't need that nigga, right!" she barely whispered.

Falicia opened her locker. "Mylena, I don't want to have this conversation right now." Mylena propped her half naked body in front of Falicia's locker.

"Well, when do you want to have this conversation? When we

get home and you're on the phone with Cash?" She folded her arms across her chest. "Or in the car while you're giving him the goo-goo eyes! Or maybe while you're passing him *your* hard earned money! When, Falicia? When do you think we should have this conversation?"

Ready to put an end to their discussion, Falicia grabbed her gold and black two-piece halter outfit. Then grabbed lotion, body spray and heels and headed for the bathroom allotted for the dancers. Mylena locked her locker, and was hot on her trail. "Or should we talk about it while you're standing upstairs in his face grinning, after he's been sitting around trying to see how much money you making?"

"He does not do all that!" Falicia stopped mid-step on the stairs.

"Girl, please!" Mylena looked disgusted. "If that's not the case, then please tell me why in the hell is he always here! Nigga ain't got no job."

"He's here for my support!" she fired back. "He makes this environment more comfortable for me." Falicia rolled her eyes and finished mounting the stairs.

"Please! Tell that shit to someone who don't know you. It was your lil ass who convinced me to dance in front of all them strangers in Rome, Burning Sands, and even now! You ain't shy about your body. So . . . real shit, Falicia. This ain't you! You have always been the one, out of the two of us, to get a nigga to break bread. It's you who have these dudes paying for our hair, getting our nails done, and paying for our pictures and drinks at the club. Now, you giving this kat your money?"

Falicia watched her storm away, her thick rear jiggling from side to side. Mylena was right about everything. But there was something about Cash that made her question if her big sister really knew what she was talking about. *Am I like the rest of them?* Falicia wondered. *Is Cash really here to clock my money? Am I falling for a . . . A pimp!*

Sereniti Hall

"Fantasia, what are you doing?" Cash asked as he drove the girls home after they finished dancing for the evening. Falicia looked up from counting past her $350 mark. Reeses cut her eyes at her, then turned back to the window. He repeated his question. "What are you doing?"

"I'm counting my money." *How in the hell did he know?*

"For what?" His quick gaze held her to him. He flipped on his signal and headed up a residential street. Falicia didn't care what he said, or how cute he was, anything past $350 was going in her pocket.

"What do you mean? I want to know how much I made." They exchanged stares as he jetted across an intersection and pulled into a gas station.

"My name is Cash, baby. I know what it sounds like when someone is counting it. I know what it smells like and what it feels like." He opened the door and got out. Chocolate Drop followed. He headed inside the store to pay for the gas. Chocolate Drop grabbed the pump. Falicia used the opportunity to separate the $350 from the rest of her earnings.

"I need some cigarettes," Chocolate Drop yelled at his back.

"That ain't nothin' new," Reeses mumbled.

Falicia glanced to her left. The poor girl Chyna looked as if she'd rather be somewhere else. For some reason, Falicia kept feeling Mylena's eyes boring a hole into her face. She heard Chocolate Drop and Cash exchanging dialogue after they both re-entered the vehicle, but she was too busy counting money to really tune in. The car jerked them as it left the gas station in a rush.

"They're all gone! And I need some more. Shit!" Chocolate Drop said. "Is that too much to ask for?" Cash tilted his head. He seemed just as surprised as everyone else that she had just cursed at him.

"Well, that's yo' fault," he said.

"Well, it's just a pack of fucking cigarettes! Can you go back and get me some?"

"Who the fuck you talking to like that?" Cash asked, voice as calm as ever. He ran off the interstate and hit brakes. Falicia had never witnessed him so annoyed. She sat back and waited to see if she would be introduced to the Cash that Reeses told her about. Chocolate Drop stared ahead. "So now you don't hear me talking to you? I'll tell you what . . . disrespect me again, and I'll put your muthafuckin' ass out. And you better be home by the time I drop everybody off!"

Reeses leaned closer to Falicia and whispered, "He's done it before. And I wouldn't even care if he beat her stupid ass again."

The rest of the drive was quiet and within ten minutes, Cash had pulled into a subdivision filled with townhouses. Cash, Reeses, and Chocolate Drop, all got out.

"I'll be right back," Cash told Falicia and Mylena.

Falicia didn't need to be present to know Cash was in there beating Chocolate Drop's ass. Mylena said something, but Falicia's thoughts were more on Chyna, who seemed detached and spoke very little. From what she could gather, Chyna made a lot of money and had her own townhouse. *Why does she look so damn unhappy though?* Falicia wondered.

Cash finally returned to the car and dropped Chyna off next. The girl barely said good-bye once they pulled up to her place. Something was definitely up with her.

"Falicia, what is this?" Cash held the stack of money Falicia had just handed him in the air. They had just finished their shift at Dancers Elite and got into his vehicle.

"What do you mean?" She had been withholding some of her money all week, sticking to her 'anything past $350' rule. It was beginning to make little sense to her why she kept giving this nigga all her hard earned money. His other bitches relied totally on him to pay their bills, supply food, and purchase their weaves. Falicia still lived under her mother's roof. All Cash did for her was transport her and Mylena to and from work. Her life outside of Cash was totally different from the other girls. She went to school and was still her mother's little girl.

"I'm trying to figure out why you only made $370 on a Friday night. I know you had more than thirty dances, Falicia. You had twenty while I sat in there."

She glanced at Mylena, who sat up front with Cash. "So, Cash, what are you saying?" Falicia asked as she eased to the edge of her seat. "Are you telling me that you only come to the club to spy on me?" She and Mylena locked eyes.

"I'm telling you . . . This—" He held up the money Falicia gave him. "Ain't you!"

"Well, your other bitches also suck and fuck for money. And I don't do either."

"And I'm cool with that, but these dollars ain't adding up."

The disappointment in his eyes cut her. She had betrayed him by holding back on her earnings. "I need to go get my nail fixed." She extended her hand so he could see it was broken and so that he would change the subject.

"Falicia, you just got your nails done," he replied. She smiled. "What are you smiling about?" he asked.

"You! You are just so fine." They'd never had sex, but she felt that he touched her every time he stared at her.

"I'm not giving you any money to get your nails done again."

"It's only one nail, Cash."

"Your lil butt keep spending money on miscellaneous shit."

"You expect me to walk around like this?" She held up her hand. He chuckled, which she concluded meant yes. "Okay." She blew him a kiss on her way inside the house.

Falicia and Mylena got up earlier than usual the following morning. To their surprise, Letty agreed to watch Mylena's sons that afternoon. So they headed to their favorite nail salon.

A Treacherous Hustle

An hour into their mission, Falicia's nails were now perfect. The sisters then walked the short distance across the street to Greenbriar Mall and wasted no time hitting up the department stores. Several stores later, they were trying to decide if they should add to the shopping bags they were already carrying, or call it quits.

They decided to hit up Foot Locker and tried on various pairs of sneakers. Three steps out of the store with matching Nikes for Mylena's boys, she and Falicia spotted Cash on the opposite side of the mall with his homie. Falicia smiled at Cash and waved.

"Bitch, are you serious?" Mylena spat.

"C'mon." She pulled her sister over to him. Falicia's heart raced as his eyes danced over her hand that once held the broken nail, and then at the bags she held with both hands.

"What's up? You been shopping?"

Falicia looked over at her sister. "Well, Mylena wanted to . . ."

Cash stepped up to her and looked inside one of her bags. "What were you saying?" He stood so close she could smell the herbal product in his locks. "You got your nail fixed, right?"

"Yeah, it's fixed." She extended her hand.

"Call me before you go to sleep tonight." He nodded and walked away.

Her day of fun had just fizzled out. The surprising thing was, once Falicia called him, he never mentioned her treachery, or asked about the nail. But the following work day, Mylena riding with them to work was suddenly an issue. Cash claimed that riding out to his aunt's house for her to babysit Mylena's sons didn't benefit him. Pressure was building between him and Mylena. Falicia knew it would burst eventually.

CHAPTER 9

"But I always go!" Falicia complained. Cash had shot down the idea of her going to spring break in Daytona Beach with her girls because there was "money to be made." He didn't understand that they'd gone to Daytona during spring break for the past three years straight.

"Falicia. You heard what I said," Cash said.

She became silent. Mylena came in the room and flipped up her sundress, showing off her new yellow thong bikini set. Falicia threw her hand over her mouth to keep from laughing in Cash's ear.

"Get dressed," he said. "I'm on my way to get you." Cash was beginning to move Falicia in the wrong way. Whatever he said afterward got filtered out of her ears quickly.

That night he picked her up in a chameleon painted convertible and cruised to the townhouse he rented for Reeses and Chocolate Drop with the top down. He escorted her inside, explaining the empty place had two levels, three bedrooms, and two bathrooms. Falicia eyed a huge spot with the plaster caved in. *Reeses said her sister knocked holes in the wall. She didn't lie.*

"I need to get these fixed," Cash said. *And get some new carpet,* she thought, turning her nose up at the badly stained beige carpet.

"You need to repaint in here too," she added. "And they need some furniture. All that money they make, and they don't have nowhere to sleep or sit?"

Cash laughed. "Falicia, I moved them into a new apartment. This is for you, if you want it."

Immediately, Falicia ended her inspection of the townhouse. "Wh . . . What? But what about my sister? I don't know . . . I can't just—"

"Your sister is grown, baby!" He stepped closer, taking her hands into his. "I'm talking you and me." The gesture sent warm chills throughout her body.

Sereniti Hall

"Cash, I need some time to think about this." Letty already suspected that Cash was a pimp because he usually had a lot of females in his car. Falicia knew that announcing that she was moving in with a man who wasn't hers would set Letty off.

Mylena also argued with Falicia about the possibility of her moving. "He only wants complete control of your money and you for that matter!" Falicia wasn't denying that, but Mylena didn't realize she was doing the same thing by staying with her sons' father, Alexander. Even after he put his hands on her and refused to buy her anything. Mylena had to fend for herself, yet she endured the mistreatment Alexander dished out because she loved him and wanted to be loved.

Falicia, too, had a yearning to be loved! She hoped her internal and external beauty was enough to captivate Cash, even in the midst of him dealing with other women. Maybe it was a false hope, but it's what she was banking on. She wanted him to long for her presence so much that he would consider another lifestyle for her. That he'd discover that only her love and affection was what his life had been missing.

Could anyone blame her? What woman doesn't hope that she's that perfect one? That one who changes the game! What young girl being raised in poverty doesn't hope to be rescued from a life of struggling and misconceptions of love? The fact that he never pressured her for sex meant a lot. She took that as a sign of admiration and respect. The gesture penetrated her heart and made room for him. Cash had given her the very thing she wanted from her parents—admiration—but they came up short every time. They were both trapped and blinded by their own lives, which is why her mother Letty always misunderstood her daughter's behavior.

Falicia was naïve and insecure. But more vital than that, she failed to comprehend that nothing in the streets was free. Even Cash's admiration had a price tag attached, and it just might be more than she bargained for.

Although she had fallen hard for Cash, she wasn't willing to submit to his every command. She was young and still wanted to have fun, and sometimes she had to resort to trickery to maintain that part of herself. "What's up?" Cash asked in a sexy voice.

"I just called to let you know . . . I don't feel up to going to work tonight."

"What's wrong?"

"What's not? My stomach is doing a number on me. I keep going to the bathroom, and I've been throwing up."

Cash offered to bring her something, but she declined. Once they hung up, she felt free! Yet guilty.

For half of the day, she and Mylena hung out and had fun, talking, shopping, and eating. Feeling adventurous, they hit the tattoo shop. Falicia got her navel pierced, and Mylena settled on a tongue piercing. Overly dramatic and in so much pain, Mylena caused a huge scene that had Falicia laughing until she cried.

"I miss doing stuff like this with you," Mylena said, sounding tongue tied.

"Shut up!" Falicia said. "I don't know how you gone dance with a sore tongue."

"Watch," Mylena said clearly.

The club was just about to get into money-making mode. Falicia didn't have her bar fee up front because she had spent so much throughout the course of the day, but being that she and Mylena arrived so early in the afternoon, the fee was only thirty dollars. She went straight to the bar and put in an order for a double shot of tequila. Her drink arrived in a shot glass outlined with salt and a lime wedge. She craved that taste in her mouth. One gulp, and she was ready to put on a show.

Falicia looked over at the mirror behind the stage. *Damn, I'm glowing.* Her neon green outfit glowed beneath the black light, shoes and all! Quickly she peeped out the room. She had definitely snatched the attention of a few men, which meant she could be seen from any angle. The thought excited her, but it also made her a little paranoid. All the money she was about to make was the thrilling part. However, the idea of Cash slipping in while she was making all the money, brought on the paranoia. He could have slipped in while she was downstairs and ducked off in one of those corners.

"You enjoying yourself?" Falicia set her focus on her first potential customer.

"As a matter of fact I am. This is my first time here," the guy said.

I know that, she thought. *I'm here every day.* "Are you serious?" is what she actually said.

"Yeah! I am." He grinned.

"What is that you're drinking?" she inquired.

"Oh, this . . ." He held up his drink. "This is just a little Crown Royal on the rocks—well ice." He grinned even harder.

"Do you mind if I buy you another drink?" she asked as she slid into the chair next to him. Judging by his expression, he was confused.

"Pardon me?" *He must have thought he didn't hear me correctly,* Falicia thought.

"Drink." She pointed to his glass. "Would you like for me to buy you another one?" He gazed at her in amazement. *Got him!* She chuckled to herself.

Most dudes came to the club with the impression that dancers only wanted their money. And for the most part they were right. So when the dancer switched it up on a man with role reversal, the man would feel more comfortable engaging in his fantasy, that yes, it was quite possible a beautiful woman was really interested in him!

"Well . . ." He was trying to gather his words. "Actually, I would like another drink, but I would prefer to buy us one."

Sucka, she thought.

"I don't know. It's a little early . . . I don't want to get too wasted and you end up taking advantage of me." With one finger, Falicia poked him directly in the small area that showed his exposed chest. He flinched a little, and then began looking for the waitress.

"I think it's only fair we enjoy one together," he said. Falicia smiled at his efforts to get her to drink. More than likely, he'd want to know what she would do when she got drunk. Minutes later, the waitress brought their drinks and Falicia downed hers. Shortly after, she was on her feet dancing, hoping to take him into the VIP room. Falicia danced her way into the third song, which happened to be slow. Plus, she had just gotten completely naked.

"Would you like me to stop?" she asked while standing in front of him. He immediately nodded no.

As the song's lyrics played, she turned and looked intensely into his eyes and wound her body slowly. She allowed her fingers to glide over her private parts, adjusting her expression as if he was the one touching her. She let the sensual lyrics leave an impression on his mind. Taking a step closer, she raised her right leg and used her knee to gently massage his manhood. His lips made contact with her stomach. Teasing him, she pulled back and rolled her lower body while still hypnotizing him with her gaze. She brushed her breasts against his face. His excitement for her intensified; it oozed from him like pheromones. Falicia returned to a full stance and turned around. Looking back, she gently made her ass cheeks clap. Seductively, she rolled her ass in his face as she bent over trying to touch her toes. Her fingers grazed over her vagina, and then she rested her behind in his lap. For a few seconds she ground her backside against him, and then raised up. With her backside close enough to his face so that he could smell her, Falicia flexed her muscles and made her vagina breathe.

The ability to take over one's mind under such circumstances was exhilarating. She turned back to face him. His half-open mouth told her that she had him at her disposal. The look into his enchanted eyes aroused her. She stepped around his right leg and moved down as if she would straddle it. His hands rested on his thighs where he had maintained them throughout the entire time. Briefly, she squatted down and allowed her wetness to slick his hand, before stepping away. His eyes rushed to inspect his hand. His fingers glistened with her wetness. She proceeded to give him a lap dance, occasionally resting her head against his body, taking his hand and making him touch her stomach. By the time the song ended, he had two questions: "Had he gotten her wet like that?" and "What was the procedure to obtain the VIP room?"

This night seemed to fall in her favor. By midnight she had already landed two VIP sessions, both $200 upfront. Also, Cash hadn't shown up and made her out to be a liar. Nothing out of the ordinary had transpired except William, a frequent patron, kept requesting her to dance for him. Normally he would get one or two dances from her, and that's it. She really didn't care to deal with William too much. Something about him was sneaky and maybe even treacherous. Absolutely messy, for sure. He loved talking about one dancer to another one. But what was so weird about the night was that he paid so much attention to Falicia, when he usually preferred light-skinned bitches.

William did a lot of talking, even as a dancer performed. Normally, Falicia would just smile and nod to his chatter, but for whatever reason she was actually listening tonight. Maybe the bottle of Moet she had in the VIP room got her a little too tipsy and clouded her judgment. For hours this man had been trying to convince her to trick off with him. By then, Falicia was officially drunk and horny.

"Fantasia, come here!" He reached out for her after she finished conducting business with some dude that sat at a table next to him.

"What, William?" She knew what he wanted, but she just thought it best to play dumb.

"You thought about what I said?" He tried to pull her into his lap.

"William, stop. How many times do I have to tell you that I don't want to sit in your lap?"

"Okay, okay." He held his hands up, as if surrendering. "Let's talk about you meeting me outside in the parking lot so I can do that pussy some good."

"I told you I don't trick off."

"Who said it's tricking off? I just want to give you a couple hundred dollars because I support the cause. I do it all the time! I know you been in here working hard to survive."

"I don't know about that. I don't have sex with strangers."

"Strangers? Girl, I ain't no stranger! I been coming here for months! Think about it. How long we been doing this?" He pulled up a chair and gestured for her to sit down. As soon as she did, she regretted it. William leaned in closer. "Listen here . . ." He pulled out his wallet and peeled through a bunch of hundred dollar bills. "Here go $300 right here. You can take this and go get dressed, then meet me outside and I'll give you a hundred and fifty more. I'm just trying to enjoy myself and show you a good time at the same time."

Falicia looked around the room. Her sister Mylena was focused on the dance she was giving a customer. No one else was paying Falicia any attention. *If I do this, it would put me at a couple hundred shy of a thousand dollars. I have never taken that much money home before and it will be all mine,* she reasoned. *But can dude be trusted? He did say he does this all the time, but what if he tells somebody? How in the hell am I going to get out of this club without someone knowing what's up?*

William placed the money in her hand and stood up to leave.

"Wait!" she called after him, but he ignored her and kept walking. Discreetly, she stood up and headed toward the front door. It was no use yelling. She wouldn't be heard over the music.

William was seconds away from leaving out the first door that led to the tiny space between the security door and exit door. "Get him!" Falicia called out to the bouncer.

"What?" he yelled back.

"Get him!" Falicia pointed at William as she stood at the door, knowing she couldn't go any further in her costume. The guard turned to see who she was talking about as three dudes were entering.

"William!" she yelled out, making one final attempt.

"What's the matter? He didn't pay you?" The bouncer looked at her hands and noticed the money balled up in her fist. "He left without getting his change?" he inquired, looking at her instead of going after him.

"Naw . . . neither. I'm cool," she responded as she gave up the chase.

"Yo, lil mama, that's your man?" one of the three men inquired.

"You funny." She did her best to smile as she acknowledged them. "But as cute as you are, you should be." Falicia turned and walked straight to the dressing room at a normal pace. A few dancers were in and out changing costumes, or counting their money after getting off stage. Falicia opened her locker and just stood there. Trying to find the guts to put on her street clothes to go meet this man outside.

"Fantasia, you don't hear them calling for you?" The house mom interrupted her thoughts.

"Ma'am?" She wasn't sure how long she had been standing there.

"DJ Cali's calling you." She eyed Falicia suspiciously.

She locked her locker and ran upstairs with the money still in hand. *Maybe he came back to get his money.* She hoped.

"You called for me?" Falicia asked, almost running into the DJ booth.

"Yeah, you next on stage," he said.

"I'm not ready." She started to panic as she glanced around, thinking about Cash possibly being in the club. *All of this shit is blowing my mind. I don't even feel my buzz anymore.*

"Well, get ready. You got one song before your set." He set his focus back on his tracks. Falicia didn't waste time looking around. She ran back down the stairs, freshened up, and changed costumes. Then she threw all her money in the locker and ran back upstairs. The DJ was introducing her as she walked up. The first thing she did was scan the room. When she didn't see Cash, she let the Ying Yang Twins take over her body and began twerking something.

By the end of the set, she had a few guys waiting for her to come dance for them, and William had walked back in the door. There was no longer room to question herself. Falicia headed straight to the dressing room to retrieve his money and give it back to him. Before doing so, she gave the bar a final glance. For some reason she felt as if she was being watched.

"It's Cash!" Falicia joked the moment her cell phone started ringing. She, Mylena, and the boys had just reached their front door.

"You ain't even looked at your phone. How you know?" Mylena replied. "Then again, it really might be his thirsty ass."

"It is Cash. For real!" Falicia said, shocked by the incoming number. She took her key out of her purse and handed it to Mylena.

"Don't answer! Don't answer!" Mylena urged.

A car door slammed. And so did Falicia's heart. Cash stood beside his convertible. Mylena and Falicia exchanged surprised gazes. Neither woman saw him pull up, or turn on their street.

Once Mylena opened the door, Falicia laid her nephew on the couch, then headed back out. *Shit!* "Mylena, I'll be back."

"Falicia," Mylena stated firmly. "Girl, forget him and just come on in the house."

Sereniti Hall

"No . . . I have to go talk to him." She hated to see the disappointment she knew would be in his eyes. A dead weight settled at the bottom of her stomach, but she wasn't afraid.

"Hey," she said with an anxious grin. *Damn . . . nigga was sitting outside waiting for me to come home. Damn!*

"You don't look sick to me," Cash stated, looking her over.

Falicia stared at the ground. "Cash." A knot formed in her throat. She swallowed. "I lied to you."

"I knew that."

"Then, why didn't you say something?" Her eyes finally met his.

"Because, I wanted to see just how far you would go." He leaned against his convertible. "Come here." Falicia stood in front of him, dying to lay her head on his chest and forget about everything.

His brow creased. "Is that a piercing?" She flinched as he reached out to touch her navel.

Falicia lowered her head, suddenly ashamed of her belly ring.

"It makes you look cheap," he said. "Had I known you back when, you never would've got that tattoo either." He remained calm and cool as usual. "And it could be this streetlight, but it looks like you got contacts in your eyes too." Annoyed, Cash laughed under his breath.

"I . . . I don't even know what to say." Her phone rang. She checked the display. It was Mylena. "Cash, hang on for a minute. I have to take . . ."

"Don't worry about it, Falicia. I'm done fighting your sister for you." He pointed at her phone. "I tried, baby. I tried to put you up in your own spot. I don't ask much of you, and I tried to look out for you and be honest about shit. But this . . ." He shook his head. "What I do understand is that I'm on one side and your sister is on the other and we both pulling you in two different directions."

"Cash . . ." She grabbed the door as he got in his convertible. "I'm sorry." She meant every word. "I love you," she confessed.

"Yeah," he replied, as more of a question than a statement. He flashed those beautiful pearly whites that grabbed her attention in the beginning.

"Do you have to leave, right this second?" She needed him to stay.

"Why? You don't wanna be with me."

"Now you know better than that. It's just that you don't understand that I still want to live my life." Hot tears wet her face. He wiped them away.

"You wanna spend the night with me?" he asked.

"You want me to?" she answered, even though it was a few hours short of dawn. Her cell phone began ringing the instant they pulled off.

"Mama, don't worry. I'll be back. Everything is all right."

Falicia ended the call, not sure if she was upset with Mylena for waking Letty up, or relieved that she cared so much. Cash took her to his spot in a quiet suburb with manicured lawns and two-car garages. After getting a tour of his immaculate place, they lay in his bed. Falicia fought off her excitement; she was finally about to know him in this way. They talked. Touched. Kissed.

As he was in the midst of thrusting himself inside her, Cash withdrew. Got up and took a shower without a word. Leaving Falicia bewildered. Did he want her to think about what she would be missing, or was the 'P' better than he expected?

Whatever the reason, she would never find out what Cash's pipe game was really like. Nor did either of them speak on the subject as she rode around with him while he took care of a few things. The closer he got to her house, the more choked up she became. He pulled into park and turned down the music.

"Baby girl, stop all that crying. I'll be around." He grabbed her hand and kissed her forehead. "You know you'll see me."

"I know." *I just hope I didn't make a mistake that I can't take back.*

CHAPTER 10

If I'm already enjoying the luxuries of life, then what is the purpose of school? Falicia asked herself once her new high school decided she'd have to repeat her freshman year. She had already assumed the profession of an exotic dancer and felt she was doing well without an education. Maybe she could just get her diploma online. All she needed was a computer. She walked into her second period math class wearing black silky capris, a silver satin button-down blouse with half sleeves. Her black, strapped-up six-inch spiked heels clicked across the floor as she took her usual seat. It was evident she didn't dress, talk, or carry herself like the other girls. Within seconds of the class beginning, Falicia placed her book on her teacher's desk and walked out the door. Ms. Young hurried behind her and stopped her in the hall. "Ms. Blakely, do you mind telling me why you're returning your math book?"

Out of all the teachers in Therell High, Ms. Young was the only one she could relate to and who seemed to understand her problem with the entire arrangement. Falicia shook her head, not wanting to have to wild out on this woman if she didn't get out of her face. Finally she explained her plan to Ms. Young about finishing school online.

As if challenging her, Ms. Young folded her arms beneath her breasts. "Does your mother approve of this?"

"Ms. Young, I don't understand why you out here drilling me, when you got a classroom . . ." Falicia exhaled dramatically.

"*While* I *have* a classroom," she corrected her. "You can finish."

"I'm done." Falicia looked at her.

"Ms. Blakely, I'm just going to be direct with you. What concerns me is that you were once very motivated, doing all of your assignments, coming to class, running track, getting outstanding grades, and then you just started missing school. Attending maybe, once or twice a week, and now you're withdrawing?"

Sereniti Hall

Yup. Ms. Blakely is shutting the hell down.

"Is there something going on at home that you want to discuss? I mean, you really don't carry yourself like other teenage girls. And I've noticed that you wear heels that I feel are only appropriate for a grown woman."

"I—keyword . . ." Ms. Young had struck a nerve. "I've been wearing heels since I was twelve, in modeling school in Florida. *And.* I was raised to believe that it's okay to be me. Now if you'll excuse me, I need to get to the dean's office."

"Falicia, listen." She reached out for her hand. "I'm not trying to judge you. I just want you to understand that it's a dangerous world out there, and some people can get the wrong impression of you, or assume you're older than you are. I just want you to be careful. You're a beautiful girl, and you can be whatever you want. Don't forget that. You have so much to offer this world, and you're smart. Just apply it." She took Falicia in her arms and hugged her.

Something about Ms. Young's tone burst through the fragile wall Falicia barricaded herself in. It served as protection from people's opinions that she never asked to hear, or the judgment, because they didn't understand her and her uniqueness. Falicia had gotten so used to people talking at her and not to her that she wasn't sure how to respond to Ms. Young. She did, however, recognize there was no reason to keep her nasty attitude and no reason to disregard everything Ms. Young was saying. Surprisingly, Falicia hugged her back. Quickly. But it was still a hug just the same.

Inside the dean's office, he tried to lay the guilt on even thicker because he had her mother Letty on speakerphone from the moment Falicia first arrived. "Well, Ms. Ford, I hate to inform you that there is nothing we can do. According to the law in the state of Georgia, a student can withdraw herself from school legally."

"Now that's a bunch of BS!" Letty was a tone or two from yelling. "I'll tell you what. I'm going to call the police on her ass!"

A Treacherous Hustle

"The police?" Falicia was on her feet before she knew it. The dean signaled her to hush. *I can't believe my mother. Why in the hell would she want to send me to jail?*

"Ms. Ford, it won't do you much good. She isn't breaking the law."

Falicia just could not believe the things she was hearing her mother say. She was already losing respect for Letty because she felt she was weak. It used to piss her off if she cried when they had arguments because Falicia did everything in her power not to let her mother see her tears. Tears were a weakness not meant to be viewed by the world. Some people preyed on the weakness of others. During most of her adolescent years, she felt she was in the jungle. She never knew what would appear next.

Therefore, she refused to stay and hear another word. It was urgent she go because despite how Falicia felt, Letty Ford was still her mother, the woman who chose to give her life rather than terminate it. If Letty could sacrifice nine months of her life to give Falicia the healthiest body she could, the least Falicia could give in return was her respect. It was obvious mother and daughter didn't understand each other. In Falicia's mind, Therell High School was a done deal. She had to get on her grind; school was very far from lining her pockets in any way, shape, or form. And with her attendance, having to redo ninth grade for a second time was straight up bullshit. She practically laughed in the dean's face as she made her exit.

By the end of the week, she was done with everything and everybody and spent most of her time in her room. Falicia walked into the kitchen and grabbed a glass of orange juice. She was halfway up the steps when Letty called her back downstairs.

"We need to talk." Letty said those four word Falicia hated most.

Falicia lagged behind Letty's broad rear and flopped beside her on the couch. It had been a long time since she'd taken a long look at her mother. One look into Letty's eyes, and Falicia's emotions sank deeper. The rims of Letty's eyes were red. She had been crying. Falicia closed her eyes and sighed.

"I just want you to know that the lease will be up in a couple weeks. And I'm sorry, but you have a choice to make, Falicia. You can either come with me and go back to school, or stay with Mylena, who's probably about to be out on the streets."

"But what about my nephews? What's going to become of them?"

Letty slammed her hand on the arm of the recliner. "That's not your concern, Falicia! They are not your children. Let their damn mother take care of them! If you get your narrow ass out of the picture, she'll get off her ass and handle her business. It's not your responsibility to get up and feed them breakfast, while her ass lays in the bed and sleep. Or always feeding them some damn noodles or a hot dog . . . them damn boys need a nutritious meal!"

"She needs help, Momma, some type of direction. Not thrown to the side because her actions don't meet your expectations." She spoke more for herself than of Mylena.

"Well, you got a couple of weeks to decide what you're going to do." Letty turned on the television.

Falicia headed upstairs, ready to get to work and even more ready to get out of the house. But if she left, where would Mylena go? This is when she really missed Cash most. From time to time, she did see him and they made small talk, but he kept it moving. She had to make this decision all on her own.

CHAPTER 11

Two weeks later, Letty moved from Continental Colony quickly, as if she was on the run, but Falicia didn't tag along. She hooked up with DJ Cali at the club where she worked, and at first it was all gravy. For Falicia, being with him and staying at his home gave her a sense of peace, but soon everything went typically bad as the work and relationship curse usually does. He was cheating and fronted on her in front of other employees. As expected, they parted on bad terms. She was ass out, occasionally staying with friends and maybe a night or two at a hotel where the guy was expecting to hook up, but she wasn't interested. Now Falicia had arrived at home sweet homeless.

She tried to get her own place, but only possessed a state ID. She needed her birth certificate and social security card, which Cash still had in his possession. For several months she hadn't seen even a glimpse of Cash. Where was he when she really needed him? Her stepsister Mylena was now living in a hotel with her boys.

A late night call from Mylena's eldest son, Jarvis, worried Falicia and forced her to change her unstable living arrangements. She moved into a hotel room one floor below Mylena, mainly to ensure that her nephews were being cared for properly.

The cab fare to and from work along with the cost of the hotel nearly depleted most of her funds. Falicia couldn't save a penny for her online diploma, or the dream apartment she and Mylena planned to one day rent. Eventually, she gave up her hotel room and decided to stack her paper until she could put herself in a better living situation.

Just the previous night she stayed with Big Al, who did security at Dancers Elite. She didn't know why she seemed to be attracted to guys who only worked where she worked. But Big Al was different. Falicia considered him a "good man" and knew she wasn't mentally ready to be the type of woman he needed in his life. So they remained friends, and because he knew she had nowhere to go, he allowed her to stay at his place with no strings attached. Plus, his ex-girlfriend kept popping in and out of his life, and she was the type that a person would catch a charge behind with her fly ass mouth.

Big Al worked for Big Boy security and was frequently hired to assist other security guards for the R&B group, Jagged Edge. His ringing cell phone woke Falicia up from her spot on his couch. A client needed him to come right away to accompany them somewhere. He called Falicia a cab and escorted her out the door because he was unable to drop her off at work. A password was required to access all entrances and exits, including the parking garage on the busy street not far from Centennial Park in Downtown Atlanta. They hugged good-bye. "I'll call you if I can't make it back tonight," he promised.

An hour later, she remained in the same spot on the sidewalk waiting for a cab. A black Escalade rolled up to the stop light. *Damn that SUV is sexy as hell!* she thought. *Especially with the rims . . . gotta be twenty-fours. Wonder what the driver lookin' like though.* He let down the window as if he'd read her thoughts.

The driver sported a pair of glasses that reminded her of something Gucci or Cartier would make. A smile crept on his face, a creepy one. Falicia wasn't impressed. *If he didn't have that truck, no chick would give him the time of day. Ugh!* The light changed, and he slowly proceeded. She turned her back to him, dialing the number for the cab company. Fifteen minutes later, she was still on the corner without a clue where she was. Had she known the area, she would have started walking.

Nearing the point of tears, she tried the cab company again, but was lied to again. The Escalade stopped in front of her. He leaned over to the passenger side. "You all right, Miss? I noticed you been out here for a while." He smiled. "Do you need a ride somewhere?"

"... I'm fine, thank you. Just waiting for my cab."

"Okay . . . So do you think I can at least get your name?" He sounded a little defeated. Falicia laughed.

"I apologize. Didn't mean to be rude. I'm just a little irritated standing out here in this heat. Unique. My name is Unique."

"Miss Unique, I can't sit here much longer. This is a busy street. Why don't you jump in, and I'll take you wherever you're trying to go? It doesn't seem like your cab is coming."

Hesitant, Falicia looked around for any sight of her cab. "C'mon," he said, pushing the door open. "Toss your luggage in the back." Again, she looked up the street, but then got inside when not a single cab was within her sight. He took no time pulling off. "So where you headed?" he asked, racing toward the interstate.

She quickly assessed him. Nice linen pants suit, expensive jewelry, and a nice SUV. A picture of a little girl was taped to his dashboard. "Dancers Elite off Marietta Street," she answered. Although she had yet to learn her way around Atlanta, she knew where he should be going. "Umm . . . this is not the way," she stated as he drove past the exit.

"Yeah, I know. Just chill for a minute. Gotta handle something."

"Handle something? I thought I stressed to you that I need to get to work."

"It won't take long."

Falicia remained silent, watching him take her farther and farther away from where he promised to take her. "Look, all I'm trying to do is get to work."

He exited some miles away on Union City and drove down some back roads where nothing but warehouses could be seen. She did her best not to come off as afraid. He might've gotten off on stuff like that.

Several more minutes passed, and he pulled into a parking lot for a public park. An elderly woman was walking her dog. Big, beautiful trees were clustered together, so she couldn't see directly

Sereniti Hall

into the park. Falicia turned back, gazing behind them, trying to remember the way back to civilization. He stopped when his Escalade could go no further, then backed his truck between two oversized trees to the left of the trail. "Come here!" he demanded as he crawled into the backseat and unfastened his belt. Bewildered, Falicia gazed at him. His once compassionate expression turned stern. His eyes danced around in his head, like he was spaced out on a powerful drug.

"Sir, please don't do this. You don't have to do this." She bit her lip to keep from crying. "You don't even know me." *Don't show weakness.*

"What?" he yelled. "I *said* come here!" *What is he about to do? What does he want me to do? Where am I?* Several thoughts flooded her mind. Falicia looked past him and out of the back window. She spotted a road. *Yes! If I can just get out of here.* She eased her hand on the door handle, keeping her eyes on him.

"Unique! Don't make me have to say it again!" He pulled down his pants. She yanked on the handle. The door didn't budge. Her heart began thumping with urgency.

"Sir, please. I don't want any trouble. Would you please just . . ."

"Shut the fuck up and get back here like I said! You want me to go under this seat?" He bent down and reached his hand under the driver's seat.

"No!" She nodded. "Don't."

"Then bring your ass here!" He pulled her to him and yanked down her panties. Forcing her on her back, he spread her legs wide and hissed, ogling her vagina. "Ooh wee, you sure do have a pretty little pussy!" The stranger stared at her, eyes full of lust. "How old are you?" He stuck his finger in her. She tried to close her legs. He pushed her dress up further and stared at her stomach.

"Do you want children?" The man took a condom out of his pants pocket and put it on. "I'm going to enjoy this," he bragged, lying on top of her.

She placed her hand on his chest to prevent him from making contact with her breasts. "Sir, please don't do this. You're a nice looking man. You seem successful. You probably could have any woman you want. You don't have to do this, not like this. Please." Something in his eyes shifted. He was considering her words. She tried to ease away, spotting her purple panties. She reached for them. He snatched her arm so hard it felt as if he pulled it from its socket.

"Who told you to get up? You think I'm playing with you?" Those crazy eyes had returned just as fast as they had left. "I see what the fuck is going on here. You can't be nice to bitches! You want me to go up under this seat?" He reached down.

"No, no, no!" she said, adamantly.

Falicia wanted to live. To see her nephews again, so she lay back and closed her eyes, daring herself to show any emotion as he violated her to his satisfaction. After he busted one, then his sick ass pulled off the condom and dropped it in a cup from a fast food restaurant. Reaching in the side passenger slot, he grabbed a baby wipe and offered the package to Falicia, who grabbed a few and attempted to wipe herself.

As if nothing had ever happened, they were back on the road within minutes. His cell rang, and he threated Falicia before answering. He took the call, but then rushed the caller off the phone. Again it rang, and he hurried to end the conversation as he drove up to a Motel 6.

"Listen, I need you to drop me off. I have a family to go home to." Falicia tried to remain rational.

"You don't want to stay with me, after what we just shared together?" His eyes danced again as confusion spread across his face.

"I can't spend the night with you. If you have any type of compassion, I need you to drop me off."

"Shut up!" he yelled.

Sereniti Hall

"Would you want someone to do this to your daughter, your sister, or even your mother? Please, just drop me off at the bus station." She was sure she looked as pitiful as she felt. *I just want out of this SUV and away from this man. God please, if you can hear me, please!*

The deeply disturbed man put the SUV in reverse and drove her to the train station. Falicia hopped out and never looked back. Once she was safely on the train, she exhaled. *I don't wanna think about this shit. I'm still going in to work.*

Falicia's ex, DJ Cali was the first person she made eye contact with when she ran through the door of Dancers Elite. He knew her well enough to know that something was wrong, but she was too ashamed to say anything. "What's up?" he asked as she rushed past him.

"Just send me a drink," Falicia said.

"You all right?" he asked, but received no response.

As much as she wanted to call her sister Mylena, the humiliation wouldn't allow it. And for some reason, Mylena hadn't come in today. Foolishly, Falicia shared in the blame with her assailant. *I mean, hell, it was my fault. I was the one that got into the vehicle with a total stranger.* The truth was simple: she made a poor decision entering a total stranger's car. It wasn't her fault that she was raped. Nothing justifies a human being violated. No means no, and Falicia had every right to say no.

As if the day couldn't have gotten any worse, Big Al called Falicia to let her know he wouldn't be back in the city that night. The club was practically empty and presented her with another dilemma. Near closing, Falicia barely had a hundred dollars. She got dressed and headed outside as if she was waiting for a cab. In reality, she hadn't an inkling of where she would stay that night.

CHAPTER 12

"Fantasia, how long did they say it would be before your cab gets here?" Jerry, one of the bouncers, asked Falicia, calling her by her dancer name.

"Umm . . ." she stalled, trying to figure out what to say. "Actually, I'm not waiting on a cab. It's cool though. You can leave. I'm fine waiting out here alone." She called Big Al and Mylena and neither of them answered.

Jerry seemed well-mannered and respectful toward women in general. In the past, he had expressed his desire to get to know Falicia better, in hopes of pursuing a relationship. He finally took notice of her broken disposition. "You okay?" he asked.

Falicia couldn't stop the tears from falling. He comforted her with a strong embrace and offered his place for her to rest for the night. For the most part, he was a gentleman, until the following morning when she was awakened by him rubbing on her backside. In her opinion, with the exception of his cologne and the way he dressed, nothing about Jerry was attractive. Big from chest to stomach but small from hips to feet. Still devastated by the rape from the previous day, she tried to contain her boiling anger as she declined Jerry's advances. Unlike her attacker, he understood no and left her to go back to sleep.

She awakened to an empty bed. Jerry had called while he was at school and informed her that he'd be there in an hour. She had no idea that he was in college. Falicia checked her phone and received two messages. One was from Big Al, and the other was from Sid, a twenty-five year old cat who had been coming in the club for as long as she had been working there.

Sid was Falicia's height, heavyset, low haircut, and had a beautiful white smile. Falicia complimented him on it a couple of times, but she never approached him for a dance.

Sereniti Hall

Usually Sid came to the club with a local rapper and a bunch of other dudes. He loved to drink, and when he had too much he would wild out! He was either spending every single dollar in his pocket, putting his hands in places on the dancer's body where they shouldn't be, or trying to bury his face between somebody's ass. A perfect example of why she didn't fuck with young, immature ass men. He flirted with her often, telling her what he was going to do once they went out. She knew he was full of shit!

What didn't escape her mind was the few hundred dollars Sid usually blew at the club. She returned his call pronto, and somehow a simple conversation ended in her confessing that she didn't have a place to stay. He cured her problem within a few hours. When she met up with him, he handed her a key to room 212 at the Suburban Lodge. She entered the room and exhaled. *Surely, shit is about to get better,* she thought, trying to drive the hopeless feelings away.

Falicia scanned the decently furnished room and saw a few items that belonged to Sid in the closet. *Guess, I'm his new roommate.* "Since Sid wanna play house and shack up with me, he can be the man of this house and maintain the bills. I've gotta save my money," she said as she headed for the shower. From their earlier conversation, she naturally assumed he'd be leaving the place to her alone, and she'd just maintain the rent, alone.

By the time she got out of the shower, Sid was present and was kicked back watching TV. He hadn't gotten drunk tonight and seemed to be chilling. Falicia really hadn't considered the time he might be coming in, nor did she ask when he was at the club. So she a little taken aback when she walked out of the bathroom with just a bath towel on, and he flashed this goofy grin. "Why you smiling like that?" she asked, hoping he wasn't thinking things were about to get heated. She barely knew him.

"What you mean? A man can't smile?" he replied.

"Yeah, a man can smile . . . if a woman can be told she has to share her bed."

"Oh, okay! I see how you do." What else could he say? She sat on her side of the bed moisturizing her skin. As she put on a pair of boxers and a wife beater, she refused to look over her shoulder. She knew he was looking, she wasn't about to entertain him.

"Good night," she said and slipped under the covers. She lay in her favorite position on her stomach as she cuffed her pillow.

It wasn't long before Sid followed suit and lay close to her in an attempt to hold her. Falicia didn't protest nor encourage his gesture. She just lay motionless, listening to sleep overtake him as he snored softly. *I am not trying to get used to this shit; he is merely a convenience. Someone who's helping me get through a rough chapter in my life. However, it feels nice, and so far he is being the perfect gentleman.*

By the end of the first week, they both realized they needed some food in their small refrigerator. Falicia slipped into a flower print strapless dress that stopped at her ankles with a low split in the back. She wore a pair of flat sandals that matched. Normally, she would have worn heels that were at least a couple inches, but Sid had already volunteered to go with her, and she didn't want to look taller than him on their first outing. They hit the block and walked the short distance to a convenience store.

The second they walked in the store, Falicia realized it was a bad idea to have Sid tagging along. With each stare or compliment she was given, she witnessed him getting more bent out of shape.

"What the fuck is your problem?" she finally yelled at Sid as they walked out of the store. She was embarrassed by the sudden change in his disposition.

"Who the fuck you talking to like that?" he snapped.

"Why are you talking to people like you've lost your mind because someone is staring at me?"

"These motherfuckers don't have no business looking at you!" he protested, as if he was seconds away from having a fit.

Ooh, I wish I could smack his whining ass back into his

mother's womb, she thought. Instead, Falicia just picked up the pace and walked ahead of him. Ignoring everything he said. She wanted to get inside before she flipped. She refused to look like an ass, outside fussing with this jerk while walking down the street. If she engaged in a yelling match with him, an onlooker may not know which of them was the fool, him or her. And she prided herself on being a lady in the streets.

They got back to the lodge, and Sid caught up with her, mounting a couple stairs at a time. Mr. Craig, their next door neighbor, was standing in his doorway. Falicia had run into him a couple of afternoons on her way to work. He struck up a conversation one day, stating she could pay him to take her wherever she was headed, instead of paying for a taxi. He seemed respectful, but Falicia saw that same look in his eyes that James, her old sugar daddy had. A couple of nights she made it home before Sid, and Mr. Craig would call her to make sure she made it in safely. He even invited her to dinner, but she declined.

Sid had heard their exchange regarding dinner and irately asked, "So, this old ass nigga wanna fuck you too?"

"Excuse me?" She cursed herself for even responding, for lowering herself to his level.

"Every time I turn around, somebody staring at you like they fantasizing about my bitch."

"Your bitch? Who you calling a bitch?" She was seconds away from losing it.

"It's a figure of speech, Falicia!" he yelled.

"Well, use that shit with the next motherfucker. Don't talk to me like that. Sid, I'm getting sick of you talking about people looking at me. I'm a stripper. Why in the fuck would your insecure ass even try to date a dancer if you worried about the next man digging your girl?"

"For your information, I ain't insecure!"

They continued to exchange words to the point where Mr. Craig called to see if she needed him to come over and escort Sid out. Falicia assured him she didn't and promised she didn't feel threatened. The mere act only added fuel to the fire, but she decided she had heard enough. She went to the bathroom, cut the shower on, and sat on the toilet, leaving Sid alone to think about how stupid he sounded fussing. By the time she came out, he was asleep.

It was clear he liked the idea of having an adult entertainer as a girlfriend, but couldn't handle it mentally. One evening while working at Dancers Elite, Falicia shot Sid an evil eye. He stood tall. Proud. Full of himself and smiling like she should be impressed. Jagged Edge's song, "Let's Get Married," blasted. If she could, she would have climbed up the pole and disappeared in the ceiling. *Why in the hell is this man dedicating this song to me in a booty club?* she fumed, and headed to the opposite side of the stage. Over the last month, whenever she danced for any particular man for too long, he got jealous. He'd sit near the VIP room to watch what she was doing. And he was constantly walking up on her, demanding she dance with him to stop her from entertaining a potential client. Falicia ordered another shot of tequila and headed to the dressing room. After counting her money, she called a cab, then got dressed.

Sid caught sight of her as soon as she exited the sweaty room. "What's up? Where you going?" He tried to embrace her.

"I'm going home." She squirmed out of his reach.

"Baby, why would you do that? The club is *packed*."

"Suddenly I got a headache and don't feel like being bothered. Besides, you don't seem to be concerned about fucking with my money. So what does it matter?"

"Whatchu' mean?" He waited for an answer. "Well, I'm not ready to leave," he said, hoping she would reconsider.

"By all means, please stay and enjoy yourself. Put some bitches in your face. Do whatever you feel you need to do, just excuse me because I'm ready to go."

Sereniti Hall

By the time her taxicab pulled up in front of the lodge, she was in a better mood. Once she reached the lodge, she jumped in the shower, hoping he would stay gone all night. No sooner than her head hit the pillow, Falicia fell into a deep sleep.

"Arghh, arghhh!" She awakened to Sid hovering over her, grunting as he climaxed.

"What the fuck!" she questioned as he collapsed on top of her. "Are you serious?" Falicia tried to force him off her. "Sid, get off me!" He held her down, breathing heavily. "I can't believe you did this shit." He didn't budge. "I said get your big ass off me!" She kicked him.

"Damn!" he complained, and rolled on his back. "Won't even let a brother catch his breath."

"Nigga, is you serious! Fuck you and your breath. Did you really just have sex with me in my sleep?" She punched him. "What type of man can fuck somebody in their sleep and the female not even feel it?"

"Man, shut up with all that."

"Shut up? I wish . . ." Falicia went to use the toilet, and then wiped herself. "Sid, did you just nut in me?" She flushed. "Your bitch ass had better not nutted in me!"

"Man, just sit on the toilet. It'll come back out. I do the shit all the time."

"You do what shit all the time?" She panicked. "Bitch, you be fucking me in my sleep all the time?" He didn't answer. Her stomach cramped. "I can't believe you did this! What the fuck is wrong with you? You should be ashamed to admit you be fucking people in their sleep, and they don't even know about it. With that lil' ass dick."

"Whatever . . . you know I be in there. You just be tryna play sleep! I told you to just sit there. It'll come out." Falicia could feel herself slipping. She wanted to fight, cry, throw up, or maybe even die. *God please,* she begged, barely above a whisper.

"I tell you what, motherfucker," she yelled out the door. "Your ass better be gone by the time I come out this bathroom, and I mean that shit." She slammed it as hard as she could, unable to fathom that this so-called grown ass boy was trying to get her pregnant. A light bulb went off in her head.

"Bingo!" she said aloud as she spotted the trashcan. She used her index finger and thumb to pick up the used condom. She stood up from the toilet, cut the faucet on, and placed the condom beneath the running water.

"You've got to be kidding me!" Fear gripped her as she watched two very tiny streams of water trickle out the tip of the condom. She heard stories where females did shit like this. But a dude?

Falicia was still in a daze. She showered, then slipped on a fresh T-shirt and panties. She changed the sheets, then crawled in bed, grateful Sid took heed. She yanked open the nightstand drawer where they kept condoms in different colors. Grabbing a handful, she hurried back to the bathroom and ripped open a condom. Water ran through it. She tested the other two, and water trickled through them as well. *How long has he been poking holes in them?*

She texted Mylena that she wouldn't be coming in to work. Falicia desperately wanted to feel her mother's arms wrapped around her. She dialed the first five digits, then ended the call. *What would I say? Would she even want to talk? Was she at work?*

Around ten, Sid began calling her cell, but she ignored each call and set her attention on a movie. An hour later he called, and she answered, "What's up?" Loud music played in the background.

"Baby!" he yelled into the phone. "Can you hear me?" She held the phone until it dawned on the idiot to go somewhere where he could hear. Why call someone when you know you can barely hear the person sitting at the table across from you?

"Can you hear me now?" It sounded like he had stepped into the restroom.

"Can you hear me now?" she questioned, being sarcastic.

"Baby, where you at? The club getting pack."

"That's good. I'm not coming," Falicia answered dryly.

"You not coming? Why?"

"Because I don't feel like being bothered, Sid. Damn! I have a right to take off if I want to."

"All right. I didn't call to start a fight."

"Okay, that's good to know."

"Well, if it's cool with you, I would like to stay and hang out."

"I'm all right with that."

"Well, all right, baby. I hope you get some rest and shit. I'll see you later tonight." He sounded so sincere. For a few quick seconds she felt bad for snapping on him. She took a deep breath.

"Enjoy your night."

"I'll try without you." His remark made her smile a little.

"Tell my sister I love her."

"I will."

"Good night."

He paused. "I love you," he said. Those words took Falicia by surprise. She didn't know what to say, so she didn't say anything. Instead, she just hung up the phone. First the song, then him coming in her, now his confession of love. Sid was moving way too fast. He didn't even know her. *Would all of this love still stand if he knew I was only sixteen?* She decided against spending her night concerning herself with this grown boy and his fleeting feelings. She exhausted herself with TV until she fell asleep. It was a good sleep, until she got a call some wee hours of the morning.

"Hello?" she answered, groggily.

"So you want me to fuck dat nigga up?" Sid's words slurred.

"What?" She struggled to make sense of what he was saying.

"I . . . I know you got a nigga up there! I'ma fuck his ass up, too!"

"Sid, what are you talking about? I'm trying to sleep."

A Treacherous Hustle

"Sound like you fucking to me!"

"You know what . . ." Falicia considered telling him how she really felt, but what would it accomplish? And to think she had just started to believe that maybe she should give him a chance. All that sweet shit he said earlier was gone out the window. "You so stupid. I'm going back to sleep." She hung up the phone.

Bam!

Falicia woke up and sat up in the bed. Sid burst into the room. "Where that motherfucka at?" He staggered in the door with a bottle of brandy. Reeking of the alcohol he spilt on himself. Sid struggled to grab a hold of the door and close it. Falicia sat in disbelief, her heart pulsating.

"Bitch ass nigga, come out wherever you are! I know you got somebody in here!" He lunged for her and lost his balance, falling into the chair by the table.

"Grow your dumb, insecure ass up!" she screamed. He flipped the table over, with a rage in his eyes that she'd never witnessed. She darted inside the bathroom and locked the door.

"I'm a fucking man!" he yelled. She waited in the sanctity of the bathroom until finally all she could hear was a Western playing on the television next door. *What kind of craziness have I involved myself in this time? Will my life ever be stable? I need a break from this crazy ass nigga. Where can I go?*

CHAPTER 13

Things between her and Sid were only getting worse. They argued about money and his constant disillusion with her cheating, so much so, that she had actually made it real and hooked up with her ex, DJ Cali. Even though her money wasn't hitting on much of anything, Falicia jumped on a Greyhound bus with Mylena. She needed to get away and clear her head and have some fun in the process. They headed to Jacksonville where they met up with Tiny and Ko-Ko and hit the road to their spring break destination, Daytona Beach. Once there, dudes and females were everywhere. Pimped out rides, live performances, and plenty of people stuntin' in front of their hotels. That entire weekend, Falicia and her girls ate overpriced food, did a lot of dancing, met interesting people and took a lot of pictures.

Instead of heading back to Atlanta when their trip was over, she found the comfort of her grandmother's house in Jacksonville, Florida too difficult to leave. Back in her old room, in her old bed, she felt a peace she hadn't felt in a long time. And there still was the rape. As much as she tried, she couldn't erase it from her mind. *If I ever lay eyes on that nigga who raped me, I'ma kill him.*

Trying to put it behind her, she let another call from Sid go to voice mail and attempted to sleep. A door closing made her go to the window. Falicia reminisced on the time she and her best friend Ko-Ko snuck into an adult club with her favorite aunt, Tasha. Aside from men feeling on her, her halter top was snatched off, and she was nearly raped by two men in the bathroom while trying to put it back on. If it hadn't been for a nice guy who showed up and kicked the dudes out, she probably would have been sexually assaulted. But even the nice guy wasn't so innocent; they exchanged numbers and a few nights later, fourteen-year-old Falicia had sex with a grown ass man who had no clue she was a minor. The experience made Falicia easily conclude that all dudes in the club were only there for sex.

A simple blink brought her back to her perch in the window at her grandmother's house. A tilt of her head found Rob-G standing on his back porch wearing nothing but a pair of shorts. She rolled her eyes, knowing what he was up to. He waved her down. She shook her head. He made a sad puppy-dog face. She sighed and slipped out the back door to meet up with him just like old times.

Without a doubt, when she got back to the ATL, she was going solo. Because she wasn't the one for games, and Sid's time had run out. A little ass dick with a fucked up attitude never did anybody any good. And Sid's young ass didn't know how to eat pussy right. Nor did he take the time out to learn. Rob-G, on the other hand, had a hunger that always needed to be fed. He wasn't selfish and was always willing to feed. Until he'd sexed her, she never knew how many positions the human body was capable of fucking in. That's why she never thought twice when it came to hooking up with him. Rob-G knew how to please and please and please again. And again.

After their sex session ended, Rob-G sat on the side of the bed with his feet on the floor. Falicia thought, *Damn, it's funny how some things never change. He's probably trying to figure out how to tell me that he's about to go handle some business, or that he's having company tonight, but I'm not that same little girl in his bed from a year ago.* Falicia had long accepted that "they" would never be and was fully aware it was best to merely enjoy the benefits he offered in their forbidden arrangement. Her feelings were a non-factor to him, so why waste time feeding them motherfuckers? At this point, he had a need and so did she. Period! And in this moment, she had some other shit on her mind.

"Falicia." Rob-G kept his back to her.

"Save it," she said, knowing the routine. "Don't even worry yourself. I'll be gone by the time you get back." He eyed her over his shoulder, surprised he didn't have to almost fight her to get her out of his bed.

"No. I want to talk to you about something else." She crawled up behind him and rubbed his back and massaged his shoulders. Just like any man, he liked feeling like a king in his castle.

"What's up, Rob?" she teased, pinching his side. He didn't flinch. His silence made her uncomfortable. She sat beside him and tried to make him look at her. He sighed heavily, but he wouldn't meet her gaze.

"You're pregnant."

It took her a minute to register what he'd just said. "How can you tell? I know I'm gaining a little weight, but that's only because for the last month since I've been here, I've been laying up, cooking and sleeping a lot. When normally, I would be dancing." She told him all about her career and she marveled at how it thrilled him to know she was making big bucks.

"Your six-pack gone."

She popped him in the head. He ducked. "Were you not listening to me?"

"Falicia, you have always had a six pack."

"So what are you saying, Rob?"

"You pregnant. I know what pregnant pussy feels like."

After about two months, Falicia's time in Jacksonville was coming to an end. She really wasn't sure if she wanted to go back to Georgia, but her money was running out. A decision had to be made quickly because she already had resorted to stealing some groceries a few times. Every day, she and Sid had been fussing about when she was coming back and him leaving the room up until about two weeks ago. Now she was right back at square one: home sweet homeless. Falicia felt she was wearing out her welcome staying with her relatives, except her grandmother, but her drug-influenced uncle, Tracy, had long ago gotten on her nerves. Likewise, she had this new pressing issue about possibly being pregnant at hand. So, she decided to go pay her dad a visit before she dipped. He may have struggled with drugs all of Falicia's life, but he was her dad and she loved this man! She hadn't seen her daddy in over a year. After ten minutes of being in his presence, he was just staring at her.

"Dad, why are looking at me like that?" Falicia asked, starting to feel apprehensive.

"You pregnant?"

Falicia almost choked. "Excuse me?" He repeated himself, looking dead ass serious. "Daddy! No, I'm not pregnant!" she answered swiftly. "You gotta be doing something in order to get pregnant." He backed off, but he eyeballed her the entire time. Unconvinced.

Why would he say that? I haven't seen this man in a year, and all he can do is suspect I'm with child. She was beyond ready to get back to Atlanta, where a few major problems awaited her presence! Stacking her money back up and dealing with Sid about the back rent at the lodge, as well as getting her belongings. *A pregnancy test will have to wait,* she thought as she boarded the Greyhound bus back to the 'A.'

Back in Atlanta, she sent word to a couple of people to let Sid know she was back. He hadn't shown his face at the club and refused to answer her calls. Finally she got a hold of him, and he agreed to bring her, her things. One week she received her clothes, and the second week he returned her costumes. She knew he was trying to get a rise out of her, but she wouldn't fall into that trap. When he refused to return the erotic pictures she had taken professionally, that only made her not want to fuck with him at all. And just the idea that he could possibly be the father of the child she was carrying made her dry heave.

Falicia hadn't had a regular menstrual cycle since she'd stopped taking her birth control pills three years ago. That's one of the reasons she ruled out pregnancy in the first place. Nevertheless, she decided to go ahead and quit prolonging what she needed to know: Was she pregnant or not?

Throwing on a cute top and some cargo pants with sneakers, Falicia caught a cab to Grady hospital. She walked into the hospital reception area when they unlocked their doors, eager to get a pregnancy test out of the way so she could head to work. She was sent across the street to the children's hospital with the insurance card Letty always made her carry. Falicia had become so lost in the adult world she quickly adapted to, that she forgot she was only sixteen and could quite possibly become a teenage mother. The moment her name was called, she was given a cup and told to pee in it. Falicia proceeded to the bathroom and did just as she was asked.

Sitting alone waiting for the results, she was petrified. "Ms. Blakely . . ." the female, black American doctor said. She closed the exam room door. "Congratulations. You're pregnant!"

"I'm gonna need to take this test over." Falicia crossed her arms like she meant business.

"Ma'am, we're one hundred percent sure. You're going to be a mother. You're several months pregnant. You need to begin prenatal care right away."

Frustration clothed her like a shawl as she stood up and left the hospital, her mind numb. She was going to have a baby! Sid was the first person she delivered the news to.

"Well, if you keep it, I'll help you. But I ain't paying for the whole thing."

"This is what you wanted." She hissed like a snake, feeling her anger bubble.

"Girl, you make plenty of money. You can—"

She walked away, praying not to bash him in the head. She needed her mother's embrace desperately.

Sereniti Hall

On Mother's Day, Falicia took Letty out to dinner and the mall. She treated her to whatever she desired, including her favorite drink, Brandy. They had such a great time that Falicia decided to put the pregnancy news on ice. She didn't want to ruin their day and besides, she was grateful she could do something nice for her mother.

Just when she was on a natural high from spending quality time with Letty, and getting her money stacked back up to a reasonable amount, some drama popped off at the club between the owner and a few hot heads. A bullet hit a metal pole and small fragments were embedded into Falicia's leg. She didn't go to the hospital because the owner of the club didn't want any heat coming down on his spot. It was the first time Falicia worried about the safety of her baby. She had to tell her mother right away.

It was close to six when she grabbed the card she purchased the day before at a CVS store. 'Momma, I'm sorry,' is all she could write inside of it. She stood in the room Letty arranged for her in her new house, as if she knew Falicia would come home sooner or later. *And this is how I'm repaying her for giving me a place to lay my head,* she thought as she left the card on the kitchen counter for Letty to find once she started dinner.

Inside on the right hand side, the card read: *Congratulations, we're having a baby!* Falicia left the house with a kiss to her mother's cheek. She hurried out the door to her awaiting cab.

Inside the bathroom stall at Dancers Elite, Falicia cried the same tears she did on her ride home from the hospital. Her heart beat fast, anxious about how mother would react. And if her first words would be, "I told you so."

As 8:00 p.m. approached, she couldn't resist the urge. She called Letty from the pay phone downstairs in the coatroom, just in case she wouldn't answer because Falicia's number popped up. The second Letty answered, Falicia cried into the phone, "Momma, I'm so sorry. Ma, please don't be mad at me. Please don't."

"Boo-Boo, I'm not mad at you." Her voice broke.

"Then stop crying."

"I'll try. It's just that you're so young, and you have the potential to be anything you want. And what about school, track, and modeling? But don't try to answer now. We'll talk when you get home."

"Okay, Momma. I love you."

"I love you too."

Falicia dried her eyes. Her favorite waitress tapped her shoulder. "Fantasia, I been looking all over for you. This dude sent you a drink." She held up a shot of tequila.

"You can have it."

"What? You feeling okay? Can't believe you don't want your lemon and salt." She jerked her head like Falicia did when she requested her drink when she was ready to turn up! It made her laugh.

"And by the way, from now on when someone orders me a drink, instead of putting alcohol in the glass, can you just put ginger ale in the glass, and we can split the money?"

"So you want it to look like you getting drunk? What made you decide that?"

"Girl, when that liquor get in me, I be all horny and shit." The women giggled. "Tell the gentleman that purchased the drink that I'll be with him shortly. And I still want my lemons and salt." That was the best part of the drink. She mimicked Falicia about her preference. "I need to take care of you," she stated, then beamed down at her belly with excitement. She'd just addressed her baby. It was becoming *hers*.

Just as she promised, Letty waited up for Falicia with a cold glass of milk and her favorite chocolate chip cookies. It was something they did back in the day when either one needed cheering up. Letty opened the pack and put four more on Falicia's saucer.

"Falicia, I just feel you're so young, and your life is barely beginning. I think abortion would be the best option for you right now."

She shook her head, battling a new batch of tears. "I can't, Momma." Even Mylena said she shouldn't keep it.

As she was getting ready for bed, she looked down at her expanding six-pack. "You should be a boy. I always said I'd only have boys." She caught herself talking to her baby again, and even though he or she never said a word, she was starting to love it. A life growing inside of her made her put on her poker face every day and get her money.

Sid met her coming off the stage. "So what you gonna do?" he asked. Three weeks had passed since Falicia had seen his punk ass. He rubbed her ass. "So can I get a dance?"

Falicia didn't show her hand like she could have. She kept walking, her mind on something more important. With a heart burdened by pressure, she located some numbers for local abortion clinics. Letty had become adamant that it was the best option for her. Having a mere conversation about the possibility of destroying her flesh and blood sent chills down Falicia's spine when she discovered that the trimester she was in put her at risk of losing her life as they took her baby. She hung up the phone within a second.

Anxious to tell Letty it wasn't safe to have the abortion, she sat in the living room anticipating her arrival. The moment Letty came home, Falicia didn't waste any time.

"Momma, God has a purpose for everything and giving my baby a chance at life is what I feel I need to do." A few tears fell down her momma's cheeks. Letty sniffled.

"If that's what you truly believe, I'll support you one hundred percent, Boo-Boo," Letty replied.

"I don't know much about God, Momma. But his presence is

undeniable. All of this just feels . . . way beyond me—like my child's purpose is way bigger than me. And I won't destroy that."

For the first time in years, they hugged and cried together. Falicia hadn't felt this close to her mother in quite a while. Knowing she didn't have a moment to waste, Falicia worked every shift she could and most times fell asleep in the cab on her way home. Especially when Mylena was with her.

Her son was draining her energy. Even though she hadn't received any prenatal care, she just knew it was a boy. His little butt kept her tired most of the time. The combination of fried food, as well as the scent of perfume, cologne, liquor, and smoke, kept her nauseous and her head throbbing. The nausea was affecting her performance, and she found herself having to work harder than ever.

Good and bad days determined her earnings, but either way she decide to dance as if every day was going to be a good one. Who knows, maybe her customers would come back on payday.

"Fellas, I've got Miss Fantasia on stage, and no one has set them titties free!" DJ Uptown, who was on shift for the night, said into the mic.

Falicia danced consistently, but Dancers Elite wasn't as packed as it could have been. This resulted in her money being funny. And she didn't have time for laughs. Her baby would be coming and so would his many needs. By the end of her first song, she would have at least received twenty dollars, ten for the top and ten for the bottoms. Yet tonight, she remained fully dressed. If she knew she could leave the stage without being penalized, she would have. The entire place was dead.

"Fantasia, we've got a gentleman over there waiting on you?" he announced as the music changed. If looks could kill, she would have strangled Uptown.

"I'm ready to go!" she stated as if he could read her lips.

The request was from a group who had been sitting in the cut. It

Sereniti Hall

was about five or six dudes and one dominant lesbian all piled up in the corner. She hadn't had a chance to go over to their area because every time she was free, everyone in the group was occupied with a dancer. Two of the dudes sat with their chairs pulled up to the side of the stage. Those were usually the kind of men who were ready to make it rain!

Falicia's eyes lit up with hope, and she danced over to a brown-skinned man with a short beard, sporting FUBU gear, white Nike Air Max, and a platinum necklace. He smiled real playa-like, but his front tooth was chipped. Out of obligation, Falicia shook her money maker, but wasn't too fond of his money falling on her backside. But it was raining hard.

"All right, fellas, I'm about to slow it down for my booty on duty," Uptown called out and started her final song. "You don't wanna miss out on your chance with this hot, sexy chocolate. They say big things come in small packages. Sometimes." Falicia turned toward him with a death stare. "Freaky Thangs" by Ludacris hit the speakers. He knew she liked the song.

"Smile," he mouthed. "Ms. Fantasia, how much you need?" he asked, bobbing his head to the beat. She started dancing as though she wanted to be there, keeping her focus on the money piling up. With five fingers held up as her answer to DJ Uptown's question, she slow-rocked her hips to the beat.

"All right, fellas, just five more dollars each, and we can see that pretty lil cat." DJ Uptown encouraged the crowd.

"She should've been naked already!" one patron shouted.

The dude who'd just tipped her left the DJ booth, moving with ease, the way only a nigga full of confidence did. Falicia walked up to him and began slowly rolling her middle to the song, looking at him the entire time. He flicked several bills at her as he held his stance. She released the tie on one side of her bikini bottoms, exposing her vagina as she made it breathe for him.

"When you get off stage, come see me," he instructed, leaving her with two hundred dollars' worth of tens and twenties. No singles.

A dancer named Cinnamon was dancing for him when Falicia finally approached him. Cinnamon's back was to him when she walked up. He leaned around her and made eye contact with Falicia. "I'll be back," she said politely. She didn't want her girl to think she was hating on her.

Cinnamon was brown-skinned, slim, with just enough butt and nice breasts. Falicia teased her about having a perfect shape for a white girl. She even moved like she only danced in predominantly Caucasian clubs. The dancers at black clubs twerked. Made that ass bounce. White clubs seduced, rolled, and slow winded.

"Naw, it's cool. You can dance for my cousin over there. Zeke." He pointed to one of the dudes who had been sitting near the stage. It made sense. Their broke asses were with him. He must've paid their way in and for their dances too.

One look at Zeke and her gut immediately told her to stay away from him. *I'll just handle my business and make ol' boy forget about his dance,* Falicia reasoned.

Zeke had already been the loudest in the club all night. A couple of times the bouncers had to stand behind him so he would get the message. A new song began. Since he wasn't paying for the dance, she decided to tease him in the hopes that he'd ask her to dance for him again. Zeke, however, had busy hands. Falicia had to place his hands on the arm of his chair several times. She let her shorts fall to her ankles and stepped out of one leg when the first song was almost over. Just as she bent over to pick them up, he licked from her vagina to the crack of her ass within two seconds. Falicia spun around and slapped a spark from him.

"You nasty motherfucker!" she yelled. "Bitch, you don't know me to be putting your mouth on me!" She glanced at the crowd surrounding them, then turned to the fly ass dude who'd invited her over to dance for his cousin. "This nasty mother—"

"Calm down, lil mama?" he interrupted. "For my sake, please forgive him."

"Just give me my money so I can get the fuck from over here."

He started peeling from his knot. She tried to remain calm, but her ass felt wet, and his cousin had the audacity to be sitting there laughing. That upset Falicia even more. He handed Falicia forty-dollars when he only owed her ten.

"That's for your inconvenience," he said. "Don't pay him no mind." Falicia looked from the guy to Zeke, who still had a giggling problem.

"What! It's funny, nigga?" she asked, grabbing the closest chair.

"Bitch! You gone hit me?" He was up like he wanted to fight. She was ready to rumble!

Falicia swung the chair at him with hopes of going upside dude's motherfucking head. Big Al picked her up and carried her away from the commotion. She still held the chair in her hands when he placed her in between the two front doors.

"I can't believe that nigga licked me! I don't know what his nasty ass got." Big Al took the chair from her and walked her to the dressing room. "Call me a cab, Big Al. I'm ready to go." He nodded and shut the door.

Falicia grabbed her washcloth from her locker and ran over to the counter with their hygiene products on it. She grabbed rubbing alcohol and poured it down her ass crack. The liquid set her pussy ablaze. "Son of a bitch!" she screamed.

Mylena hit the corner running fast. "What's the matter?" She pulled her hair back and flipped it in a ponytail, ready to scrap.

"My coochie is burning! This nasty nigga!" Falicia hopped on two feet.

Mylena burst out laughing as Falicia now stood with her legs apart, back humped, fanning and trying to blow away her agony. At first Falicia was pissed at Mylena for laughing at her, but then she saw herself in the mirror and cracked up laughing too. Outdone for the night, she finished separating her money, and got ready to leave.

Cinnamon walked up to her. "So you leaving me?"

"Girl, I'm so over this shit for the night. That nasty . . . That bitch could have given me an infection or something that might affect my son."

"Son? Wait. When did you find out what you're having?" Cinnamon put her hands on her hips. Falicia rolled her bag toward the door. "Wait. You can't leave. The dude I was dancing for upstairs paid me a hundred dollars to come get you."

"Well, you better give it back because I'm trying to take my ass home before I have to bash somebody's head in."

"Please," she begged as she blinked her long lashes.

Falicia shook her head at her antics and laughed. "All I know is when my cab comes, I'm out."

"And I forgot, he said he didn't care if you were dressed, he just wants you to come talk to him."

Falicia stopped by the DJ booth, paid him his tip, and then went to the bar to retrieve the butter pecan ice cream the bartender, Tommy had waiting for her. She chopped it up with Tommy, enjoying each spoonful. One glance at Zeke left her disgusted. Mahogany, a dark skinned, pretty, plus size, but bad ass dancer was dancing for him, and his face was buried in her ass! Falicia prayed he didn't have a woman to go home to.

Finally she made her way over to dude who requested she come and talk to him. Someone got her a chair, and she sat next to him while someone danced for him. "What's up?" she asked.

"From what I hear, you didn't want to come chill with a nigga." He was soft spoken and made a lot of gestures with his hands.

"Yeah, you heard right, and you need to put some bass in your voice talking to me." He was amused by her directness. "And I won't be in your presence much longer. My cab will be here any minute."

"Now that's cold . . ."

"What's cold?"

"You just sat down, and you already trying to run off before I even get the chance to change your mind."

"Can't always get what you want," she stated.

"So is that the case here?" He was smooth. Still there wasn't a line he could tell her that she hadn't heard before.

"Was that the case when you asked me to come over to dance for you and you sent me over to that muthafucka—"

"Wait, wait, wait." He threw his hands up and mumbled something.

"What! That was some disrespectful shit. For real, I'm not one of these simple minded 'hos. I prefer to invite people to my body." She finished her ice cream.

"You know what? You got heart, lil mama. You got heart, but I didn't call you over here to fight. For real. Can we start over?" He extended his hand, waiting for her to shake it. She didn't budge. "Really? So that's how you do a nigga? That's fucked up!" They laughed together.

"I'm Ike." He extended his hand again.

"I'm Fantasia." She smiled.

"Nice to meet you, Falicia," he retorted.

"What? Who told you that?" He took her by surprise.

"I got my ways of finding out what I need to know and already ordered your favorite: wings, extra hot, and wet flats." He grinned mischievously.

"Who told you my name and what I like to eat? Cinnamon?"

"All you need to know is I know a lot about you. So. Are you going to grace me with your presence while we eat?"

Falicia was slightly impressed and decided to entertain his company. He even paid her to sit with him. She chilled with Ike until the music went off and the lights came on. Somewhere between getting her things together and counting her money,

Falicia lost Ike's number. It was the first night that she had made over seven hundred dollars, and she had Ike to thank for most of that.

She put an extra pep in her step in hopes of catching him in the parking lot. "Shit!" she shouted after almost tripping over some dude stretched out on the pavement with blood all over his face. "Oh my God!" The guy was barely conscious, holding a broken beer bottle.

The moment she eased away, her attention was drawn to a Champagne colored Lincoln that seemed to be chasing a guy running up Marietta Street. Some dude wearing an orange hat and shirt stopped the car and jumped out. *Didn't Ike have on an orange hat and shirt?* she thought.

"OMG, that's Ike!" Falicia said to no one in particular. Ike two-pieced the guy he had been chasing, and the guy hit the ground hard.

"I gotta go make sure he's all right," she told Big Al, whom she hadn't seen standing there before. She made her way toward the Lincoln.

"Baby girl, what you doing out here? You don't even know him," Big Al said. He grabbed Falicia by the arm and no sooner than he did, the police pulled up and made Ike get on the ground. The Lincoln pulled up directly in front of her. The man who had given her a chair to sit next to Ike in the club was now driving. She asked him for Ike's number, and once it was in her hands, she smiled.

"I'm definitely going to call him as soon as he makes bond." The cops had placed an uncooperative Ike in handcuffs and put him in the back of the police cruiser. Falicia was impressed.

CHAPTER 14

The club was poppin! It was perfect for the new Falicia! After last night, she saw things with a different perspective. She had been nickel and diming the game. Bitches were really leaving the club with close to a thousand dollars a night, if not a stack. She had to step her game up and do it quickly before the baby put her ass on temporary rest. She was like a beast trying to get hers, and not everyone wanted to align with her plans. Some niggas were turning her down.

"Yo, ma, you cute, but you're a little too skinny for me."

Another dude replied, "You sexy, but I don't like my women that dark." And then there were others who simply said, "Naw, I'm good right now."

Falicia learned quickly that she had to toughen her skin. So instead of taking it personal, she made them think twice about not breaking bread with her. She'd find someone who sat close to the guy who'd turned her down, or who was within eyesight and gave him all she had, while glancing in the direction of the one who rejected her.

She was dancing for a guy when a gang of dudes walked into the club and caught her eye. Ike and his crew were back in the house. Ike walked up to her. Falicia lit up like a Christmas tree.

"Let's go . . . you know what it is," he said as he walked up to her and pulled her into his embrace. The fact that she was in the middle of a dance made her a little uncomfortable.

"I'll be over there when this . . ."

"What?" He smiled, and then looked behind her. Ike went in his pocket and pulled out a ten dollar bill and place it on the bar next to dude's drink. He grabbed Falicia's arm and escorted her to the middle of the room. She mouthed, "Sorry" to the dude she was dancing for. He didn't look too pleased, but he was playa about it.

Ike sat in the cut and pulled her into his lap. "I didn't think I would see you anytime soon," she confessed.

"As long as I got money, can't nobody hold me down," he replied.

Falicia stared into his eyes. That was her personal motto. What spoke volumes to her most was, regardless of what was going on in her life, nobody could hold her down.

Thanks to his contributions, she had another good night. When the club closed, he tried to convince her to go to breakfast with him and his friends.

"What's the problem with you accompanying me?" he asked for the third time. She leaned against the wall outside the dressing room. Normally, customers weren't allowed in that area. Jerry looked the other way when he saw Ike escorting her.

"What business do I have leaving with you at this time in the morning?" she asked, smirking.

"Because after we eat, I just wanna rub you to sleep."

"Really?" Falicia hadn't met one nigga who could lay next to her and not at least attempt to sex her, and here Ike was speaking of rubbing her to sleep.

"Most, definitely. Baby girl, please believe . . . pussy ain't a matter for me. I just want to spend some time with you, and then rub you to sleep just like I said."

Regardless of what Ike confessed, nothing about her leaving with him was ladylike. If she said yes, she'd be breaking her own morals. *I'm not just some booty call, and I won't be handled as such. Plus, I'm pregnant with another man's baby. So there's no point in investing my time into something new.* And the last thing was the circumstances in which Falicia met him. She felt she'd make a stronger impression by declining his offer. Besides, he had money and could get any bitch he wanted. She gave him her cell number and bid him goodnight. His disappointment was apparent. Falicia hopped in the cab, shutting herself down for the night.

A Treacherous Hustle

She had just walked in her bedroom, closed the door, and kicked off her shoes when her phone rang. Falicia answered immediately to keep from disturbing Letty, who had to get up soon.

"You straight?" Ike inquired, before she could say hello.

"Yeah, I am. Thank you for checking," she answered while undressing.

"No doubt. Shit, for real I wish I could know you were straight every day, all day."

Falicia didn't say a word, just tried not to smile too damn hard. She wasn't certain what she had done, but she was beginning to feel like she might have lucked-up. They talked for almost an hour, as she listened to him clown with his folks at IHOP and brag about talking to her. At some point he got too raunchy for her taste. He kept talking to her while pulling his penis out in the restaurant and promptly got kicked out. He thought it was hilarious. She did not.

Sometime after she had fallen asleep, he called her again. "I know you sleep, but I wanted to hear your voice before I went to sleep." It was after six in the morning. Falicia rolled over on her back.

"Okay, well you should probably get off this phone and go to bed."

"You right, but it's going to be hard because it seems like you should be next to me."

"Whatever, Ike. Besides, it's too early for you to be running game. I'm going back to sleep."

"I ain't running game. I'm keeping shit real."

The more they conversed, the more she yearned to tell him about her baby, but for some reason she kept pushing him away. Yet he kept calling and popping up at the club. Here she was, going back and forth with Sid about their son, and Ike popped up in her life and showered her with all this admiration and attention that she had been dying for. A man eleven years her elder. By the time she built up the nerve to tell him she was pregnant, she had already rehearsed the exact words she would speak to him over a thousand times.

"I already know that," he responded nonchalantly. "Baby girl, I told you from day one I did my background check on you."

"But who—"

"Now, you should know that I'm not going to reveal my source. But I do know you from Florida. You got an older sister that works with you. You used to fuck with a nigga named Cash. You pregnant by this young cat named Sid. And that overall, you're a good girl. "

"Oh, okay." Falicia was impressed.

"Let me explain something to you. I been knowing all this shit, and it doesn't change my stance. I want you, and therefore that means everything that comes with you. Shit, how I see it, if you be mine, your baby is my baby. Everything concerning you, concerns me. You feel me?"

Falicia was at a loss for words. With a nigga like this on her side, she wouldn't have to struggle. She and her baby would be straight. With the knowledge she had about how to satisfy and keep a man, she would have dude wrapped around her finger. Things were starting to look up. Her son just might be raised in a family setting after all.

"So, what are your plans for Sunday?" he asked. "I know you ain't gonna keep telling me no."

When Sunday arrived, Falicia was a nervous wreck. This dude named Andrew was the only "date" she had ever had, but he was just something to do whenever she was bored. With Ike, this was different. They shared a mutual interest, and he was not only a man, but a well experienced one. He represented everything she should probably stay away from. Ike sold out to the streets and was married to the game, reckless as fuck, and weak for her. The perfect ingredients for a bitch like her who was striving to get more out of life than what poverty offered. She wasn't sure what to wear because she didn't know where they were going.

"What's up, Sunshine?" he asked. "I'll be there soon. I got to drop one of my workers off something to eat, and then I'll be there."

"Okay, but I was calling to ask where we were going?" She opened her closet door and stared inside. Everything was getting too small.

"It's a surprise. So wear whatever you want to wear. Ain't no motherfucker gone tell you, you can't come in because of the way you're dressed. If you want, you can be naked. I got somewhere we can go for that too." They laughed.

She mentioned her date to Letty and sat outside on their tiny patio with her to waste some time, until Ike arrived. She called him several times, but didn't get an answer. By the time the sun set, she wrapped her hair and got in bed. Pulling out her coloring book, she began her therapy. Letty came to check on her.

"You all right?"

"Yes," Falicia answered, without looking up.

"You only color when something is on your mind."

"I just don't understand. Why would he say he would be here shortly if he wasn't?" Letty stared at her as if she could feel her daughter's disappointment.

"You know, Boo-Boo. Something could have come up."

"I know. But that doesn't change how I feel. He could have called."

Sometime in the wee hours of the night her cell rang. "What?" she answered.

"Sunshine," Ike said.

"Why you calling me now?" she snapped.

"Baby, come on. Check this. I know you probably mad at a nigga, but under no circumstances would I leave you hanging like that. As soon as I pulled in the drive-thru, I was ambushed. Police everywhere. You would have thought I was wanted for murder or some shit."

"So you locked up right now?"

Sereniti Hall

"Yeah, in this holding cell with all these muhfuhs."

"Then why didn't you call me collect?"

"Because I got my cell phone with me."

"Then you should have been called me by now then."

"Baby, I . . ."

"Fuck your excuses, Ike. Don't come half-stepping with me."

He took a minute to answer. "You right."

Ike explained that because he was already on probation in Fulton County, he was being transferred from DeKalb County to the area of his offense. He wanted her to visit him.

Falicia wasted no time, and started catching the train to see him once a week and looked forward to being in his company. Something for her finally felt real, something they might not have done had he not gotten locked up.

Ike sat opposite the glass smiling at her, as if her presence was the most awakening thing that existed. It was the perfect time for her to get to know him. "So, tell me all about who you really are."

"What you mean?"

"I wanna know about Ike."

"What about him?"

"Who is he?"

"You mean you don't wanna know about me as Slim, the dope boy, or the dude that demands his respect in the streets?"

"No, I don't."

He smiled. "So you wanna know about Ike Newberry. The one who stayed in group homes and was subjected to various forms of abuse before he was adopted, and was always compared to his adopted brother." His face still held a smile, but his eyes didn't.

Falicia lost her smile as well.

"You still wanna know more?"

"Yes."

"A'ight then. I was labeled as a trouble maker instead of being viewed as merely trying to find my place in life. Or labeled as the one who turned to the streets because the streets accepted my kind." He finished with a shrug. She was surprised that he opened up to her so easy. Every conversation they had was profound.

"Soooo, I'm gonna be straight up. I'm really worried about getting too close to you because it seems like everything I love gets taken from me. Like my momma, for instance. Some dude always steals her from me. That's one of the reasons I'm here in Georgia now. That shit always leave me feeling like second best, and I hate that," Falicia said.

"I feel you." Ike nodded as if he understood.

"Got drama with Sid, my baby's daddy too. But I ain't trippin'. 'Cause I'ma take care of my baby without him. No matter what." Falicia gave Ike the chance to know her in her most vulnerable, authentic state. A state she had only revealed to one other man. Also, she disclosed how she justified being a dancer with the intention of using the money to finish school.

"I'ma change all that for you one day," Ike said, filling her with hope. "Did I tell you I got caught at the age of twelve bending my teacher over her desk, giving her what she was begging for?"

"What! No. And never mind, I don't even want to know." Falicia frowned. They laughed a lot. He showered her with affectionate words and began to express what he wanted to do to her sexually. She blushed. Grinned. He stared into her eyes. Licked his lips. Glanced down. Stared at his hand. He lifted his shirt. His erect penis was pressed against his stomach.

"What the fuck!" she blurted out and threw her hand over her mouth. He chuckled. She didn't find it funny and looked over her shoulder to see if anybody else was watching. He flashed it again. "Why in the hell is it so big?" she asked, her face twisted and turned like something was stinking.

He caught his breath. Her discomfort was hilarious to him. His horny ass made his horse dick jump under his shirt. Her frown deepened as she shook her head.

"I don't know what makes you think you putting that thing in me. It is huge!" Her vagina already hurt just thinking about it. She didn't even know they came in that size.

He rubbed the glass as if he was touching her. "I'ma take it easy on you, Sunshine." He sat back and made his dick jump again. "Because you ain't ready to handle all of this man."

What she should've regarded as pure disrespect got brushed aside because of the words he spoke about who he had been as a child and who he had become as a man. She ignored the small voice that warned her to be careful. Instead, she left there feeling as if she had won the love lottery.

From that visit, a series of visits started, and she grew to love Ike's mind and his pain. She had pain too. Maybe he could fill her void and she, his. If this new love felt so right, why wouldn't the nagging voice inside of her head stop?

CHAPTER 15

"The next visitor for Ike Newberry," was announced over the loud speaker.

Falicia passed a female who made it her business to see what she looked like. The chick tried to be discreet, but the second Falicia heard her man's name, all discretion went out the door. The woman was close to her height, if not an inch taller. Her straight, silky hair might've been real as it danced on her shoulders. She was thicker than Falicia with nice legs exposed by a split in her gray skirt. *This bitch checking me out!* Falicia turned up and strutted like the model she was, until she was out of sight.

"Don't worry about her," Ike expressed, once she later questioned him about her.

"I'm not. I just wanted you to know that I peeped that. In the meantime, I need to get off this call. Cinnamon can't take me to my doctor's appointment tomorrow, so I need to find a ride."

"Let me handle it."

At 8:30 a.m., a car pulled up in front of her house and blew the horn. *This nigga making it happen, even from a jail cell*, Falicia thought, locking the door. She wasted no time being courteous to the female she saw at the jail visiting Ike. Never would she allow a broad to know where she was mentally.

"Good morning," Falicia said in a cheerful voice.

The brown-skinned woman returned her greeting. "Morning. So where are we headed?"

Falicia politely gave her the address to her doctor's office, oblivious to her relationship with Ike, yet confident she was about to piece it all together. She took immediate notice of Falicia's neutral-colored, form-fitting dress and her neutral four-inch sandals. She smiled at her chauffeur.

"I'm Falicia." *Good thing I dressed cute.*

"I know . . . I'm Velvet," she said in a dry tone.

"So how do you know me?"

Velvet kept her attention on the road. "Ike talks about you all the time."

"Does he?"

"Yeah," she admitted, as if she really wasn't thrilled about driving Falicia around, or having a conversation with her.

Falicia eyed her white top with a lace front. Ike made a big deal about her wearing a skirt when she visited him. And Velvet had one on. It was either a coincidence, or there was more to the arrangement than she was aware of.

"If I'm not mistaken, I saw you at the jail," Falicia replied.

"You did."

"Well, if Ike told you about me,"—She sat back—"I wonder why he failed to mention you." Falicia delivered a bomb and sat back to watch it explode. Velvet sped up. "Did he tell you we're having a boy?"

"That's his baby?" She looked confused and repeated herself. "That's his baby?"

"He didn't tell you?" Velvet grabbed a pack of cigarettes from the side door compartment, accelerating the car. Falicia laughed inside and pretended she was searching through her phone. She had definitely shut it down, but she expected to see her in the near future.

Velvet became a face Falicia saw almost daily. She picked her up for work and took her home at night. She didn't have any kids and was at least seven years older than Falicia. Velvet learned the dope trade from her father and was trusted to handle Ike's business while he was in jail. Eventually, Velvet grew comfortable with Ike's arrangement and began to open up. Falicia kept her cool and waited to learn what she needed to, unlike some people who lost their cool and jumped the gun the second they heard or saw something contrary to their perceived impression. The game taught Falicia how to sit back and watch shit unfold. To play the background and offer advice whenever asked, or she deemed it necessary.

As had become the norm, Velvet was just chatting away while Falicia took it all in and decided to offer her opinion.

"Well, I personally feel you should make a man wait some months before you have relations with him," Falicia suggested.

Velvet gasped. "Girl, months?"

"This ain't no 'ho he's dealing with. So treat me accordingly," she boasted.

"But how in the hell do you do it? I be too horny," Velvet replied.

"Well then, don't be surprised when that dude treats you like the next bitch or booty call." Falicia reflected on her previous relationships in Florida.

Velvet exited the interstate on Marietta Street, bypassing the ESPN center, a familiar landmark only minutes from Dancers Elite. "I feel where you coming from, Falicia. And it does make sense."

"Plus, if you rushing into bed with niggas, you subjecting yourself to catching something. Ike's ass will definitely be getting an STD test when he gets out," Falicia added, purposely throwing out bait.

"Oh, he straight, girl. I just got checked and don't have nothing. So he good."

Falicia's temperature soared. Her armpits got sweaty. *I could just about box with this bitch. So this nigga got the bitch he's fucking, catering to the needs of the bitch he wants to have a future with!* Falicia thought. She put her purse on her shoulder with grace. "Well, that's good to hear."

"Yeah . . ." Velvet pulled into the parking lot that Dancer's Elite shared with Bar One.

"Thanks for the ride." She opened her door. "But don't worry about coming to pick me up tonight."

"Are you sure?" she expressed, heedless of Falicia's insult.

"I have something else going on. So you don't have to pick me up tomorrow either." Falicia exited Velvet's car and removed her bag from the back.

Velvet turned around, anxiously.

"Falicia, I really don't mind. Growing up in the game, it's nice having another woman to talk to."

"That's sweet, I suppose. And I appreciate you taking me everywhere I needed to go."

"Aww . . . You're welcome."

"But this is our last time." Falicia closed the door and walked away.

"Falicia . . ." Velvet called out of the window. "What do you want me to tell Ike?"

"Tell him that I'm glad to know he's free of STDs."

Ike became relentless with his collect calls over the next days, disregarding her refusal to accept them. She didn't have time to be a part of anybody's equation. She took a chance and was willing to try again with him because he appeared different. Instead of sitting around the house disenchanted, Falicia accepted a lunch invitation with Miles, an older cat who faithfully came to Pin Up's to spend his money on her.

Falicia hadn't danced there since she came back from Florida and found out she was pregnant. He picked her up from the Underground bus station, ecstatic to see her. She enjoyed her first meal at the Cheesecake Factory, and afterward convinced him to take her to get her clit pierced.

Miles may have been in his late forties, but he was one sexy ass black man in her eyes. Mocha skin, fine curly hair tapered close, and brown eyes. And he was around five eleven, medium build, and bow legged. In addition, the tailor made the suits he rocked indicate "success," and that shit made him sexier! The tattoo shop sat dead center in the hood. Miles stood tall but out of place in his tailored pants, button down shirt, and Stacy Adams. He flashed her a bright smile when she led him inside by the hand.

"How you doing, Black?" stated Alex, whose body was full of piercings. He always came in Pin Up's getting dances and promoting his business. "So, you finally decided to come give me back some of my money." They hugged.

"Not really, because Miles is giving me this lil present. And it's bad luck to give a man his money back." Alex looked at her like: Where you hear that from? The trio laughed.

Miles, stepping outside to take an incoming call while the self-proclaimed "king of body piercing" led Falicia to his booth.

Alex sanitized everything, and besides a little rip to the hood of her clit, Falicia felt nothing else during the piercing. Once her clit was pierced, she passed out a few sexy flyers of her and Mylena advertising her birthday bash. She quickly left with Miles at her side. They headed back to the car. As they walked, Falicia laid her head on his shoulder and smiled up at him. Miles always told her how much he loved her big brown eyes.

"I got something for you," she teased. His eyes lit up as if to ask, "Is it sex?" He opened her door. When he got inside, she said, "This is for you." And put her panties in his hand. "I don't have any use for them right now."

"Woman, this ain't fair. How you gone dangle loose carrots in the rabbit's face?"

"Who said I was just dangling?"

He grinned big and didn't say another word as he pulled out of the parking lot and drove to the Downtown Westin. Although she and Miles had a great afternoon, her heart was filled with thoughts of Ike the entire time.

Later, when he pulled in front of Dancer's Elite, he took her hand and placed a large number of bills in it.

"What's this for?" she asked.

Miles kissed the back of it. "For all the money you missed out on, giving me the best afternoon I've had in a long time."

Falicia shared his sentiment on her way inside and did her thing all night like she had a lot to celebrate. Which began with trying to put Ike Newberry out of her mind. And his flytrap, Velvet. He rang her phone all morning, every morning for a whole week. She snatched up the phone around noon on the eighth day.

"What is it?" Falicia answered.

"Sunshine, what's up?" His tone was chill, but full of questions.

She rolled her eyes. "Why you keep calling here like this? I'm—"

"So that's how you talk to your nigga?"

"Naw. Actually, I have more respect for my nigga because he respects me."

"Baby . . . Come on now. This how you're gonna be?"

"Baby, nothing! You can call me by name." She grabbed her cup from the nightstand and stomped downstairs.

"Chill wit' all that shit. I'm trying to figure out why you haven't accepted any of my calls?"

She snatched open the refrigerator, pissed off to the point where she wouldn't spare his feelings. "Because I don't want to talk to you." Somebody laughed on the other end. She frowned. "Who you call me through anyway? How you gonna give somebody I don't know, my number?"

"He's my homie. But hey, check the move. Shit ain't what it seem. You tripping on a nigga without fully understanding what's really going on."

"Well, until you ready to fill me in, stop fucking calling me. Because I don't appreciate a bitch telling me that my nigga ain't got shit because *she* straight. Fuck you and that busted bitch you sent to cater to me."

"Sunshine, chill the fuck out. Now!"

"Nigga, don't tell me what to do. Tell them motherfuckers that work for you what to do." She hung up. Seconds later her phone rang. "What!" she shouted, wanting to fuss some more.

"Baby, don't hang up this phone. Just come see a nigga so I can explain what time it really is."

"If I can make time, I'll come."

"What?" He was stunned.

"You heard me. If I can find time."

He burst out laughing. "Girl. I'ma fuck the shit outta you! You gone feel me."

"Whatever! I don't know what makes you think—"

He laughed even more. "Fuck you talking about? That's my baby and my pussy."

"No, it's not . . . I'm only giving myself to the one who doesn't allow other people to tell me shit about them that I don't know." He was quiet for a second.

"You right . . ." She finally filled her cup up with juice, then closed the refrigerator. This call had been long enough. Falicia sat at the kitchen table and propped her feet on the closest chair.

"Damn right, I am. And don't be calling here unless I come to see you."

"You out your fucking mind. I'm gon' give you a pass because you in your feelings. But you got an appointment Friday, right?" She glanced at the dates she marked on the calendar hanging on the back door. *How the fuck does he know this?* "I'm sending somebody through there. He'll be there by eight. If it's too early, give his ass something to do until you need to head out to see about my son."

"No, I'm good. I—"

"Shut that shit up, Falicia. And be up to see me this week."

"We'll see," she said, trying to play hard. "Bye." She clicked the mute button, pretending to hang up.

"No. Later, Sunshine. Not bye."

"That's her?" she heard a dude say on the other line. "Shorty sound like she a trip."

"Nah, man. She the one," Ike replied.

"Straight up?"

"Fuck yeah. Ain't met one like her." He sounded as if he was smiling. "But I'll holla at you later. 'Preciate you, man."

Falicia held the phone to her heart. *Did he say I was the one?* Damn she couldn't help but feel special. She hadn't been singled out like that outside of running track and modeling. But this was something else. He was a twenty-seven-year-old man with money, power, and respect, boasting to his friend that his sixteen-year-old secret, outshined all the bitches he came in contact with.

Most young girls raised in the hood dreamed of having a thoroughbred by her side. Someone to take them from rags to riches. *Wow*, she thought. *This nigga can take me and my son where we deserve to be.*

CHAPTER 16

The next couple months sped by without Falicia's permission. Final preparations were made for her party and Falicia needed the date of the scheduled party to hurry and arrive because she was beginning to gain weight in areas that might indicate that she was with child. Letty made her infamous potato salad and crab salad, but couldn't be convinced to come celebrate with them. The house mom grilled the ribs, pork chops, and burgers. To set the night off, Falicia bought blue jeans of various shades from a thrift store, a hot-glue gun, some cubic Zirconia stones, and thread from Walmart. Then she cut and sewed shorts, G-strings, skirts, halters, and tube tops for the dancers for the birthday stage set.

The sisters began their night with Mylena dressed in a revealing red patent leather body suit with devil horns, a tail, and a pitchfork. Falicia graced Dancer's Elite in a white leather corset with a halo. They danced for the packed club until the birthday set, the time when all of the dancers, including Mylena and Falicia, put on their outfits, got on stage, and fascinated pussy-thirsty men into making it storm for the birthday girls only.

Following an outstanding performance, the dancers left Mylena and Falicia on stage alone. Phil, Cinnamon's baby daddy, pulled out a ten-dollar bill with his gaze stuck between Falicia's legs. With his eyeballs still transfixed on her vagina, Phil slid the money up Falicia's thigh and under her garter.

"Happy Birthday, Falicia." Phil licked his lips.

Cinnamon stood next to him, glowing with his child. She wasn't showing yet, but decided to stop dancing. She smiled and shook her head as if she didn't seem to mind. He continued cheesing at Falicia. She locked eyes with another dude by the stage, leaving Phil behind with whatever depraved thoughts he envisioned.

Right when the night seemed to be slowing down, Big Boi

Sereniti Hall

showed up and turned the club out, stunning Mylena and Falicia that he was actually in their neck of the woods, partying with them. The sisters agreed their party was worth their every effort on their way home. Since this was close to her beginning her maternity leave, Falicia had wanted to give her patrons something to remember. Her only complaint was that the house mom cooked the ribs too long, and Ike couldn't be there.

On the following Friday, Shy, the dude Ike said he would send, picked Falicia up to start her work week all over again. He was a high-yellow guy, around six feet tall and 180 pounds, down to earth and quiet. As she was getting to know him, he mentioned trying to holler at her, and getting her to dance for him before she had even met Ike. Shy had soft, nappy hair that he wore in a fro, unless he rocked cornrows. And judging by the way his clothes hung from his body, he had a decent build, but he wasn't her type.

Shy made himself more available than Velvet, whether it was taking Falicia shopping, picking up her nephews, taking her to work, or to her doctor appointments or to see Ike. Even if she just wanted to chill, he was there if he wasn't at work. Regardless of his motive for always being on go-mode, when she called him, he was faithful to the point that her midwife and doctor thought he was her unborn son's father. Shy stopped his car in front of Dancer's Elite.

Falicia stared at the door. "I can't do this today, Shy."

"You sure?" he asked several times, before he burned rubber on his way to the Cobb Galleria mall. After browsing around, he purchased a Sean John denim jumper that everybody was rocking. Falicia got some ice cream.

Their next destination was a refined subdivision boasting apartments and townhomes. A heavyset, dark-skinned woman approached the window with a Shih Tzu in her arms.

"Hey, you," she said with a broader than necessary grin.

"How you doin', Tracy? That's a nice dog," Shy commented. "When you get that?"

She eyed Falicia. "So who's this? Boy, I can't never keep up with you."

"This is Falicia. I'm keepin' her company until Ike gets out."

Tracy threw her hand over her heart. "Ohh! I miss that nigga!" Falicia turned to her slowly. Tracy got louder. "I can't *wait* for him to come fuck the shit outta me!"

Shy started letting up his window. "Woman, you stupid."

"No I'm not. I tell him all the time. Shit, can't nobody lay the pipe like Ike does."

Falicia sat back, appalled. *Did this bitch just say Ike?* She cut her eyes at Tracy, sizing her up. There was nothing attractive about her, not her broken-off-ass relaxed hair, her big flat face, or her damn body. All she was left to assume was that Tracy had money, but that didn't change the infraction brewing that another bad-body bitch was claiming Ike was fucking her.

Shy wrapped up his conversation and got back on the expressway. Falicia glanced at him. He glanced back. *He wanted me to hear that.* Those words resonated in her spirit. She wondered if Shy was trying to look out for her, or himself. Another unsolved mystery was if Ike really thought he could use Shy to keep her pleased and to keep his eyes on her.

After she cursed Ike's ass out for not being one hundred with her about his dealings in the street, she decided she needed a little company of her own. Falicia wasn't buying his excuse about what he did before she came into the picture. They both knew he still had 'hos wishing on a star, and the more she hung with Shy, she grew to better understand the life they lived before she came around. Shy had no problem taking her around other dudes whose living arrangements and after dark activities reminded her of LA. What his actions didn't reveal . . . he would eventually tell her.

But in the meantime, Mr. Shaun White had become a regular guest at her mother's house.

"I wish he was my grandson's daddy," Letty often remarked

about Shaun, a senior in high school that had become a regular guest at their house. There were plenty times when Falicia came home and Shaun would be in the living room with Letty eating dinner and watching a movie. She didn't have a problem heading to bed and leaving her daughter alone in front of the television with him. Falicia stretched out on the sofa with her head in his lap.

Their late nights alone lead to conversations that made Falicia giggle like seventeen-year-old girls giggle. It was cool to talk to a dude without him trying to lay her down. Falicia began seducing him. Within weeks, his young and inexperienced sex game was upgraded. They were fucking at least twice in her room, or in the living room on the sofa, the floor, or against the wall.

She had turned that smiling, well-mannered young man into her personal freak with just enough wood to fill her and leave him thinking about what he was going to do to her next. And what she was going to do to him. Watching him bust his first nut made her feel like she was in control again. Empowered. She had no plans of ever relinquishing control again. And then there was Ike.

Even though she wasn't feeling Ike as much, and there was plenty she would have to see from him to believe anything he said, Falicia gave him her word that she was coming. Still Falicia went to see him whenever she could, but it had become a task. Shy worked during Ike's hours of visitation, so it left her using Marta.

"You got too much leg showing," a deputy stated one afternoon as she tried to visit Ike. The split in her dress stopped at her knee, and she wore a dainty button-down sweater to cover her arms.

"Oh my God!" Falicia cried. "I'm pregnant and had to walk to the train station, and then catch a bus that dropped me off here." She was obviously very pregnant.

"Walk her out," he said to one of the women deputies. Falicia bawled all the way home. By the time she got back home, Ike had been blowing up her phone and was so mad when she told him what happened, he snatched the phone out of the wall.

"That nigga is wild." Shy laughed when she told him what happened.

He picked up Mylena's boys, dropped them off, and then stayed for dinner. After she put them to sleep, they stepped in the sun room so Shy could smoke a blunt. She opened a window as soon as he lit it up. In his zone, the nigga started talking like they were having pillow talk.

"Yeah, this nigga met Velvet like a year before you came into the picture. She good at selling dope, but man, she has cost Ike a lot of money."

Falicia opened a second window, curious to know how and why. Shy blew a ring of smoke into the air, laughing to himself.

"Man, I'll never forget that time when . . ." He shook his head. "Damn. So we at the hotel where Ike trappin' at, right? And I'm chilling. Next thing I know this chick came racing out of the room with a bloody sheet wrapped around her, screaming like her ass is on fire. I look up and this dude is in the door with a straight razor. Chill as hell like it ain't shit." Shy laughed and shook his head. "This nigga was in bed with Velvet, slicing at her skin with just-below-the-surface kind of cuts, while her ass was sleep. Freaked me the fuck out! But Velvet still keep coming back for more. And he keeps dealing with her because she is reliable and does whatever he says. She be causing him losses though. And Velvet ass is too emotional." He put out his blunt. "But you . . ." Shy poked her shoulder playfully. "You are the best thing Ike could have ever met, Ms. Falicia Blakely."

Falicia grinned on the inside. *I know I am. I just hope he is my best thing. That crazy bitch must've lost him a lot of money. How can I get rid of her stupid ass?*

CHAPTER 17

"Baby, it's all good!" Ike said.

"Really?" Falicia sat straight up in bed.

"Hell yeah! I'll be wrapping you in my arms real soon," Ike said into the receiver. "I got a week left in this bitch, and then I'm out this motherfucker on the seventeenth. But it's only one thing I have to tell you."

"What?" She didn't like the sound of his tone. "What, Ike? Don't tell me you have to go to another county?"

"Nah . . . nah, nothing like that, baby. But do you remember how I snatched that phone out the wall?"

"Yeah," Falicia answered, holding her breath because she wasn't sure what he was about to tell her.

"Well, I have to go upstairs to lockdown and spend the rest of my time there until I leave."

"Okay, so what are you saying? What's so bad about that?"

"That means I won't be able to call you."

"Damn, that's effed up."

"Yeah, I know."

"But at least you'll be here when the baby is born."

"Hell yeah! That's the move right there."

Shortly after they ended the call, the excitement Falicia experienced when she first met Ike slowly began to rekindle. Standing in the mirror gazing at her growing belly, she couldn't avoid grinning or deny the anticipation of knowing it was almost over. That idea of Ike being released melted away all the pressure between them. Now he could prove himself to her and prove he was a man of his word. In spite of her happiness about Ike coming home, there was still Sid's ass to deal with. They were still at odds.

Falicia didn't understand why her mother had purchased everything their son would need. The house she and Letty lived in wasn't big enough to give him his own nursery, so they put all of his stuff in Falicia's room, and it was beyond cramped. The instant she pointed it out to him, after slapping his hand off her ass, all Sid could think of to say was, "What?"

"You haven't given me a penny, that's what. But I'm not about to waste energy on yo' ass. But I am going to make sure my son is straight. Yo' bitch ass went through all this to bring him into this world and just because *we* ain't up for discussion, you act like my baby ain't up for your consideration."

"Yeah, okay," he stated, and left with a shrug.

Her final days toward her due date were moving fast. Falicia wasn't sure what had become of Shy. He wouldn't answer her calls. As usual, Cinnamon came through for her and she and her baby's father, Phil, picked her up. They decided she'd spend the night, and then go to her appointment in the morning.

On the way there, Falicia mentioned having anal sex with Ike to Cinnamon, who had asked how things were progressing between them. Somehow Phil injected himself to their conversation. Falicia ignored his stupid ass. Most of that entire evening was a bad idea. She had to set Phil's wanna-be-a-rapper ass straight because he kept coming at her on some sexual shit whenever Cinnamon left the room. She finally had enough when he removed the curtain while she was showering. She snatched a towel and covered her body.

"Sorry ass nigga! You got the wrong bitch. Step to me like this one more time, and Ike's gonna fuck you up. I said I liked yo' music, not yo' busta ass!"

"How Ike gonna fuck me up?" Phil laughed. "He's in jail. What he gonna do? Beat my ass from his cell? So you might as well go ahead and let me taste it. I won't tell. If you won't."

Falicia glared at him. "Bitch, we'll see. He getting out December 17." The smirk dropped off his face. It was only a few days away. "Nigga, you still standing there?" Phil left the bathroom with urgency. "That's what I thought."

Headed to her doctor's office, Cinnamon did most of the talking in the car. Falicia halfway listened. Her thoughts were too busy trying to figure out how she would tell her friend that her baby's daddy was trying to fuck her right under her nose. She decided to wait until she spoke to her mother. Letty would tell her what she should do. Or Ike, since he would be out soon. She began her count down. In seventy-two hours, her man would be home.

The night before his release, Falicia could barely sleep. With Ike being gone and discovering that she was loyal, yet not about anybody's bullshit, made them closer than she was to anybody. Even the sun seemed to be shining extra bright when she woke up on the morning of. The first thing she did was check her phone. By two o'clock, she was beginning to panic. She dialed 411 and got the number for DeKalb's information.

"Ma'am, I have an Ike Newberry, but I'm showing he was released December the eleventh."

December the what? Falicia thanked her for her help, anxious to get back to what she needed to do. It all began to make sense to her. She cried as she realized he hadn't wanted her to know his release date so he could spend time with some fat bitch, which explained Shy's instant absence. The hurt caused more questions such as: Why would he lie about getting out? Why even tell her a date at all? Hurt soon turned into concern. She called every county jail in Atlanta, in case he had gotten arrested again. She tried Shy's phone. Disconnected. His parents . . . Bingo!

"Hello?"

"Hello. May I speak with Mrs. or Mr. Newberry?" Falicia asked politely.

"Who's calling?"

"My name is Falicia. I'm calling in reference to Ike Newberry." She heard the phone shuffling and someone whispering.

"Hello!" A man's voice boomed through the phone.

"Is this Ike's father?" Falicia asked, hoping to get some answers.

"Who am I speaking with?" He sounded irritated.

"Sir, I do apologize for disturbing you and your wife. My name is Falicia Blakely, and I'm looking for your son, Ike. We have a son that will be born any day, and he was released from jail this week, but I haven't heard from him. I'm only calling to inquire if you may have heard from him. I don't mean to cause any problems, and please forgive me if I have done so." She sighed. It took everything in her to maintain her composure. There was a few seconds of silence, and then he finally responded.

"Ma'am, you sound like a very decent young lady, it's unfortunate to hear you are bearing a child into this world by Ike. You have upset my wife by calling here. I have to ask you never to call here again, and if he has disappeared, that is probably the best thing that could have happened for you and your unborn child. Now excuse me, I have to tend to my wife." Just like that, he hung up the phone.

I can't believe my ears! How could someone say such a thing about their child? And how did I upset his mother by merely asking if I had the right house? Falicia thought about all the stories Ike told her about his parents treating him indifferent and being misunderstood. She just couldn't believe those people and found herself crying, and simply overwhelmed with everything. Although she was confused, one thing was for sure. She would love her baby the way she wished the people she loved most, would love her.

Her "get over Ike quick" remedy was calling Shaun over and making up for wasted time. She'd also heard that sex would make her baby come faster. So she was ready to try all suggestions. Falicia was riding Shaun backward, following Cinnamon's advice. A gush of water warmed her thighs.

"Honey, if you really want to have that baby," Cinnamon had suggested as they walked back to her car. "Let him hit that thang from the back, that's how."

"Girl, whatever!" Falicia had responded.

"I'm dead serious! I'm telling you, my girlfriend has three kids and she says it works."

"Nigga, did you nut on me?" Falicia asked Shaun, trying to stand up.

Shaun sat up and helped her get off of him. "I was about to ask you the same thing."

When she stood, fluid rushed down her legs. She burst out laughing.

"Momma!" she yelled, getting off the bed. "Momma!"

"Falicia, wait!" Shaun scrambled for his clothes.

She cut the light on, observing his toned body and his hairy ass that matched his chest. More liquid rushed down her legs.

Inside the maternity ward, the nurses busied themselves with getting her ready for delivery while she called her sister and asked her to let Cinnamon know. By the time Sid walked in the door, Falicia was about to go ham. Almost an hour had passed, and her midwife hadn't responded to any of their calls.

"If he ain't red, he ain't my baby," Sid announced.

Falicia's head turned to Mylena like the girl from *The Exorcist*. "What!" Falicia asked. A sharp pain struck her body. She gripped her stomach.

Her midwife walked in the door with Cinnamon just as the team rotated the bed, got all the linen out, and positioned her to spread it like an eagle. She cursed out everybody in the room, screamed out in pain, and almost broke Mylena's hand squeezing it. Yet, in the midst of her agony, her son's first sound calmed her.

It wasn't a cry. It was a grunt. Her midwife placed him in her arms. Sid cut his umbilical cord. She couldn't stop staring at him. He was the most beautiful being she had ever seen. She got lost in his tiny red face, cute and serious, identical to Sid's. When they locked eyes, she was in love. She kissed the top of his head. Checked to see if he had all his fingers and toes. Her midwife scooped out of her arms. Letty walked through the door right as they were cleaning him off.

"Oh, I'm right on time. Oh, look at my baby!" she exclaimed while Falicia's afterbirth was being removed, which was more excruciating than delivery. "Oh, look how he got his lil fist balled up!" Letty added, disregarding her daughter's screams. She watched over the nurses' shoulders as they cleaned him up. "He's going to be a boxer," she continued as though she couldn't help herself.

Through groggy eyes, Falicia watched her mother, sister, and friend crowd around Sid, sitting in a rocking chair holding their son. She drifted off to sleep with a smile in her heart and didn't wake up until the nurse came to educate her on breastfeeding. She jerked her head left, expecting to see Sid nowhere in sight. *I knew he was going to leave. Predictable ass.* Just then, Sid entered the room with the baby still in his arms and sat back down. *Maybe . . . just maybe he gone do right,* she thought.

As she suspected, Sid coming to the hospital was just for show and perhaps to intentionally irritate the hell out of her. He kept changing their son's name every time he signed the birth certificate. What gave him the right to think he could just up and change it when he hadn't done anything to prepare for him to come into this world?

He shook his head for the third time. "Well, I'm not feeling this name." Falicia snatched the paper from him and sat on her bed. She was going to be checking out of the hospital in the morning and he was still playing games.

"Whatever," he said and stormed out the door. She shook her head and began a new form, turning it in without his signature.

Later in the week, when she and her baby were settled in at

home, she called Sid to discuss the necessary arrangements that needed to be made, like childcare while she worked and his basic needs. "Well, he's too small for me to look after, so I'm gonna have to catch up with him, when he gets a little bigger," Sid said.

"Amazing! Fucking amazing!" Falicia sat back in her chair shaking her head. "Well, Sid. I guess I must have missed the memo that said it was all good to pick and choose when you want to tolerate your child. That you worked so hard to get."

"Yeah, okay. Here we go."

"Already went and been back twice. Peace, nigga!" Falicia hung up, done with his ignorance.

Three weeks had passed them along into late January when she noticed that her desires had begun to change. She didn't want her body exposed. Sex was the furthest thing from her mind as well, so she had no need for Shaun. And as for Ike, Letty eventually told her, "He called the night you went into labor, and I told him you were at the hospital about to give birth."

Falicia repeated her mother's exact words to Cinnamon, adding, "If that ain't some shit!" In a few weeks, she'd be back at work taking care of her own.

"Do what you gotta do, girl. Get that money," Cinnamon stated. "Shiiit, at least your son's here now. I'll be so glad when my baby gets here."

"Uh huh," Falicia said, eager to get some things off her chest. "You would think that would have motivated his ass to get back in my good graces. But it didn't. So it's all good. It don't matter anymore."

"It will be all good. Take care of yourself and your son."

"Exactly!" Falicia replied. By the middle of the year, she and Letty planned to buy a bigger house together anyway.

They were definitely going to need it, especially with how fast Mylena's boys were growing. Falicia invited them over after getting Man on a scheduled feeding and nap times. Man was her nickname

Sereniti Hall

for him. She thought loving her nephews was the capacity of her heart, but after spending long nights staring at Man, holding him while his tiny fingers gripped one of hers, she knew no love exceeded what brewed in her heart daily.

During his naptime, the boys sat in the middle of the floor playing quietly with their race cars, while she joyfully slaved over a hot stove. Suddenly, the phone rang. She thought it was Letty checking up on them. This was her first time going out ever since Falicia had moved back home. Letty had gone out one other time with Falicia before her pregnant belly started showing. They had gone to a biker's bar. A few of Letty's friends mistook Falicia for her younger sister, blowing Letty's head up. Men were trying to buy her drinks and get her to dance. Falicia declined, only interested in eating hot wings.

"Boo-Boo, come dance with me," Letty asked.

"Okay." Just as Falicia was getting ready to hit the floor, she recognized this dude from the strip club, whom she had been playing pool with. And judging by the way he kept looking at Falicia, it made her uncomfortable. Like he might possibly tell other patrons her business. Stripping wasn't something Falicia wanted anybody questioning her mother about.

Still, her friends seemed to be enjoying her presence. Everyone but her stepdad's sister, Cheryl. "That's my baby, and I would rather she be here with me, where I know she's safe than be out in the streets sneaking around with God knows who!" Letty snapped as they stood fussing at the back of the club.

"That's not the point, Letty. She's a child, and she needs to stay in a child's place. She ain't got no business in here. Period," Aunt Cheryl retorted.

What Letty said next was drowned out by the DJ announcing somebody was blocking another car and the owner needed to move their car. She leaned over the table, closer to Cheryl's face. Falicia had no clue what Letty said, but imagined she'd informed Aunt

Cheryl that Falicia's innocence was no more. Indeed she was already leading a grown woman's life, so why handle her any different? In hind sight, Falicia wished Letty would have agreed with Aunt Cheryl. Just because Falicia thought she was grown and conducted herself as such, didn't change the fact that Falicia was still a child. And there were lessons she would learn over the years through experience that would gradually lead her into maturity. Not all of them were good.

CHAPTER 18

"What's the move?" the male voice questioned Falicia from the opposite end of the line.

"I know you not calling me like we just spoke yesterday," she responded. Her nephews, Jarvis and Damian wanted to know who was calling.

"It's Shy, baby. It's Shy," she answered with a lie, only to quench their nosiness. She kissed them on their cheeks and sent them to wait at the table until she finished cooking.

"It's been a lot going on . . ."

"Who you telling? You don't know the half . . . On the real though, that don't excuse your disappearance. Nigga, you waited until I could barely get around to bail on me."

"I know. I feel you. I got to find a way to make it up. Did you have the baby? Did everything go smooth? Do you need something? Tell me what you doing, maybe I can swing through and we can catch up?" He asked so many questions she didn't know where to start with her answers.

"Man is perfect. I'm good, and tonight wouldn't be a good time. I got my nephews over here and shit. I'm just chilling with them. Maybe another time."

"What you cooking?"

"What? Why?"

"Shit, if they over there, then you or your mother cooking, one. So what you cooking?"

"You think you know me . . ." Falicia sucked her teeth. "Stir fry cabbage, fried chicken and mashed potatoes."

"What do I need to get from the store because I'm on my way?"

Shy's gray Honda pulled up in their driveway. Music blasting. Windows rattling.

"Shyyyyy!" Jarvis and Damian squealed and raced out of sight.

"Y'all better not open that front door!" Falicia yelled, taking the last batch of fried chicken out of the grease. By the time she turned the corner and headed into the living room, Damian was on his tiptoes struggling to let Shy in. Her blood rushed to her head, seeing Ike following him up the steps, grinning his butt off like she should be glad to see him.

Ike stayed on her heels the entire time Falicia took care of her nephews and got them settled in for the night. Falicia appreciated the things he made happen from his jail cell. But she had no time for anybody who couldn't be upfront with her. "Damn, a nigga can't get no love?" he asked, trying to hug Falicia for the umpteenth time.

"Nigga, fuck you. You're a liar." She slapped his hands away.

"Baby, it's not like that. I promise you it's not what you thinking. Baby, I just couldn't come straight to you like that. Broke as fuck. I ain't that nigga. I was supposed to just hit this quick lick and be back by the time I told you. I just wasn't comfortable being up under you and my son with no money in my pockets like that."

"That don't excuse you, Ike. You could have just communicated that. You don't know what I been through. I was worried sick! I even spoke with your parents, and you wouldn't believe the shit they said to me."

Please, don't call here again, his father had said. *And if Ike has disappeared, that's probably the best thing that could have happened for you and your unborn child.* She didn't understand how a parent could say something like that about their child. Her eyes began to well. "Then you missed out on the birth of the child you asked to be named after you, who you claim to love. Nigga, I'm so glad I wasn't stupid enough to listen to you."

He tried to hold her. "Baby, I just thought I was making the best decision for us. All I could think about is getting my pockets straight before I pull up, but I'm sorry I hurt you." He reached for her vagina. "Well, how about you let me put some of that in my mouth? I know I don't deserve it, but I been wondering what you—"

A Treacherous Hustle

Falicia pushed his hand aside. She checked out his new shoes. His white Sean John jogging suit, and she hadn't ever seen his chain or earth charm before. "Naw, I'm good," she replied. "Besides, when you pulled your lil disappearing act, I was fucking Shaun."

"You fuck with bitches?" He looked surprised and intrigued. "You never told me you fuck with 'hos." Several times when she was talking to him, Shaun would massage her feet or her aching back.

"Shaun is a dude," she stated. Ike's face froze. "See the difference in keeping shit real?"

He grinned. "It's all good. How much he pay you?" he joked.

"Whatever!" She escorted him and his buddy to the door.

"So you putting us out?" Ike questioned.

"Nigga, it's in your best interest to just stop talking. I'm going to deal with you on my time. Now yes, it's time to go." Ike tried to kiss her. Falicia turned her head. He kissed her cheek, then the back of Man's head. Pain was obvious in his eyes, however, that wasn't her concern at the moment. She had her own well-being to consider.

When she got settled for the night, she discovered a hundred and fifty dollars under Man's blanket. It was a kind gesture, but it didn't suffice for her pain. She gave it to Letty for groceries, appreciating her mother for being her anchor in the midst of her storm. What Falicia could not afford, Letty paid for it, although it had been a while since she had to totally depend on anyone.

The following evening, Falicia ran into Sid, and he was acting as if he had a change of heart and was asking about seeing the baby, so she let him come home with her. Now Man didn't sleep in his crib. His crib was against the wall, and the bed was pushed all the way to the crib so he wouldn't fall out. Man usually slept between Falicia and the crib. So the night Sid stayed over, Falicia placed him in his crib to sleep. It seemed to be fine until she cut the lights out. Sid had just dozed off when Man started fussing. She made sure he wasn't wet or hungry, but none of that mattered! Man just wanted to lie next to her. Apparently, so did Sid, because he complained about not being able to get to her with Man between them, but she didn't give two fucks.

Early that next morning, Falicia made Sid hold Man, and she took a picture. But the shit that blew her the most was the question he had asked. "Falicia, do you think can you give me some money so I can get where I'm headed?"

"Nigga, you used to take care of me. What makes you think I'm going to take food out my mouth, or diapers off our son's ass and give it to you?" Her mother was glad to see his ass walking down the street. Letty said she didn't like his aura. What's sad though is that, that would be the only time her son would have ever spent with his dad, but it was nowhere near their last argument about Sid's role in their son's life.

Life for Falicia still had to go on, with or without Sid or Ike, and Ike's ass was trying to get back in, but she wasn't thinking about him. She would cut her phone off when she got home from work. By the time she got Man to go back to sleep, she was beat! She'd prop herself up against this huge pillow with arms that sat on the bed like a recliner. Many nights and mornings she would nurse Man and would fall asleep with him still nursing.

As soon as the doctor gave her the okay to take Man out of the house, she was in a cab dropping him and her breastmilk off at the babysitter. She enjoyed every minute with him, but she had been trying to stretch her money from her and Mylena's party. Now it was gone. After kicking Ike and Sid out of her life, she put in as many hours as she could at work. Oftentimes, waking up to Letty taking care of Man so she could sleep.

Ike popped up over to her house just as she was getting into a cab with Man to go get her hair done. She refused to let him take her. "Nah, we good."

"Sunshine, what the fuck? How long you going to keep my son from me like this?" He sounded so pitiful; she almost gave in.

"I'm not keeping you from him. You know where we stay." Yes, she loved him. That she could admit, but she wasn't about to be anybody's fool. Ike was full of shit, and she didn't have time for it.

She got inside and closed the door. He leaned in and kissed her cheek. "I love you, baby." *Sure you do, while you're out there fucking fat bitches out of their money.*

When the cab pulled up in front of the beauty shop in the plaza across from Greenbriar Mall, she tried to pay her tab. Ike had already taken care of it and did other kind acts for her and Man as well. By Valentine's Day, she was sold! He came by the club with presents and paid for her to dance only with him.

Accepting his invitation to spend the night, Falicia called her babysitter and got the okay for Man to stay there overnight. At the end of her shift, she got in the passenger's seat with Ike. His homeboys sat in the back as they headed up I-85 North. They passed a sign that read Clairmont Road next exit, half a mile. Ike looked at her, eyes excited.

"Baby, we almost there. I'm about to get off in that ass!" He smiled as he flipped on his turn signal, pressed the accelerator, and made for the exit. Before Ike could say "Damn!" A police officer cut his flashing lights on and pulled them over. Ike was arrested, and Falicia had to spend the night in a strange hotel with the people who were in the car, that she didn't know. Hurt and lonely, she was scared to sleep and could only imagine how Ike felt.

Come morning, somebody took her home, and Ike called by the afternoon. He wasn't getting out.

Back at square one, Ike was gone for a couple weeks before he announced he was about to get out. To her surprise, he talked a female Correctional Officer into going into the computer and changing his release date in exchange for her spending the weekend with him. Naturally, Falicia had an issue with her man spending any time with another bitch, but he explained that this was something he needed to do, in order to get back to his family.

Sereniti Hall

Ike had been released that Thursday, but she didn't expect to see him until Sunday. But early Friday morning, he was pulling up in front of her house.

"I thought—"

"Sunshine, I fucked that bitch to sleep and left in her car. So get your stuff so you can spend the rest of the weekend with me."

Falicia refused. That night when she got off work, Shy was outside waiting for her with instructions to bring her to Ike. He was at the same place she'd spent the night when he got arrested, but he was in a different room. It felt surreal. She was finally alone with him. They laughed and talked about everything. Lighting a blunt, he offered her some.

"No thanks," she said.

He stared at her, eyes filled with lust. She knew what that type of look meant. Nervous, she felt more afraid now than when she'd lost her virginity. Back then, the dude didn't know what he was doing anyway and ended up hurting them both. "Can I have a kiss?" Ike asked, outlining her face with his finger.

She nodded yes. Closed her eyes. Opened her mouth. Waiting for his lips to touch hers. Her lungs suddenly filled with smoke. Falicia began to choke and ran to the bathroom, coughing. Eyes red, face wet, and vision blurry. She burst out laughing at the image in the mirror staring back at her tight eyes. Ike entered the bathroom door to check on her, rolling. Even his ass looked weird. She doubled over with laughter. "Why you do me like that? I told you I don't smoke that stuff."

"Because like I told you, Sunshine. I don't fuck with a woman who don't smoke weed." They finished the blunt together, sitting on the bed. Ike watching her get high.

That night they didn't have sex, and neither did Falicia spend the night, but they enjoyed each other's company. It was the first of many nights that they would spend together chilling, smoking and laughing, high on 'dro.

A Treacherous Hustle

The following weekend, Ike convinced Falicia to leave Man in Velvet's care. She stayed in a lodge not too far away. Although Velvet didn't seem too happy about the arrangement, she didn't hesitate to carry out Ike's order to babysit Man. Apprehensive about leaving her baby with Velvet, Falicia put up a fight. But Ike assured her that Man would be fine, and they would get him early the next day.

They left Man in Velvet's care and went to a hotel off Fulton Industries Highway. What moved her most, was how excited Ike seemed to be about her. This was the same man that she'd seen giving people orders, knocking niggas out, and he was with her, grinning and shit like she was the baddest bitch. *Why me?* she wondered.

"Undress for me," he asked, then kissed her almost invisible stretch marks. Caressed her back and planted soft kisses on it. As she watched him undress, she hoped he would be gentle. He sat at the foot of the bed. Her stomach ached with nervousness. He stared in her eyes and laid her down. "It's gonna be all right. You know I got you, right?"

Falicia closed her eyes and held her breath. Within seconds, she wanted to explode. Her body convulsed. She had never known anybody who could work his tongue like this. *Where did he learn how to do that?*

"Ah, that feels so good," she moaned. He spread her legs and tried to penetrate her, but he wouldn't fit. He was too big, and when he removed himself from her, blood coated his penis. The sight scared the shit out of her.

"Oh, my God!" She gasped and jumped up and ran to the bathroom. Blood dipped from her as if she had been stabbed! A trail of blood stained the bed and trailed across the tan carpet all the way to the bathroom. Falicia cut the shower on and jumped inside. By the time she got out, Ike had thrown the comforter on the floor and lay stretched out, leaning against the head board.

Sereniti Hall

"You got it looking like a crime scene in here," he said, making light of the situation. Falicia smiled. "You all right, baby?"

"Yeah, I just don't understand though. I been stopped bleeding several days ago."

Again they tried and again she bled. She showered a second time with Ike. Afterward, they lay next to one another. Ike wore a solemn expression.

"Something just don't want us to be together," he finally said. "It's been something every time we try to get together." Falicia stared at Ike, watching his lips move. She thought he had a valid point. "Shit, somebody know you and me together will be unstoppable. Baby, I feel it. With you by my side, it's game over!"

She looked into the eyes of the man she had grown to love. He jumped up and grabbed his pants off the chair. "I know you getting ready to let me get up in there."

Falicia frowned at him shoving his feet in his Nikes. "Ike, I don't think I'm ready—"

He opened the door. "Baby, you know I got you, right? We really can't do shit else with you bleeding! You might as well let me bust that thang open."

In Ike's absence, Falicia tried to convince herself that she was ready to give a part of her that no other woman had been willing to explore with him, but as soon as he opened the door, her stomach dropped.

"Sunshine, I couldn't find any KY jelly, but I got some petroleum jelly and baby oil and you some tampons," he said. Her heart wouldn't slow down, and she was already throbbing from the previous attempt at regular sex.

He tossed the brown paper bag on the bed, where she lay, trying to look seductive. She took advantage of him leaving to take another shower and put on the other corset she brought for their evening. He pulled off his shirt. "You gone be straight with one of them?" He went to the sink and washed his dick and hands. Not once did she think about any of his previous sexual partners, nor did she ask him about condoms.

With tears streaming from her eyes, his seventeen-year-old secret bit her lip to keep from begging for mercy and clawed at the sheets. "I'm gonna have your body where you only respond to me," Ike promised. She lay there anticipating when it would be over. By the next day she was getting accustomed to the pain. It went from the worst feeling ever, to only hurting at first. Nothing could prepare her for the agony she willingly let this man subject her to.

As days turned into weeks and weeks into months, Ike had a way of leaving an impression on Falicia. For Mother's Day, he bought Falicia and Letty identical necklaces with a #1 MOM charm. Falicia thought it was cute. Letty swore Ike was a womanizer, and the scowl she couldn't erase let him know coming in the door that she didn't trust him. Nevertheless, she tried to be supportive of her daughter and the fact that he was being to Man what Sid wasn't.

The following week, Ike called Falicia and told her that he wanted her to visit someone who meant a lot to him. Falicia felt honored to meet anyone from Ike's inner circle. She showered and got dressed right away, and then cleaned up Man and dressed him. Feeling a little nervous yet happy, she wasn't sure what to expect from whomever she was going to meet. Ike arrived on time, and they had made it to their destination forty minutes later.

"Baby, I hate coming home alone without you and my son," Ike complained as he put his white Caprice in park and took a pack of cigarettes from over the visor. And I'm eating fast food every day because you're not here to cook me a decent meal. Here I am out in the streets trying to build for our future. And you just out here blowing money on buying your mama a house, instead of investing in us. Letting me flip the money you making."

Disappointed by Ike's comments, Falicia watched him get out of the car, lighting a cigarette. She thought they were a team, and she was dancing in the club practically around the clock. Also, she served as a middleman for Ike's hustle. He had shown her how to profile the type of nigga who would be interested in his product. And he asked her to call him whenever she came into contact with him or her. Most times, the dancers would clean her out of the cocaine walking in the door.

Impatiently, Falicia stared in the direction he had gone, anxious to introduce her to a man he considered as his Godfather. She wiped the fog away from the window. They were supposed to be headed to Letty's. Her cousin and aunt were coming for a few days, and she was anxious to see them as well as show off Man.

An elderly dude, tall and slim, dismounted some steps that were attached to the second level of a house that Andre, Ike's childhood friend owned. His swag reminded her of Sir Carter. So she wasn't surprised after he complimented Ike for her external beauty, then told him," I can see why you running around grinning, talking about she the one. But it's them white ones that you send to them whore houses that'll get you paid."

Falicia spun around, heading back to the car with Man. Days prior, they stopped by to see another one of Ike's homies that he grew up with, Ike told her on the way home, "Yeah, I had to cuss that nigga out. Telling me that he ain't sure that I'm making the best decision by being with you."

"And what the hell is that supposed to mean?" Falicia had snapped. She fastened Man in his car seat, boiling mad. "Y'all niggas don't know Falicia Blakely. I'm about to be all Ike Newberry need! Y'all bitches about to bow down when you see that I am 'the one!'"

What was so pathetic about it all was, she didn't know they were all making references to her being Ike's main whore, his bottom bitch! Her young, fast, dumb ass was about to place her life in his hands for him to mold it into whatever he was so adamant that she could become. Unfortunately for Falicia, she would be his scapegoat, the muscle behind the moves he orchestrated.

CHAPTER 19

"What's up, Slim?" a junkie yelled out to Ike as they sat at the stoplight. Ike grinned and threw back his head. Falicia cut her eyes at him and frowned.

Finishing up a Wednesday night birthday set, she was in the dressing room trying to hurry. This young girl who looked under age was packing up as well, dramatizing an encounter she had with a pimp that she didn't want to work for. He had snatched her off the street and threw her in the trunk of his car.

"Girl, hurry up and tell me what his name is," one of the dancer's interrupted. "So I'll know to stay the fuck away from this crazy ass fool!" Others nodded.

"All I know is that they call that muthafucka' Slim. And I hear that maniac is still around. All I can say is that it takes a bitch badder than me to deal with his ass. He tricked me into that shit anyway. I met this nigga trying to get to the mall. So he and his boy take me shopping, right? I figure it's no big deal. Next thing I know, they put me out on Metropolitan Avenue and tell me I better make a damn quota. I'm like. Hold the fuck up. I didn't even know I was working for you." The girls cracked up laughing.

Suddenly Falicia stopped giggling, remembering Ike nodding when being addressed as Slim and when she visited him in jail once, he told her his street name was Slim. Before that, it did dawn on her one night while she and Ike were having dinner, that he was the same "IKE" as was tattooed on this girl named Candy's breast. Out of curiosity, Falicia later asked her, "So what's up with you and Ike?" Candy stared at her vacantly and walked away.

As if piecing together pieces of a puzzle, she remembered a few occasions when she couldn't get Ike on the phone when she called, but he was very adamant about her answering when he called. The thing that tripped her out most, was the night he called, and she was so excited about how profitable her night dancing at the club had turned out.

"Ike, I made almost nine hundred dollars, baby! Tonight was a good night!" Falicia was so happy and excited.

"Yeah, that's the move. Well damn! You did good." Ike sounded like he was impressed.

"It is, right? I'm stepping up," she said, beaming with pride.

"So . . . check this. I'm over here at Crystal Palace. How about you catch a cab and bring me that? I'm out here working on something and I need that."

Falicia snatched the phone from her ear to check the number, making sure she was talking to the right person. When did their lines get crossed? She didn't give her money to men. They gave her their money. She wasn't feeling that shit.

"Okay, I'll be there shortly. Ahh, before I hang up, when you going to give it back?" she asked as if she honestly intended to give it to him.

"Shit, for real, it takes me no time to flip it. But you know I'm good for it." He didn't answer the question, but who gave a fuck? She hung up the phone, put it on vibrate, and went to sleep. *This nigga tried me, but he'll figure it out*. At some point after she had fallen asleep, her phone began vibrating and it was his ass.

"Ahh, what's up? Where you at?" Ike asked.

"I'm coming." Falicia spoke into the phone, not trying to hide the fact she was asleep.

"You sure you still coming?" he asked again, like he didn't believe her.

"Yeah," she answered and hung up the phone.

Falicia cut her phone off and early the next morning she got up and put on some blue cargo pants and a fitted top with some multi-colored blue Nike Air Max and headed to the mall with Mylena to buy her nephew a birthday present. Later, they took Mylena's boys to Chuck E Cheese. Falicia didn't return Ike's calls until she was on her way to work that evening. She told him how she spent her time earlier in the day.

"I thought you told me you was coming," Ike said.

"Didn't you hear what I just told you I did!" she replied, permanently ending any more dialogue about 'her' money. No pimp named Slim or Ike was going to get one cent of her hard earned cash.

For one reason or another, Ike landed back in jail and this time Shy started coming back around. Eventually he moved into their sun room so he could be available whenever she needed him. Falicia hustled even harder and took on performing at private parties and dancing at another strip club, Pin Up's.

Once Ike got out and got a whiff of all the money she was bringing in, he started inquiring about how she was spending her money and making an even bigger deal about them being under two different roofs. Falicia felt torn between staying with her mother and moving in with Ike. Letty and Falicia had gotten really close! They laughed together and finally enjoyed each other's presence. She had become the woman Falicia had longed for her entire life. Letty didn't judge her. Mother and daughter had gotten to a good place. Letty could have anything that was Falicia's, accessories, shoes, or money. Many weekends she would ask Falicia what she wanted to eat for their Sunday dinner. She would tell Letty, "Just go in my purse and get what you need." Oftentimes Falicia laughed when Letty did go in her purse because who needed a hundred dollars to buy a ham or some collards greens? She loved Letty so much and so did her son. Letty had been nothing but supportive, and assisted her with raising him. Even helped with picking out his name.

Ike pushed and pushed Falicia to move in with him until she finally broke down and said yes, although she didn't give him an exact date. She also never asked if he was aware of a pimp called Slim, who had a rep for mistreating women. Instead she woke up

Sereniti Hall

the next morning and came up with the bright idea to explore "some new things" with her profession. Falicia asked Ike to take her to get her butt hole pierced. Somehow her "great" idea to grow their funds thrilled Ike, who encouraged the guys in the tattoo shop to come and see Alex give her a second piercing.

"You can't tell me I ain't got the baddest bitch around," he bragged to his boy as they were on their way out the door. He was the first one Ike called to come and see. He slapped Falicia across her rear. "We about to take it to another level, baby." Falicia grinned, thinking Ike just wanted other dudes to see his bitch and make them wish they could have what's his. But that wasn't the case in the least.

Ike lit a blunt while taking her home. He expressed how no one had been down for him like her. "Kiss my son," he said, dropping her off in their driveway. Falicia wanted him to come inside to say hello to Letty, hoping she could see what she saw in him.

"There's money to be made," Ike expressed. "I can't get you the crib you deserve sitting around chit-chatting.

She kissed his cheek and headed inside to the smell of Letty throwing down in the kitchen.

"Guess what," Falicia said to her mother, who was busy cooking dinner. Man was in his playpen in the middle of the living room where Letty could keep an eye on him. "I have something to show you," she teased.

Letty eyed her daughter, grinning wide, eyes tight. "Hell no, Falicia Rose!" She turned her attention back to her task. "I heard you giggling on the phone the other night talking about how you been letting that man do you in your ass. It's sickening. So, no I'm not guessing anything. Because nowadays I never know with you." Letty picked up a glass from the counter and turned it up.

Falicia burst out laughing. Letty gazed at her with contempt as she doubled over. "And I know he got you smoking weed. Look at you. Standing there laughing like that. When I don't see in the least bit what is funny. And just so you know. That spray you been using ain't hiding shit!"

"Okay and . . . You used to smoke, Momma. So stop acting like I'm committing the ultimate sin. Besides, this is more important."

"First, you pierced your navel, that shit got infected. Then I catch you in the mirror staring at your pussy and for whatever reason you put a ring down there. Now you want me to see some more stupid shit . . ." Letty checked her pots.

"Momma, just look. Damn!" She moved toward her mother, but she pushed her away. Falicia tried to pucker up and kiss Letty. "Ma, stop acting like that."

"Stop now." Letty shook her head and tuned Falicia out. She stirred her collard greens. Once Falicia turned her back to Letty and pulled up her dress, Letty spun back with her ham in her hands. Falicia held her butt open, grinning at her over her shoulder. Showing her, her new butt ring.

Letty's face froze with shock. Then speed-raced to disgust. "You nasty black bitch!" She tossed the ham back on the stove. "I'ma kick yo' lil muthafuckin' ass! You don't invite nobody to ass unless you want it kicked!" she threatened as she gave chase.

Falicia grabbed Man and raced upstairs, locking them in her room. Letty was still pissed. "That's some sick shit, Falicia! I don't know where you get that from—doing sick shit! You don't get that from me. You got that from your daddy." She continued to fuss as she headed back in the kitchen.

She didn't open her mouth anymore until she saw that Falicia had opened her bedroom door and was packing some of her and Man's things. Falicia wasn't completely ready to move out, so she left some stuff at home. She was still anticipating buying the house with Letty and didn't want to leave her high and dry. When Falicia revealed her plans, Letty said even less.

"Momma, don't worry. I'm still going to buy a computer and finish school online."

Without a word, Letty headed back downstairs. Her silence, nevertheless, spoke volumes. She got up from the sofa and poured herself a drink, draining her glass, then refilling it. Grabbing the bottle of bourbon, she headed upstairs to her room and didn't look back.

"Baby, every parent is like that when their child leaves home," Ike stated. "And like we agreed the other night. You have to live for you. For us."

Falicia glanced around the tiny room. She envisioned a decent-sized apartment and them going shopping for furniture and house stuff when he insisted he'd found them a place. Not living at a lodge hotel room with a kitchenette. Plus, it wasn't even at Clairmont Lodge, where Ike trapped out of.

"Why are we not at the Clairmont?" Falicia asked.

"Rule number one: You don't hustle where you lay your head," Ike said. "Anything can happen, so you never bring what you do to your home front." Falicia didn't care for the arrangement, but didn't want to come off as if she was nagging.

As the days passed, she gradually began to see the perks of staying with her man. She woke up to new outfits he wanted her to wear that day. Ike scheduled her hair and nail appointments. And he made sure she stayed by his side, learning how he orchestrated his business. Come nightfall, after work, he would run her bath, bathe her, then lotion her entire body. Making her smile at the way he pampered her.

"Rule number two," he told her one day as they were smoking a blunt after dropping Man off with the babysitter. "Nobody in these streets should be able to come tell me anything about mine that I don't already know."

"And vice versa," Falicia replied. He stared at her and put his eyes back on the road. "Shouldn't no bitch be able to tell me anything about my man." She handed him back the blunt and sat up straight. "Well, I wanna tell you something. I've been thinking about what you said. When you was like, imagine how much more money I could be bringing in, if I was to take some of them dudes up on their offer to pay me for sex."

"Mmm hmm. What about it?"

"I feel like it's cheating. I mean, you my nigga. What I look like fucking the next man?" He removed one hand from the steering wheel and reached out for her. Falicia put her hand in his.

"First of all, baby. I'm not some young, insecure ass nigga. I know what we out here trying to do. It's money to be made, and I respect the way you feel it's necessary to obtain it. You not cheating on me. We doing this shit together, you feel me?" She nodded, forehead wrinkled. *Is he saying what I think he's saying? Or is it the weed?*

"I ain't stuttin' these lames," Ike continued. "Ain't no nigga out here can do to your body what I do. That's my sweet lil pussy." He leaned down for a peck on the lips.

"Shit. But these busters willing to pay five, six hundred dollars to see what that sweet lil thang hitting like. Hell yeah, I want you to get that. That's what you make sometime after a whole night . . . and you could make all that in thirty minutes. Sheeeiiiiiit . . ." Falicia didn't say much else and neither did he. It sounded good and easy, but she didn't feel that way. She'd taken pride in the fact that she hadn't lost sight of her self-worth. Falicia was the one out of twenty dancers to decline having sex for money. But wasn't this love, the kind of love that required sacrifice?

CHAPTER 20

Ike was growing impatient with Falicia's resistance to turn a trick. "So tell me everything that happened?" he asked her as he was driving home.

"So, I asked him what he was trying to spend," she said.

"You don't ask them that when you trying to trick off. You tell them what price you want. You ask that when you sling dope."

"Oh okay . . . so he was like $150. I told his ass there was no way I was giving up anything for $150. So he said $200, and I countered his ass with $400. He went down to $250. I wasn't about to keep going back and forth and just told his ass if he ain't willing to pay $350, then we ain't doing business."

"Mama, what made you drop your price?" Mama had become a name he started calling her because of the way she looked after her son and Ike.

"Well, because he started off talking under two. I knew he wasn't willing to part with five."

"That's understandable, but you don't never start low when you're negotiating anything. Always start higher than you expect to receive, that way as you're compromising, you'll end up getting what you really wanted, if not more. You feel me?" he corrected.

"In other words, I should have said seven, and then possibly talked him down to five or around that number."

"Exactly!"

Falicia finished recanting her story, taking a deep breath. "So, he was game for the $350. Long story short, I asked if he had a condom. He didn't. He asked if I could go find one. Now baby, considering this would be my first time, I was already nervous as fuck. Paranoid. Hoping no one would find out what I was about to do . . . you know, degrade myself." She said that last part quietly.

"What?"

"So I went to the dressing room to see who I could ask for one. But it was too embarrassing, and I couldn't bring myself to do it. I did ask him to get one from the store and come back. He said okay, but he never did. So other than that, it was a normal night." Falicia looked over at Ike, who remained quiet and concentrated on the road.

Three minutes passed, and he pulled into an apartment complex. She wasn't sure where they were, but there really wasn't any telling with the way Ike moved. He probably had to make a drop or pick something up. "Mama, get out." Ike got out of his car and walked around to her side. Opening her door, he extended his hand to assist her. She grabbed her purse and stepped out.

"You're such a gentleman."

"Leave that," he said.

Falicia tossed her purse back on the seat, then closed the car door. Sure, they were in the hood, but he knew best. So that's why she trusted him.

"Bam!"

The impact of Ike's slap was so fierce, she immediately tasted blood. "What the fuck, Ike?" She threw up her hands and arms to protect her face. Without a word, Ike pounded her like a heavyweight champion, landing paralyzing body shot after body shot. Suddenly he stopped.

"Now get back in," he said as calmly as he told her to get out. He opened her car door.

She got in and pulled down the sun visor. "Ike, you busted my lip!" she shouted. He mumbled something. "Yo' motherfucking ass busted my lip! Damn! Why would you do that?" Falicia was hurt, confused. She didn't know which one hurt worse, her face or her heart. "You sittin' there. You don't hear me talking to you?"

"I said I don't want to hear it." He spoke barely over a whisper.

"You made my lip bleed, Ike!" she yelled again and considered acting a fool.

A Treacherous Hustle

"I said I don't want to hear about it, Falicia!" he yelled back.

Normally, she would have got back with his ass, but something about the look in his eyes gave her chills. She just sat back with her arms folded after she slapped the visor shut. He began fumbling with the CD player, and their favorite song started playing softly from the speakers.

Is this bitch-nigga serious? Bust my fucking lip, and then wanna play a love song, she thought as she distracted herself with the streets of Atlanta.

"Come here," Ike said sweetly. Falicia looked at him and rolled her eyes.

"Fuck you!" is what she wished she had the courage to say.

"Baby, come here," he asked again, removing one hand from the steering wheel and extending it for hers. She looked down at it. "Baby, come here." Ike looked so kind and loving, as if he wasn't even the same person who had just tried to rearrange her face. "Baby, I love you. Please, come here." Logic entangled with her emotions; she felt herself getting overwhelmed. He slowed the vehicle and pulled Falicia to him, holding her like he needed her.

"Mama, you know we out here trying to get this money," he said, pulling off. "So one day you won't have to be out here in these streets. We will be somewhere laid up, where I can keep them babies in you. And it's like you just let somebody go."

"So you beat my ass because I wanted to protect myself and you? You busted my lip, Ike. You made me bleed."

He considered what she said. "It's my fault. I should have put some in your bag." He stroked her arm like the man she had grown to love. "Mama, I'm sorry I got so upset. I won't do that to you anymore." She couldn't hold her tears back. "Remember this?" He played their favorite song and took her hand.

Wiping away Falicia's tears, Ike exited his car at a gas station on Metropolitan. A black Lexus pulled opposite of his ride. A buff black dude with dreads got out. They bumped fists. Falicia turned and checked on Man, grateful he wasn't old enough to witness what had just transpired. He was still fast asleep. Every rib hurt and her stomach felt like a hole was left in it. Ike opened the door and hopped in with a grin.

"Baby, that's Blue. My re-up man."

"Okay." She nodded as he watched Blue get into his vehicle. He supplied Ike with coke and had stopped by the other night.

"So I'm gonna need you to go get that for me."

"Huh? Well, if he got something for you—"

"Yeah, he do. So go get it for me real quick and take your phone." She glanced from Ike to Man. Something didn't feel right.

"Hurry up, baby," he encouraged.

Falicia walked up to Blue's car and got inside. His head jerked back, shocked to see her. "Ike told me to come get something from you," she stated.

The guy started laughing. "Really? That damn Ike." Falicia looked over at him. Ike was driving away with Man. She blinked, in utter dismay.

Blue called him on his cell. "For real, man? I told you I'm tired, Ike . . . come on, man . . . you stupid." He ended their call and sat for a moment.

"Well, Sexy Black." He looked Falicia over with lust. "I guess you're going with me."

An hour later, Falicia dismounted him and he rolled over like a baby, fast asleep. An ache sat in the pit of her stomach as she stared at him, snoring lightly, hand on his dick. A little smile on his face. Had she been his woman, their souls would have intertwined when he reached his climax. They would have been as one. And had she gone with him on her own accord, she could've stroked her ego to know she knocked him out like that. But she felt degraded. Worthless.

Barely awake, Blue asked her to hand him one of the two grocery bags that set on a recliner full of balled up bills.

"This it?" Falicia asked, holding four hundred dollars in her hand. "You in here knocked out and this the best you can do?"

"I always give Ike's girls that. Just let me go back to sleep."

"Well, I ain't them. I'm the one." She stood over Blue with her hands on her hips. He chuckled and handed her another hundred dollars. "Close the door when you leave."

She went to the bathroom and cleaned herself as best as she could with no rag. She located her cell phone and called Ike. He was there within twenty-five minutes.

"What's the matter wit' my baby?" Ike asked with a wide grin as Falicia got in and closed the car door and stared ahead, afraid to look his way. He'd set her up. She was hurt. And she was ready to kill.

"I'm just ready to go home and bathe," she replied.

"Baby, what happened?" Falicia reached in her bra and handed him the five hundred dollars that he was more concerned about. Had he been that concerned, they would have discussed it first. He counted the bills. "That's my mama."

She closed her eyes, wanting to sleep the moment away. She spun around, looking in the backseat frantically.

"Where's Man? He should've been here so I can see him."

"He with Velvet, baby. We leaving him there for the night."

"Well, we'll go pick him up, please."

"Well, baby, we leaving him there for the night."

She jerked her head, glaring at him with deadly intent. "Why?"

"For real, I just wanted to be alone with you. Shit, I need some time alone with my woman."

"Well, if that's what you really wanted, why in the heck would you tell me to go get something, and then you drive off, leaving me with a total stranger. That shit wasn't cool."

"I can see how you can feel like that. But baby, I saw an opportunity, and in this game you just gotta know when to act on instinct. That's all it was. That nigga got plenty of money to spare, and I figure he might as well give us back some of what we give his ass all the time."

"You could have just told me that, instead of making me feel like some . . ." She didn't want to say it.

"My fault. I could have just told you what the move was."

"If we really out here doing this shit together, why does it feel like it's just me? Why are you making all of the decisions?"

"I say what's what because I know these streets. Either you trust me or you don't."

Falicia shifted in her seat and turned toward the window. She placed her focus on the exit that led to Velvet's lodge, wanting to see Man more than ever. Ike threw question after question at her, anxious to know how everything went down.

"This nigga had what?" he asked when she mentioned the two bags of money. "Damn, baby, why the fuck didn't you rob his ass? Shit! I can't *believe* you missed out on another pay day!" He bumped her aside when they arrived at their apartment in the lodge. She glanced at him, setting her purse on the table. Grabbing a pair of sweats and a T-shirt, she left him pacing in front of the television with the remote. She needed the hottest water she could stand to wash off her disgust from the day. Ike's erection was at full attention when she walked out of the bathroom. Dog tired.

"So tell me again, why didn't you rob dude's bitch ass?" He massaged his erection, eyes fixed on the door.

"Because he's your re-up man," she reiterated. "Blue knows where you stay, where you sell your dope, and the people you hang with. That's stupid. And besides, that's the first rule you told me not to do. Don't bring trouble to your front door." He cut his eyes at her, staring hard and long. Her heart jumped.

"Come here," he said.

Falicia was still hurt from him going Floyd Mayweather on her. She longed to know what made him do that. But she didn't say it. Still confused and apprehensive, she sat on the bed beside him. He pulled her to him. She got on her knees to ride him. He pushed her head down and pressed his erection against her lips. She had never performed oral sex before. The more she tried to resist, the harder he pulled her hair until her mouth opened.

Once she cleaned up her vomit, he repeated the process, determined to teach her how to breathe and not throw up each time he shoved his massive organ down her throat.

"Make me nut, bitch! Make me nut, Mama!" he commanded until the wee hours of the morning when she was too exhausted to hold up her head. "I ain't gonna stop until I get this nut out!" She had fallen asleep with his penis in her mouth and woke up the next morning in the same position. Again he repeated his actions from the previous night, making her feel just as low as she felt the night prior.

Funny, she had always thought sex with your mate was supposed to be consensual and enjoyable. *Maybe this wasn't really sex.* Whatever it was, she didn't have a name for it.

Now that Falicia had evolved into that bitch who sucked Ike off until her stomach released all its contents in a supersize, fast food cup and rode him beyond her legs' ability to withstand the tightness in her muscles, she had mastered how to use her body to get results the average woman didn't think about. Now she knew how to "fuck a nigga so good he looked forward to giving her his hard earned money."

"Baby, he doesn't want to do it in his car," she told Ike. It was near closing time for Body Tapp.

"Well, you better convince his ass to do it there because I don't want you to leave."

It had only been a couple months ago that he had taught her a harsh lesson on not missing out on any money. Now she got dressed and hurried upstairs. Blue wasn't sitting at the bar anymore. One of the bouncers was standing outside when she proceeded to the parking lot, looking for him.

"Fantasia, you gone for the night?" he asked. It was a little after three in the morning. The club closed at four.

"No, I'm going to pick up something. I'll be back." She jumped inside Blue's Lexus with the agonizing pain of having to sex a man she didn't know. Blue put his key in the ignition. "You sure you don't want to just do this right here?" she asked, glancing around for a hint of Ike.

"Hell, naw. I deserve this second chance. And if you play nice, I'll shoot you an extra hundred." He handed her five crisp hundred dollar bills and pulled out of the parking lot. Her stomach sunk more as he whipped into traffic, rocking to a reggae beat.

Inside his shop, Blue escorted Falicia to his office, neatly decorated with a TV on the wall that displayed views from different directions of the property, a small refrigerator, and a microwave. She walked up to the door that led inside his paint shop. Through the frosted panes, she took notice of how neat and organized he was.

"This is all right, Blue," she said, complimenting his shop. "This is a dope setup!"

He dried his hands at the small sink near the refrigerator. Her eyes lingered over his dark charcoal skin, outlining the curves and contours of his bulging muscles. He removed his shirt like he knew she was checking him out. Six pack, big erect dick, strong arms, and muscular legs approached her. Picked her up. "Do you want me?" she whispered in his ear. The way he looked at her made her pussy wet. She saw longing in his eyes. Desire maybe? She decided to stay in the moment with him. Most times she'd usually check herself out mentally.

"I'm about to show you," he promised, bringing them to the point of moaning so loud she missed Ike calling her phone. Near four, she grabbed her phone. Blue took it out of her hand, sexing her again. Falicia was having a difficult time enjoying herself. The first time it was the adrenaline of sneaking away and fucking. She felt like she was being a bad girl. Sensing she was distracted, Blue focused on her, massaging her, stroking her in the right places. She closed her eyes, biting her lip. Losing control and calling his name. Like a thorough street bred nigga that he was, his ass laid the pipe, holding her lower body with his arms and making her take it.

"Turn around," he told her at one point. Blue was hitting it doggie style. Now it was her chance to take control. She found good placement for her knees on his sofa and thrust back at him, squeezing her vagina muscles as she pulled away.

While still stroking her, he answered his phone after he looked at the number. It was obviously his baby's mother. Falicia heard her asking him to pick up things on his way home. He lied about being in the middle of a paint job and rushed her off the phone. He grabbed a remote and enlarged the security screen view, as if he expected her crazy ass to roll up on his shop.

I ain't hardly about to get caught up in no drama. Falicia quickly slid off him and retrieved her phone.

"What you doing?" he asked, almost panicking and pulling her back to him.

"We gotta wrap this up," she replied.

"I was about to say the same thing before this crazy bitch come lookin' for me." They fell back into the zone, missionary style, climaxing at the same time, a first ever for Falicia.

She wasted no more than ten seconds getting herself together and pulling Blue toward his car.

"Thank you!" she said as he pulled off once the light changed. Blue smiled, thinking she was talking about the money, but she was referring to how he made her feel like a woman: beautiful, desired, cared for, special, and willing to protect.

"Don't stop in front of the club. Circle the block first," she instructed, trying to keep the fact that she was scared to death out of her voice. Ike had been dialing her phone back to back for the last hour. But this time she was walking away with $700. A sad smile framed her lips temporarily. *Daddy gon' be so happy.* She was eager to present it to him when she almost jumped out of Blue's Lexus.

"Damn, girl, you act like you running for your life. That nigga ain't putting his hands on you, is he?" Blue asked.

"Hell no!" she stated. "I just need to get my son from the babysitter. Later. See you." She twisted away with confidence, knowing he was watching the sway of her hips. Knowing that Ike was absent allowed her to breathe easier.

"Fantasia, where the hell you been?" the same bouncer at the door stated. "Your ol' man came looking for you, and somebody told him that you left with dude in the Lexus. Why you cheating on that man?" he teased.

Her phone rang on her way inside the club.

"Baby, I'm coming. I have to pay my bar fees. I'll be right up." It was no sense in acting like she didn't know what time it was. She was shitting bricks.

"You better hurry your motherfucking ass up! And I mean hurry!" Ike yelled and hung up.

Falicia packed up for the night, counting her money and separating her tips. She was leaving with a couple dollar shy of nine hundred dollars. That was good as hell for a week night. She exhaled deeply to calm her nerves, hoping her take for the night would bring her mercy. Ike leaped out of a white van she saw parked near the club entrance when Blue pulled away. He grabbed her hand and escorted her to vehicle like a little child.

"Ike, don't do that shit out here," someone from the front side pleaded with him.

"No, Ike. Not out here. Just wait," Ike said to himself as they approached the van.

This nigga finna go psycho on my ass, she thought.

"Get yo' motherfuckin' ass in here!" he demanded as he snatched her inside.

I'm caught. Please, please, please don't let him hit me in here, Falicia prayed, looking around in desperation. "Lord, Jesus." No one noticed her legs hanging out the door, then disappearing inside the van, then the door slamming shut.

Falicia stared at his boy Andre, the driver. Another one of Ike's homeboys sat in the front passenger seat. "Good evening," she said, trembling with fear. She cut her eyes at Ike. So furious he clinched his fist and grinded his teeth. They spoke back and returned their focus on the road.

"Yeah, you lil sneaky ass bitch. I should've knocked your ass up under one of these fucking wheels. Cut on some music." He tightened his grip on Falicia's arm. "I got something for yo' slick ass," he promised, his breath hot on her ear. He let her go, pushing her away. "How much money did you make tonight?"

Falicia pulled two stacks out of her pocket and handed it to Ike. He counted it, then snatched her by the hair. "You sucked his dick?" he asked.

"No, Ike! Ike, I didn't suck anybody's dick. You're hurting me. What's wrong with you?" If there was nothing else in life that she hated, Falicia hated people being in her business. Especially, his friends, because they had already felt she was inadequate. "Ike, I didn't suck anybody's dick. You're hurting me." She raised her tone some. He looked up in the direction of his boys.

"Shut up, talking so loud!" He released her hair and tugged on his pants.

"What's wrong with you?"

"Fuck you mean what's wrong wit' me? You supposed to know!" He slapped her in the back of her head, then forced her face toward his exposed penis. "Fuck you waiting on?" He popped her harder. And harder. Slanting her head a little so she could look toward the front seat. Briefly she glanced at Andre, then complied with Ike's wishes. Tears rolled down her face as Andre looked away, shaking his head. Ike slapped the back of her head twice as hard, trying to knock out her tonsils. "And suck up them motherfuckin' tears!" She wiped them away to the best of her ability, battling to understand what she did wrong? He told her not to miss out on the opportunity to make money.

They picked up Man and the things he needed from the store. Once they returned home, Ike's anger seemed to have died. His temples no longer were throbbing.

"Take your pants off," Ike instructed Falicia as she got off the bed that Man slept on.

"Take my pants off?" she asked. His request kind of threw her for a loop, but she complied, not wanting to bring any trouble on herself. "Baby, why you want me to take my pants off?" He didn't answer, but she noticed him unfastening his belt. Falicia stopped mid stride. "What you doing that for?"

"Ike please, don't do this," she begged all over again the first time the belt whacked her. *Where was the man who was so thoughtful and considerate of me? The one I loved?* She wanted to cry because her heart broke as she looked into the eyes of this stranger. *She would have tried to understand if he did drugs, but he didn't. So what was the excuse for the mood swings?*

"So you going to beat my ass like I'm a child?"

"Falicia, I ain't gon' tell you anymore. Take them pants off." He swung his belt and hit her on the leg. Instinctively she reached down and rubbed the spot to make it stop stinging. "Why in the fuck you still got them pants on?" He swung again.

"Okay, okay," she said, holding up her hand and trying to get him to stop swinging as she pulled her pants down.

"Lay on your stomach!" he ordered and went ape shit on her for not doing what he said. And making him and his boys miss out on the opportunity to rob Blue while he was fucking Falicia in the parking lot. She buried her face in the comforter, hoping not to wake her son, as Ike gave her one lash after the other with his leather belt. When she couldn't take it anymore, she jumped up begging him to stop. He kept swinging. She ended up on the floor, then raced off into the bathroom where she hid beneath the sink.

"Open the door!" he yelled, but she wasn't even picking that as an option. Falicia stayed barricaded until it sounded quiet. About ten minutes later, she crept out and Ike was gone. It was hard to fall asleep that night, but when she did, she got in bed with Man. For some reason she just felt that Ike wouldn't do anything to her lying next to Man. If she hadn't crawled inside the bathroom and locked the door, he probably would have killed her.

Ike came home later that morning in a bloody shirt, explaining he spent the night in the emergency room because he busted Velvet's eye socket. He was so mad at Falicia, that he assaulted Velvet too. "To honor my promise of not putting my hands on you again," he assured her.

Falicia couldn't say that she was relieved about him taking his frustrations out on someone else. She was, however, thankful he hadn't busted her eye. Still, she was confused about the way he wanted her to do business. Now she was beginning to feel as if she had to tiptoe around anything involving him, except when it came to Man.

CHAPTER 21

Time was money and Falicia had grown to make the most of every bit of it. She also discovered that out here in these streets it was best for her not to be driven by emotions. Naturally, she smiled whenever she and Ike were together in the streets, or around his friends because she loved him, despite all the terrible things he did that left her confused at times. Overall, she knew he didn't have any ill intentions toward her. It wasn't his fault no one really showed him how to express himself in a positive manner, or had even made it so he'd be able to trust that Falicia had his best intentions at heart at all times like he did with her. All these were things Falicia took into consideration.

Now when she was on her grind, it didn't take long for her to see the only way to survive was to put how she really felt aside. There was no place for fear or even insecurity! These streets would eat her alive if she dared to display either. It was about rising to the occasion, being whatever the situation required, and at the moment she was evolving into that bitch.

Finally, the truth came to her. Ike had been priming her, teaching her how to fuck. True, she was already experienced in having sex, but fucking was something that a woman had to learn through experience, to master how to use her body to get the results the average woman didn't think about. With that being said, she embraced being a 'ho. Falicia just didn't realize she was Ike's 'ho! Or even "one" of his 'hos!

"Ike, don't keep giving Man all that apple juice," she fussed, headed to the bathroom for a soak in the tub.

"He good. Ain't nothing wrong wit' him drinking this juice if he wants it."

Falicia glanced back at him holding Man like he was scared he would jump up and run any second. He looked adorable. Lately, he had been mentioning her giving him a seed, which was something she considered. Her main priority was in sight, but they were far from it. They hadn't even made it out of Georgia yet.

"You are going to give him diarrhea."

"Everybody needs to shit. Ain't nothing wrong with a lil shit. Ain't that right?"

Falicia rolled her eyes and closed the bathroom door to get a little solitude. She looked forward to her baths after she got off work. It was one of the few times that she could be herself. Not Mama, Fantasia, or Unique, just Falicia.

"Hey, Mama," Ike called from the other room.

"Yes!" She smiled to herself, thinking she had two babies.

"When you get out the tub, I want a steak and bake potato."

"Ike, you want a bake potato this late at night?"

"Please." He sounded so precious, how could she say no?

His and Man's demeanor changed when she got out of the tub. Man was extra talkative, and he was anxious. She opened the refrigerator door. The jug of apple juice was almost gone.

"Ike, this was a new thing of juice. I can't believe you gave all that juice to Man," she fussed, removing steak, potatoes, and onions out of the refrigerator.

Man's jabbering became louder, although no one was talking to him. Falicia glanced at Ike, placing the items on the counter. Ike was rolling a blunt. His temple throbbed. Something was wrong. Falicia couldn't have done anything wrong. What was the matter? She buttered the potatoes, wrapped them in foil and put them in the oven. Then she went to go check on her man. She sat in Ike's lap. "What has you upset?" Falicia stroked his face.

"I gotta go handle some business. So I'll be back."

"Baby, you told me you wanted something to eat," she whined, feelings slowly being hurt.

"I do, but I gotta go handle something." He licked the blunt he was rolling.

Falicia stood up. "Ike." He gazed up at her. "I been at work all night. I'm tired. I really wanted to come home and go to sleep, but because you asked me to, I'm cooking you something to eat and you telling me you have to handle some business?! It can't wait, or you can't get somebody else to do it?"

"Naw, ma. I said *I* got some business to handle." He kissed her, set the blunt on the nightstand, and kissed Man. "I love you. I'll be back as soon as I can." And then he was gone.

Falicia wished she could have cursed his ass out or something, anything to release the hostility she now had brewing. She headed back to the kitchen to complete the task. She figured she might as well fix herself a steak, listening to Man chattering continuously, a clear sign he was wide awake. She made her plate and sat down next to him.

"What you doing, boy?" she asked, smiling at him. He stared at her, his eyes crossed. Falicia put her plate down and reached for him. He was distracted by the food. She watched him attempt to roll over. He struggled, as if he couldn't focus on the target. His lil hand kept bypassing the plate.

"What the fuck?" She picked Man up and stared at him. Waved her index finger in front of him. He giggled with excitement each time. She sniffed him. He smelled like weed. *Ike gave my baby a shotgun?* The odor was too strong to have just been Ike smoking around him.

"Son of a bitch! What type of man would get his own child high?" she asked aloud, dialing his cell. No answer. Following numerous attempts, she called the room he trapped out of. Nothing. She waited a few minutes and called back.

"Baby, I can't talk right now." A female screamed in the background. Ike hung up.

"What the hell?"

Falicia stared at the phone trying to figure out what type of scream it was. Was he fucking or what? She called back. No one answered. Relieved he left her a blunt, because she was about to flip, she headed inside the bathroom. If it hadn't been for Man, she would have walked down to his trap spot and saw what the hell was going on. She tried to call again once she was done smoking, but fell asleep hugging Man close and leaving Ike's plate in the microwave.

The ringing phone awakened her. She reached over Man and picked it up. Assuming it was Ike, she didn't say a word. Just held it to her ear.

"Sunshine."

"Hmm." Her squinting eyes tried to focus on the clock. It was almost eleven. She rolled them.

"I'll be there in a minute. Get up and get ready for work."

Falicia hung up the phone and lay back down. Her heart raced a bit, because normally when he told her he would be there any minute, she greeted him at the door with a kiss and possibly something to drink. She recounted the events that led to her current anger. Staying up all night slaving over a meal Ike didn't even eat. The bitch in the background, and then Man shitting all night. And let's not talk about him getting her son high! Ike could kiss her behind. She lay in bed with her eyes closed like she didn't hear him open the door.

"Bam!"

She was on the floor before she realized he was so close by.

"So, you gon' just lay in bed like you don't know I'm coming." His eyes were wild. Dazed.

Falicia didn't give a fuck. "You gone leave me in here all night, and didn't even have the decency to at least come get your dinner, *after* you asked me to cook it. Then you give my son a fucking shot gun. He's a baby, Ike! Why in the fuck would you even think he would enjoy being high?"

"My lil nigga was chillin'."

"Are you serious?" She was on the verge of losing her cool. "And then I call you and hear some bitch in the background screaming. If that wasn't enough, you waltz your ass in here snatching me up like I wronged you. I haven't done shit to you, Ike."

"Falicia—"

"No, let me speak. You claim shouldn't nobody be able to tell me shit about my nigga, but clearly you got some shit going on I don't know nothing about. If you don't want me, then let me be, and I can just go back home. Because all I've done is been good to you and tried to be all that you need." She sat on the side of bed that her son slept on and smiled at her precious gift. He smiled back, kicking his legs like he was swimming. Ike sat next to her. She refused to look at him, preferring him not to see how he was hurting her. Or how much she loved him. Nor how weak she was for him.

"Baby, listen. You right. I haven't been one hundred with you. It's just . . ."

"Save your excuses for someone else. Either we doing this shit together or we not. I'm out here selling my ass and shit, and you can't even be truthful with me." Falicia started crying.

Ike took her into his arms and finally confessed that he was pimping Velvet and two other girls. "It's just something I been dabbling in for a second. And the screaming you heard was, I had to dump her head in a tub full of water. She been out on the block with the other girls tricking off and two of the hundred dollar bills she brought home were counterfeit. Her ass should have been smarter than that. And so I had to make an example out of her."

He ended his confession with, "I dated a stripper some years ago, and she would just bring all of her money home to me. But Sunshine, you don't have to worry about that. You and me, we're different. Understand that. You have heart, and I can see you being a leader. The type of woman I need by my side. Who I can rely on to handle my business when I ain't present." He took her hand, kissed the back of it, staring into her eyes. "So if you just follow my lead, you will gain the respect you deserve and everyone will answer to you."

Sereniti Hall

Just when she thought things were running smoothly, Falicia got hit with the remix. "As I was saying, earlier tonight when you saw me talking to Royal, she mentioned she'd like to come back," Ike said with his latest request.

"So what you saying, Ike?" she asked, glancing at Ike over a Foot Locker sales paper. She saw some Nikes she wanted for Man and was hoping to catch them on sale.

Royal was this slim, brown-skinned girl that she danced with at Body Tapp. She knew they seemed mighty cozy. And now he was telling her that she wanted to come back home. And that she was the bitch it all started with.

"Hell no!" she quickly stated.

"Well, Sunshine, we gonna have to do something, because the amount of money we living off is just enough to get by."

She tried to suppress her rage. "I'm not about to share my bed with that bitch! Or anybody else. You the one who promised that all of that is over now. So since my body is trained to respond only to you. It should go both ways, Ike."

"Well, what do you suggest, Falicia?" Ike asked.

It was the same question he posed when they had their first conversation about her turning tricks. She closed the sales paper and lay on the bed next to Man. Feeling set up. Like when Satan presented you with an idea, then went away, giving you enough time to ponder and justify why you should carry such a thing out. Falicia tried to think of additional options.

She had been to the "track," a place where young girls, old 'hos, and crack heads walked up and down Metropolitan Avenue, practically naked, trying to pick up men in hopes of exchanging sex for money or drugs. All while trying to avoid five-o. Twice was enough to convince Falicia it was no place for her. The club scene was more of her caliber. Not long after Ike put her on a quest to figure out how to make more money, he began to make sense.

She could see a storm coming the instant Lil Jon and the Eastside boys walked into Body Tapp. Stupid money was in the building, and she wasn't going to turn down a dime. There was also no way Ike was reconnecting with Royal, or any of his other has-beens. This dude sat by the pool tables, right next to the stairs that led to the dressing room. Falicia spotted his wallet on the floor, next to his feet. Her first instinct was to give him back his wallet, but she recalled the night she tricked off with Blue.

"Why didn't you rob him?" Ike had asked. Then later tried to shove her tonsils down her throat, trying to teach her how to suck his dick.

Falicia nonchalantly turned on her heels and headed to a restroom stall inside the dressing room. Closing the door, she sat on the toilet, then opened his wallet filled with hundred dollar bills. She grabbed all of them but one, leaving him enough to catch a cab or get some gas or something, so he wouldn't go home completely empty-handed. She stayed in the bathroom for some minutes, trying to calm her nerves but couldn't. Having hit ol' boy up for seven hundred dollars! Then taking the wallet to the DJ. Ike sexed her real good that night, pleased she exceeded quota.

Afterward, they lay in bed, and he dropped a few nuggets of street wisdom on her. "Ain't nothin' like hittin' a lick," he bragged. "Catching a nigga slipping and taking him for all he got. Like we was gonna do Blue. We had him, Sunshine. But we settled on that. Next time you'll recognize the opportunity."

They began a new language. She had proven to Ike that she could handle being challenged, and this brought her joy.

"We'll be like Bonnie and Clyde, Sunshine. We going places, and if you listen to me, we'll be riding off into the sunset together. Leaving this life behind." Leaving this treacherous ass hustle behind, the life she adapted to. But in the midst of her finding relief with him being in such high spirits, Ike began to freak her out some.

Sereniti Hall

Like a kid on Christmas morning, Ike sat up explaining the do's and don'ts of a robbery. "I'ma get you to the point where you'll love how warm blood feels running down your hand." She didn't say shit. Shock wouldn't let her. Sometimes the line between fact and fiction became very thin when dealing with Ike. *I hope he don't expect me to do that shit for real. Damn, I'm ready to get the fuck outta here.*

CHAPTER 22

Must be my lucky day. Catch a bitch slippin'. Falicia was gazing at not exactly a gold mine, but she'd take the golden nuggets too. She was in the dressing room preparing to go on stage, when a dancer rushed past her after exiting the stage. She had hurried by Falicia so fast, she forgot to close her locker. Falicia had always considered the girl as being very beautiful, and so did the men in the club. She was the only one who was making any real money. Thick redbone, small waist, fat ass, thick thighs, nice breasts. A dime. At first, Falicia was just minding her business, but could not resist accepting the invitation an open locker full of money invited her to. She heard Ike's words ringing in her head: "Catch a nigga slippin', and take them for all they got."

Swiftly, Falicia grabbed the dancer's bag and closed the locker, and then hurried inside the bathroom. "Daddy, meet me in the parking lot," she said into her cell phone, adrenaline pulsating through her veins. Maybe her morals weren't perfect, but she wasn't callous enough to take everything, so she left the girl with all of her singles. Her pretty ass would make all the money back anyway. She heard all the chaos that went down as she was leaving the building to meet up with Ike. He pulled up and she hopped in the car. After a brief sixty seconds, the club manager stepped outside and called Falicia's name.

"Want me to just pull off?" Ike asked, knowing she was up to something.

"Naw. Here." Falicia handed him the money she'd stolen, passing him the roll of big bills, in exchange for the shoes she left in the car.

"Fantasia!" Again, the club manager, Vera called her name. She then stepped out to meet her, hoping it would look like she had nothing to hide.

Sereniti Hall

"Yes, ma'am!" Falicia approached her manager.

"Come with me," she instructed as they walked back inside and into her office. A red, snotty face greeted her. Redbone was clearly upset about her money being missing.

"Did you happen to see her money, or see somebody in the dressing room by her locker?"

"No." She shook her head. "When you came in, I was getting ready for my stage performance. I do recall you coming in, but what happened after that, I don't know. "

"Did you take her money?" Vera asked.

"No! . . . Absolutely not." Falicia reached down in her purse and pulled out her money. "Here's what I made tonight. Three hundred dollars. You're welcome to look in my purse if you want." Falicia extended it to the dancer.

"No, I don't want to." She sounded defeated. "I just don't understand . . . It's just not adding up. Somebody took all of my money out of my locker."

"I can understand that. Do you want to check my purse or me?" Falicia asked the manager. Vera nodded no. Looking around, Falicia noticed a TV with the dressing room on it and all of the VIP rooms as well. "Hey! There's a camera right there. Just run the tape backward, and we can see who did it." She sounded more certain than she felt.

"Can't. It's not recording," Vera answered.

"Damn! All this would have been squashed if it did." She sounded disappointed, but on the inside she was rejoicing. "Well, do you need to borrow some money? Do you have something that you need to handle and this lil incident will prevent you from doing so?" It was her final inquiry.

"No, I'm straight," Redbone said.

"Well, if it's okay with you, may I leave?" she asked Vera.

"Yes, you may go."

"I'm sorry," Falicia told her one last time as she walked out the door. She felt bad for doing Redbone like that, but when she got back in the car, Ike leaned over and kissed her with so much passion and zeal.

"Everything straight?" He inquired about Falicia having to go back inside. After she told him it was and what happened, he beamed. "That's my baby!" Ike seemed very pleased. She took her time handing him the rest of her earnings as they pulled off from the light.

"What's this?" he asked.

"The rest of what I made."

"How much is it?"

"Three." He gave Falicia the biggest smile.

"You must want to give me that ass tonight," he flirted.

"Maybe."

"Ain't no maybe . . . you giving me some pussy." She sat back and observed him. He was most definitely excited. Ike turned the music up and glanced over at Falicia from time to time. *I love him. I love how he looks at me, but more than that, I love how he sets me apart from the rest.*

"Mama, I *knew* you was the one." The happiness he expressed was indescribable as they headed up I-285 North.

They celebrated with a fifth of Hennessy and some 'dro that made Falicia horny as hell. Tonight, she had earned his good head. Everything after that was a blur.

In the morning her stomach burned as she emptied herself of brown stuff that she was convinced was the lining of her stomach. In that moment, Falicia vowed to stop drinking Hennessy. Finally able to leave the toilet's side, she felt better. The phone had just rung and rung. She wanted to beat the hell out of whoever it was. She stumbled over to it and picked up the receiver.

"What, got-dammit!" Falicia yelled into the phone.

"Is Slim there?" a Caucasian male asked.

"No. Ain't no damn Slim here, and quit calling this phone!" She hung up and went to lay back down. As soon as her face hit the pillow, someone started knocking on the door. Falicia wanted to flip! She cursed Ike for leaving her at his trap house alone. Quickly, she slid into her pants and went to the door to serve the baser disturbing her sleep. One look into the peephole, and she almost panicked!

"What the fuck!" she whispered as the police stood outside with their guns drawn, pointing at the door. The officer standing directly in front of the door was in civilian clothes and was looking to his right, as if watching to see if someone would appear. Falicia turned and ran and jumped back in bed. She decided that she was going to just play sleep. *I can't believe this shit! Did Ike set me up? Surely, he wouldn't have done that to me,* she reasoned as she lay there for a few seconds. *The dope's on the table next to the door. Shit!* Falicia jumped back up, ripped a piece of a trash bag from off the counter, scooped all the dope inside the plastic, tied it up, and shoved it up her vagina, then lay back down. *They'll just have to bust in and find me in the bed so-called asleep.*

The weed! She thought about the 'dro they had been smoking. She took it off the dresser and folded the ounce bag as tight as she could get it and also shoved it into her vagina. She felt like the stems could have possibly scraped her walls. After she buckled her capri pants back up, she lay back down. The banging on the door continued, and the phone kept ringing. *What should I do?* Her heart raced as she looked around the room for her phone. Her purse wasn't in sight. *I should go out the back and jump off the patio. Oh shit naw. I'm on the second floor.* This time Falicia peeped out the blinds and saw DeKalb County police cars sitting in view of the patio door.

Fuck it, she told herself as she walked to the door. "What!" she screamed at the continuous knocks to the door as if she was being awakened from her sleep. "Bitch can't even get any rest. Go away!" she yelled through the door.

A Treacherous Hustle

"Sorry, don't mean to bother you. I'm just looking for Slim," the cop answered back.

"There isn't a Slim here," Falicia said, opening the door.

"Put your hands up! Put 'em up!" the police shouted as she eased back from the door. They rushed past, bumping her into a chair that was close by. The man in civilian clothes directed his attention on Falicia.

"Where is that motherfucker!" he yelled as he flipped the table. She jumped up to get out of the way. His throwing stuff around and making threats went on for about five minutes.

"I don't know him," she replied.

The officer found Falicia's purse in the kitchen, and then dumped it in front of her. Nude pictures spilled out. Pictures she had taken for her birthday party promotion. She had them with her because she and Ike had been moving around so much that she didn't want them to get into the wrong hands.

After they discovered that Ike wasn't there, they trashed the place and threatened her some more with their pistols drawn. Falicia didn't know if it was the liquor or what, but she wasn't moved. A cop threatened to lock her up and escorted her outside. As they were walking out the door, Falicia made eye contact with the maintenance man. He nodded, letting her know he would do what he could to help. He was one of Ike's customers.

Falicia was sitting in the backseat of the squad car. Her ID and pictures were the only things the cop brought from the room. Her money and phone were still locked inside. After doing a background check, they let her go, but threatened to lock her up if they ever caught her in Clairmont Lodge again. She started walking as if she was leaving, when the maintenance man got her attention.

"Hey, if you can get my phone or call Ike, I will look out," Falicia told him.

"Yeah?" His eyes lit up like a light bulb.

"Yeah, I got some on me right now."

He took her to his room and got the keys to let her back in the room. He watched out as she ran in and got her stuff, and then returned to his room. Finally, she got Ike on the phone and he was livid. She ended up having to wait for one of the maintenance man's friends to come pick her up. She lay flat in the back covered up as he drove past the road block at the entrance of the lodge. Then he drove to the gas station on the corner, right next to the interstate and waited for Ike. Once he arrived, he promised to take care of them both. They took off on to the interstate, headed across town.

"Mama, I'm so sorry," Ike apologized repeatedly for putting her in that position.

When they finally arrived at Andre's house, Ike held her as she recounted the raid. That day, everything changed between them. They connected on another level and began to complete each other's sentences. She knew what he was asking with just a look. He knew what she wanted just by her tone of voice. Somehow they merged, and she was that bitch. Falicia became a mirror reflection of Ike. He taught her everything there was to know about the streets. About life and death.

CHAPTER 23

"So what you think about that?" he asked, blowing smoke in Falicia's face. Ike was ready to teach Falicia how to turn a woman out.

"I don't really know, Daddy," Falicia responded.

"What you mean you don't know. This is how we gon' stack even more paper. You wit' me, Mama?"

Women had begun to take an interest in Falicia, but she wasn't feeling it. Nothing about a woman turned her on in the least bit. Nothing about a woman made her think of eating her out. Or vice versa. Instead of revealing her true feelings, she shrugged and said, "A'ight, Daddy. I'm wit' it."

"Ay. Velvet," Ike said, waking her up from her nap on the couch. He sent her to take a shower.

After dinner, Falicia had to drink several shots and some, but Ike taught her how to have a woman speaking in a foreign tongue. "Damn, baby, you almost as good as me." He applauded as Velvet stumbled into the kitchen for a glass of water. Falicia wiped her lips on the way to the bathroom. He grabbed her and smacked a kiss on her cheek.

The women who were interested in Falicia, she usually brought them home to meet Ike. If he felt they could be profitable, she would take them out for a night and see how men responded to them, and learn what they were willing to do or not do for money. She gave them a chance to prove they wanted to be a part of what she and Ike were building. Some of them stayed because they were hoping to one day have Ike for themselves, or maybe even take Falicia's place. In any case, they were so consumed with desire, that they overlooked the kind of love he only displayed for Falicia. Yes, it was dysfunctional, but they were establishing a foundation for the future. Their future.

Sereniti Hall

In the midst of working toward their goal, Falicia began missing her son tremendously. Lately, Man had been spending the night over to the babysitter's house much more than Falicia preferred because she had been working so hard. She constantly complained to Ike about having a nanny that he eventually moved her, Man, and Velvet into a one-bedroom lodge apartment at Clairmont. Velvet was now Man's nanny.

After a long night at the club, Falicia and Ike had just walked in the door.

"Go take your bath, then go lay down after you done," Ike instructed.

"Excuse me? What do you mean lay down after I'm done? I'm not ready for bed." Usually he stayed up with Falicia.

He bucked. She blinked. "Are you questioning me?" Ike hadn't been violent toward her in a while. His glare dared her to try him. She did.

"I am. Since when you been wanting this bitch?" Falicia folded her arms across her chest.

"Falicia, go get your ass in that tub before I beat your ass." She rolled her eyes and went to check on Man. He was knocked out.

Taking Ike's advice, Falicia took a long soak and washed her hair. By the time she got out and lotioned herself and put on her pajamas, Velvet began screaming. Falicia raced to the bedroom door. Ike had Velvet bent over the couch doggie style, pants down around his ankles. *I can't believe his ass.* She closed the bedroom door because she didn't want to hear it. He must have gotten more aggressive because now Velvet was shrieking.

Someone came and opened the door. Falicia shut it back, knowing Ike intentionally wanted her to hear him. She was trying with all the patience she could muster to keep her composure, but the more Velvet shrieked, the more Falicia's temperature rose. She lost it completely. Snatching the door open, she shouted, "Nigga, you in here fucking this bitch? Leave me the fuck alone now! Stop opening this damn door!" For a second she thought she saw a smirk on his face. He pushed the bitch away as his dick slipped out of her.

"Go back there and lay your ass down now!" he demanded as he casually stood up.

"Fuck you, Ike! And this big-belly bitch." She tried to get her hands on Velvet. Velvet hid behind Ike, but then she eased out of the room.

"This my dick!" he shouted. "If yo' ass had made your quota, I wouldn't be touching her." Falicia's mouth gaped open. For a second she stopped breathing. *What kind of bullshit game is this?*

"What the fuck is that supposed to mean? So I'm just one of your 'hos, Ike? You only touch me because I bank every night? Is that what you saying?" Falicia laughed and cried, reality hitting her where it throbbed most. "I been good to you, nigga. Fuck you and fuck that bad body bitch you—"

"Shut up, Falicia!" he demanded. "Dumb ass 'ho—"

"No, you sh—" He grabbed her by the throat. Falicia clawed at his arm frantically, staring in his eyes, cold with death. She started kicking, desperate to live.

"Bitch, you kicked me!" He was stunned.

"I didn't mean to," she repeated, trying to get away.

"Bring yo' ass here!" Ike charged her, sending them over the couch and slamming her to the floor. She crawled a few feet but jumped up. He stormed toward her.

"I thought you said you wouldn't hit me anymore." Man began to cry.

"Go check on my son," he told Velvet. And slammed the door, putting a chokehold around Falicia's neck.

Where is my baby, my nigga? She knew he was in there somewhere. A few seconds past, but it felt like forever when his grip around her neck loosened. Suddenly, his hand grabbed hers as he forced her to touch his dick.

"Touch me!" he demanded. Petrified, she grabbed his penis.

"Mama, calm me down. Touch me!" Falicia searched his eyes for answers as she rubbed his chest and stroked him. Gradually, she could feel the tension leaving his body. He rested his head against hers. "Mama, go lay down."

She eased out of his reach and ran into the bathroom and wiped away a face full of tears. Slowly she left the room and walked into her room. Velvet held Man in her arms, gently rocking him.

"Thank you, but I would prefer if you put my baby down." Velvet complied and didn't say a word. Slowly she left the room and walked back upfront where Ike sat on the sofa.

Falicia sat on the bed crying. Man stared at her, the love in his eyes apparent, as if he was praying for her. She took him in her arms and began rocking him back to sleep. When she got up to go to the bathroom, Velvet was on her knees giving Ike head. He held a handful of hair, gagging her with his penis, staring directly at Falicia. The smugness all over his face gave her chills.

Instead of dwelling on his blatant disrespect, she finished rocking her child until he fell asleep. It had started raining, so once she had him back in bed, Falicia cracked the patio door. She lay on the floor so she could smell and hear the rain. Uncertain what Ike was doing because she wouldn't look, she dared not give him the satisfaction of even thinking she cared anymore. He had fucked up, drove her to a place mentally that she hadn't signed up for.

With a plan to leave, especially after Ike had punched her in the mouth for not getting up off the floor and into the bed, Falicia had only asked Velvet for a ride. Of course the bitch went back and told Ike.

"Baby, you scared of me?" Ike asked Falicia, although it was obvious she was shaking. He gently bobbed his head on top of hers. "What the fuck?" he said repeatedly. "Sunshine, you can't leave me. You can't leave me . . . you can't." He held her face and kissed her lip where it was busted. "I fucked up. I know I did." She didn't want to say or do anything that would cause him to get violent, so she stood there thinking of the right words to say. "Mama, you gon' take my family?"

"Ike, I love you, but I can't live like this. I can't. I'm too young for this shit." Bingo! It hit her like a light bulb. "I'm too young. I'm only seventeen years old." She knew that revealing her age would be enough to get them out. This puzzled look spread across his face.

"What?"

"I didn't tell you because no one in Georgia knows, but now that you do, nobody else has to know. I won't say anything about it. You can just go back to living your life, and no one has to know why we didn't work out. I would appreciate it if you keep quiet about it, because I have to support my child."

"That explains some things, but some things it doesn't," he responded, then pulled out his phone and called her mother.

"Hello, Ms. Ford? . . . This is Ike . . . Yeah, Falicia's fine. I just have one question for you. Why didn't you tell me your daughter was just a child?" he asked. Falicia could not make out what Letty said in response. He held the phone a few seconds, then hung up.

"Well, what did she say?" Falicia asked.

"She said because you were happy. Then she hung up."

Falicia's heart ached. That could have been her chance out. She wished Letty had told him, "Well, now that you know, bring my baby home." But her mother had no way of knowing what her child was enduring. Falicia looked down at the floor. She just wanted to get out of there. She took a deep breath. "I love you," she said again, "I'm sorry." Falicia started toward the door. Ike grabbed her and fell to his knees. Big elephant tears poured from his eyes as he held her by her waist crying, begging her not to leave him.

"Baby, please don't go. I fucked up. I fucked up, but I can't be without you. What the fuck am I living for if I don't have you and Man?" She didn't like the way that sounded. Finally she looked down at him. They cried together for a minute.

"Mama, be patient with me. You know I love you. You know

don't nobody love you more than me. At least think about it . . . Can you do that? Just think about it?"

"Yeah, I can do that." She nodded.

Ike walked her to the Blazer and opened the door. "Can I hold my son for a minute? Just in case it's my last time?" he asked. He took Man out of the seat and held him close for about two minutes as he told him how much he loved him and would miss them. After putting him back, he leaned in and kissed her, leaving his tears on her face.

Although she didn't admit it to anyone, seeing him cry like that tore her apart. *How could he not love me? Maybe he sincerely does have a problem controlling his anger.* She watched him stand in the road as they pulled away. Falicia's nerves were so shot, she grabbed one of Velvet's cigarettes, and she didn't even smoke the nasty things.

Velvet's phone rang and she answered. She listened to the caller for a minute. "Okay," she finally said and ended the call. She turn toward Falicia.

"That was Ike. He told me I better not come home without you." A tear slipped down her cheek. A sudden burst of tears fell and her body shook as she sobbed. "If you leave, he might kill me, Mama. Please don't leave."

CHAPTER 24

Life had taken on a new perspective for Ike, Velvet, and Falicia. Having money meant having power and respect and in Falicia's house, peace. Ike had accumulated a few females who were willing to do whatever she said. Falicia was responsible for their hair, clothes, and health. All of the women could spend what they wanted at the mall or other big box stores, but they had to double whatever they spent that night. Most of their dates were arranged by Falicia with men from the club, or men she met while out and about who weren't willing to pay her asking price. The man's pockets determined which female Falicia arranged for him to trick with. She made the most money in the house, so she was able to spend the most and was the most respected. Even Ike's homeboys respected her. She grew to love coming home, and they'd all be in front of the TV playing video games. Falicia would drop a stack of money in Ike's lap from a nigga she caught slipping. The look on their faces gave her pure satisfaction. Her nigga was happy, and therefore, so was she. But all good things ended abruptly when dealing with Ike's finicky ass.

He had gotten arrested one other time; it felt like it was going to kill Falicia, sleeping next to Velvet every day. His jail time ended a month later. Once Ike got home, he and Falicia talked about keeping him out of jail. "Daddy, you need to chill," Falicia said.

"That's true, but who gon' do it if I don't," he said.

"I gotchu. I'll do it. In the meantime, you just chill. All you gotta do is supply the drugs, sling dick with your white collar tricks, discipline the 'hos, see about me, and count our money."

"A'ight. I can do that," he said.

So Falicia started selling pills and powder out of the club, and that's when all these 'hos really joined the family. Ike didn't have to sling dope at all if he didn't want to. Falicia saw it as an opportunity to stop losing money on him going to jail, getting bailed out, or spending it on commissary. There was money to be made, and she was willing to go the distance to get it.

In the midst of this transition, this chick named Monie, who had just gotten out of prison, had set up shop in the hotel area near Clairmont Lodge. Several of Ike's regulars came telling him that she was trying to push dope on his territory, knowing he would give them some shake. Shake was the crumbs from dope that settled at the bottom of the bag it was stored in, or the crumbs that remained on whatever you cut it up on. Ike, operating in his calculating mind, had already established a relationship with the security guards, and paid them to go knock on Monie's door and give her an ultimatum. Either she got down with him, or she'd go back to jail. Monie chose Ike; he had her set up shop for him. He had already told Falicia that once she made him about eight thousand dollars that he was going to fuck her, as a motivating factor to keep her bringing him money.

A couple months later, Monie got sick and seemed to have just a simple cold that carried on into its second week. Instead of going to the hospital, she asked to be put up in a separate room where she could nurse herself back to health and sell dope in the small hotel next door to the lodge.

Taking her some TheraFlu and orange juice at her request, Falicia, or one of the other girls, frequently went to go check on her and renew her supply. Until one day, Ike couldn't get Monie on the phone. Falicia and Velvet went over to her room. She was gone. Not a note, an apology, or an explanation. Nothing . . . In Monie's absence, Ike posted Carlos up in the room to serve the basers that shopped at this spot. He used to be a security guard for the lodge.

Things were back in order, and a few days later a dancer named Satin asked Falicia if she wanted to take a trip to Miami to dance at some clubs down there.

"Girl, hell yeah! I ain't never been to Miami. I know I can convince Ike to let me go. If it's money to be made, he down wit' it."

"A'ight. I'll rent a car. We'll head out in two days," Satin said.

The night before Falicia left, she and Ike were lying in bed together smoking a blunt when his phone rang. At this point, she wasn't even concerned about his dealings. When she went through certain neighborhoods, or when certain niggas greeted her at the bar, they all acknowledged her as Lil Ike." So she occupied herself as he talked on his phone.

"Bitch!" Ike yelled in the phone. "You got me fucked up!" he screamed at the caller. He proceeded with his conversation as Falicia got up and went to get something to drink.

"Daddy, you all right?" she asked as she re-entered the room.

"Yeah, this dumb bitch just called trying to proposition me to leave you!"

"What! Who?" Falicia crawled behind him, rubbing his shoulders, and kissing his neck. All too familiar with how ugly things could get when he was angry, she started her calming technique before he got turned up.

"Monie ol' trifling muthafuckin' ass. Talkin' 'bout she in New York and just hit the lottery. If I leave you and come to her, I wouldn't have to work another day in my life."

"Really?" For some reason Falicia wasn't moved. "Well, did she say why she just up and disappeared?"

"I didn't give her time. I just roasted that 'ho for trying me and disrespecting your honor."

It wasn't absolutely clear that was all she said because he was extremely upset, but Falicia wasn't going to make a big deal about it. "Daddy, lay down and let me show you how much I'm going to miss you." She caressed his chest, and then his manhood. Ike was immediately aroused. He grabbed a blunt from the nightstand, took a few pulls, and then passed it to her. She hit it and gave it back, getting ready to take off her teddy.

"Leave it . . ." Ike ordered. "I want to rip it off." Grabbing her legs, he snatched them from under her, forcing her to fall on her back. Hard. With one yank, the threads popped, and she was only left in her panties. He snatched them off, shoved her legs in the air, and went in head first with much aggression, until he made her climax twice.

Climbing on top of her, he forced his way into her butt. The pain wasn't as bad as it used to be, but wherever his mind was, it didn't permit him to be gentle. He used his arms to hold up his weight. Falicia tried not to think of her agony, because Ike was frustrated and needed to relax. She just needed something to distract her mind. He was swelling inside her, making her want to run as he shifted his weight and used one hand to hold her shoulder. Slamming into her with brutal force. No longer capable of enduring the anguish, Falicia started clawing at his hand. He looked at her. She kept clawing. He sped up. She grabbed his hand and placed it around her throat. Ike snatched it away. She placed it back and dug her nails into his skin. "Do it!" she said. He realized what she was doing and tightened his grip, bringing him and Falicia to one of the best sexual encounters they'd ever experienced together.

Hearts set on "gettin' dem' dollars," Falicia and Satin drove to Miami where Ike heard there was even more money to be made, and it might be some place they could one day consider relocating. The morning Falicia and Satin left, things started on a bad note. Everything that could go wrong went wrong. A half a mile away from their exit, she was pulled over, blunt in her hand, but was lucky enough to only be given a warning.

They entered the hotel Ike booked for them and tripped out on the fact that life was pretty much the same there as it was in the 'A.' Some dude was doing the same shit, living out of a hotel room with a few whores working the track, a long road that bordered the beach. Falicia and Satin walked up and down looking for dates, men to exchange sexual favors for money.

Honestly, Falicia really wanted to dance at Black Magic in Miami; it was more like Magic City in Atlanta. She had no intention of beating the strip, but without a permit to work in the adult entertainment club, she had no choice but to pick up a few John Doe's to trick off. Easy money. She'd slide the condom on their penis with her mouth, and then deep throat it. Early on she had learned it was better to put the condom in her mouth and put it on, instead of just applying it. Because them dudes would try to debate with her, as if she was really about to put a raw, and probably filthy ass dick in her mouth, when she didn't know the dude not even a day of her life. Hell naw!

It seemed the lil trip was proving to be beneficial, until she hooked up with this dude at the gas station across from their hotel. He drove a black Cadillac SUV, claiming he was the owner of Black Magic, the very place Falicia wanted to dance. Like a naive lil girl, Falicia got in his SUV and left with him, leaving the rental car at the gas station.

"I can help you make some real money," the big, black, bald club owner had promised her. "I own Black Magic."

"For real!" she said with a sexy grin, scanning the location once more so she could remember which gas station she'd left her rental. The instant he pulled off, Falicia climbed into his lap and rode the man all the way to the club. The sex was so good he was inspired to help her make some more money and took her by this club where a few niggas came to the truck and tricked off. By the third dude, Falicia was over it. She wasn't trying to fuck the entire club. Her old man didn't spend this much time in her pussy; he preferred her ass. She wasn't about to wear her shit out for a few hundred dollars. Most dudes got played with some head. Falicia just made sure they agreed to one nut. How he obtained that nut wasn't clarified. So when she declined to do any more business, shit got crazy. She supposed the so-called "strip club owner" expected her to fuck all these men, and then just take her money.

Sereniti Hall

Things really went left when they pulled on this street that looked like an abandoned junkyard, and then another car pulled up. Her body went still as her heart pumped fiercely from nervousness. *I'm not even sure how da fuck I'm going to survive this one my damn self! These niggas might kill me.* But Falicia got real ratchet when dude told her the other men were going to take her to her car.

"No they ain't! They ain't taking me no motherfuckin' where!"

He told her this after they had been standing outside talking privately on this empty ass dark street. "They said they'll drop you back off at the gas station," he said without any expression on his face. This nigga knew better—he knew what he was doing.

"Please don't do this," she pleaded. The dude stepped back into the street to talk to the other men. They spoke in low voices. "Sir, what would you do if your sister was in this predicament? Please, help me. You know full well what they are going to do to me."

It had to be by the grace of God that dude convinced them to allow him to take her back to her car, but old boy ended up taking about four hundred dollars, which was what he had paid her. He couldn't find the rest.

That night she called Ike and told him what happened. Falicia didn't tell him her exact thoughts then, but she concluded that she was over this lifestyle. *I'm done with this shit. I'm tired of this street ass bullshit. Maybe I'll stay in Miami somewhere.* She considered the financial struggle, and she wasn't trying to make a career out of turning tricks. One thing was for sure, Falicia wanted out when she got back to the 'A.'

Before Falicia and Satin got back on the interstate, they did a little shopping. Falicia purchased Man some Jordan booties and a few pieces for herself. She figured she might as well spend some of the money she had made over the previous four nights. The ride gave her time to think about what she was going to say to Ike. It wouldn't be an easy way out, but she had to do what needed to be done.

Satin dropped her off at the lodge. Falicia called Ike to tell him she was outside. Once he came out, he grabbed her like he truly missed her. All she could give him was a weak smile, just thinking about how he had probably had Velvet, or his baby mama, sucking and fucking him since she'd been gone. Ike kept a bitch around because there were just certain things he felt he shouldn't have to do. Hell, she had even seen him order a few dudes around.

They went upstairs to a different room than the one he worked out of when she first left. There, they talked in depth about her trip, and he updated her on the activities of their dysfunctional life. "Mama, go to the back and get me that key out that coat inside pocket," he said casually.

"In a second," Falicia replied, planting a kiss on Man's head. She sniffed. Velvet had recently washed his hair and given him a bath. "Velvet, I need to talk to Ike alone. Can you excuse us?" she asked, trying to muster up the courage to tell him what she had to say. Velvet glanced at Ike and left quietly.

"Naw, baby. I need you to handle that now." She dragged herself to their bedroom. Being the 'one' was taking a toll on her. She wanted to go home to be with Letty, where things made sense. If only for an overnight visit.

"Surprise!" Ike replied from the doorway.

Waiting for her return was a small black Coach purse and a fur coat. "That's a mink, baby," he boasted. She smiled, not knowing the difference. "Baby, Fat Joe, and R. Kelly wearing them mink coats. That's some expensive shit you wrapped up in." She retained her false grin, not comprehending the big deal. She already owned a Coach purse that she bought from a booster at the club.

"Thank you."

"You deserve it, but there's more."

She tried the coat on and felt a set of keys inside. "But whose keys are these?" She held them in her hand, looking at them strangely.

"Whoever keys they are," he replied. She stared at him, ready to say something slick, but it finally registered. Ike sat there grinning, sending her on a dummy mission.

"These are my keys?" she asked, jumping up. "Are they?" Ike grinned. "Daddy, tell me!"

"You ready to take a ride in your new truck?" She practically jumped in his arms and kissed his face all wild.

She hit the alarm button, convinced she heard it respond. Taking the coat off, she threw it on the bed and beat him downstairs! She was seven years old. Joyful tears ran from her eyes. Falicia wasn't a hundred percent sure what Ike had in mind by getting her a champagne-colored Suburban, but the first thing that came to mind was to floss it. He upgraded her dress code as well. "If you look like money, Sunshine. You'll attract money!"

And she was soaking it all in. She had earned her stripes. Now she had the power to tell a bitch to come and she would. Take your clothes off and she got naked. They did whatever she said because her nigga trained them to be that way. And there were consequences if anybody disrespected her. She was his Bottom Bitch. She proved to those who doubted her that she was all Ike needed. Going back home was no longer necessary.

Falicia relished the idea of knowing that things had flipped around in her favor instantly. Dudes walked up to her with a mind to run some game, but when she turned around, they would say, "Oh, I see. You 'bout that money." She had struggled all her life, so looking like what she always dreamed of was her fuel to stay on her grind. They were seeing better days, and Ike was back to flossing like he had when they first met.

Instead of kicking it with his homies, he made grand introductions with Velvet and Falicia at his side and some of the other girls trailing behind. They took one day a week as their relax day, going from a strip club to a nice restaurant. She and the girls worked hard, so why not. Those nights usually turned into a big orgy of some type. And it wasn't like just anybody could join their family. A female would have to satisfy Falicia, taking her there wasn't as easy as they thought. And a dude who wanted to be on his team had to be able to handle several women at one time. Usually, Falicia ordered what they should do to him.

As time progressed, she began drinking so much that she often blacked out. Consciously awake, but unable to recall things that happened. When it came to being sexual, she was usually dominant with another woman. That's how Ike had taught her to be. She was the one Ike depended on to get the party started. Sometimes turning up in the back of her truck while Ike or Velvet drove. Sex. Liquor. Money and drugs. She was living the life. Waking up naked in the closet more than once where Ike left her to sleep it off. One morning she woke up with her butt piercing in the bed with her, her rear end split and needing stitches. And there were times when she would be so sore, she could barely move.

Waking up with a leg and an arm tied together and belt marks all over, she knew Ike was taking advantage of her being passed out. Not just from being high, but working around the clock. The most terrifying was waking up at the foot of the bed being strangled while he got off doggie style. Regardless of how he tormented her, and how comatose she was from last night's party, she still had to get up and go to work.

Their latest hustle included dudes from another state with all their homeboys stopping through Atlanta to enjoy the luxuries of southern hospitality. They were the ones who never knew what hit them. A room full of beautiful women in every size, every skin tone, various heights, all willing for the right price. But what they didn't expect was that while they were having a threesome, two girls on one dude, or being blown out of his mind, Falicia and her girls were leaving their hotel rooms with everything they could take them for.

Between what they paid Falicia to trick off with the girls and what she stole, it was a joy ride going home. Sometimes they left with as much as three grand plus. But as seasons change, so does the streets. A drought hit. Only a little bit of drugs, if any at all, were available to sell. Therefore, if the dope boys weren't making much money, neither were Falicia and her girls. Nevertheless, she hoped her corporate clients would come through the club and spend something. Their money was rationed and predictable. Mostly at the end of the week when they got paid, and after all their bills were paid on the first of the month. So where Falicia was able to meet her quota, the girls weren't. And those late nights—well—mornings of cruising the streets in search of coming up on some money for them, but then going home empty-handed took a toll on her. And Ike wasn't the type you could come home to with nothing. Or it would be hell to pay, Falicia catching the brunt of most of his hostility. She wasn't crowned Bottom Bitch for nothing.

Furious with the few dollars the girls brought home, he slapped their earnings off the table, his face distorted with rage. "I send four of you bitches out. And all you fucking bring me back is three fucking hundred dollars!" He turned the table over and grabbed Falicia by the back of her neck. "Somebody better get me my damn money! You bitches better hit the road. You bet' not come up short another damn day!"

On Sunday, Ike's demand stayed with Falicia all the way to Jazzy T's, the spot she and Ike chose to go and unwind. There, she could have chilled with him all night, but she knew her nigga, and 'time was money.' She could hear him in her head. Upon entering the club, Falicia had run into an old friend, and Ike's jealousy crawled all over her. He thought every dude Falicia ran into was a business proposition. She immediately sent a dancer over to Ike to calm his anger. She had barely sat down when a waitress brought her a drink. Her brows bent.

"Who bought this?" she asked. The waitress pointed to the man sitting across from her. It was Gator, a regular at Dancer's Elite and Body Tapp, who always spent money with her. He was eyeing her like his nickname implied. She texted Ike with a proposal. "The only thing," she expressed, "is that he uses ecstasy. I know because he's bought some from me."

Falicia didn't trust people whose minds were altered by drugs, but recalled Cinnamon saying that he looked out for her one night when she went home with him. So Falicia left the club with Gator.

He and Falicia had only been inside his apartment within a matter of minutes, when gut instinct put an ache in her stomach. She had an unpleasant feeling about being in his domain where different pills were spread out on the table.

"Take whatever you want," he said.

"No thank you," Falicia replied, turning her head.

"You sure?"

"Yeah." She nodded.

"Here. Just try it."

"Naw, I'm good." Twice he tried to shove a pill in her mouth. The more she resisted, the more Gator unraveled. She started dancing for him, trying to tame the beast in his altered mind.

"Get naked for me," he said.

"I just want you to relax and let me do what I do best," Falicia explained gently. "I'll get naked eventually." She glanced at the door several times, feeling like some shit was in the making. Tucking her cell phone in her boots, she set them by the door. Her heart raced as she pulled up her dress, revealing her breasts and tight belly. She danced slowly, trying to groove to the music in her head. And put this frantic nigga at ease.

Gator pounced on her like a ferocious lion and put a gun to her head. Unzipped his pants. Took out his stiff dick.

Falicia almost gasped. *This bitch already got a condom on!* "Gator, no. Don't do this shit!" He pried his erection between her legs, keeping the pistol to her head. Moaning in ecstasy. The louder he groaned in pleasure, the more enraged Falicia became. *A nigga already did this shit to me before. Not a-fucking-gain! If he kill me, then he kill me,* she thought. Like a hunter waiting on its prey, she waited for him to ease back, intending to stroke her again. She jammed her knee in his balls.

"Arrggh!" Gator dropped his gun, grabbing his nuts. Falicia pushed him off of her. He grabbed her thigh with his nails. She swung her fists and kicked at him. He punched and grabbed at anything his hands could make contact with. Scrambling to her feet, she grabbed her boots and turned the key in the door. Just as she grabbed the doorknob and pulled, Gator tackled her. Falicia kicked like a woman gone wild, determined he would not get her back inside his apartment. She bailed out of the main door.

"Help!" Falicia screamed to a lady who was getting groceries out the trunk of her car with two small kids.

Gator barreled out the door, grabbing her quickly by the arm. Falicia fought even harder to break free from his grip.

"Help me!" Falicia shouted. "Please, he just raped me!" Her dress was halfway up her body, with no panties on and her thighs were scratched up. The woman's eyes widened in terror.

"Oh my God!" The woman covered one of her children's eyes and rushed them away.

"Please!" Falicia yelled, trying to wrestle out of Gator's grip.

He slipped and fell on one knee, fighting desperately to hold on to her, his eyes wild with rage like she'd never seen. Falicia ducked out of his reach and raced away, her days of sprinting paying off.

"Excuse me, sir. Please tell me where I am," she asked, crying and looking around for Gator. She unzipped her boot and retrieved her phone.

"Hello?" Ike said.

"I'm on Wesley Chapel running down the street. Daddy, hurry. Gator just raped me!" She wiped her face with both hands and shook it off.

"That son-of-a-bitch!"

Within five minutes, Ike and Velvet picked her up. To Falicia's surprise, Ike also called the police. They put Gator in back of the police car as Falicia sat in back of the truck.

Falicia heard Gator speaking to the cop. "She a hooker. She pissed 'cause I ain't pay her!" he lied, knowing he had already given her $300 that she'd given to Ike before they even left the club together.

"He raped me!" Falicia insisted, staring at the black female detective who arrived on the scene last and handled the incident in an apathetic way. It didn't matter what Falicia said, or the fact that she could show her, her wounds.

"Go to Emory hospital and get a rape kit, ma'am," the female detective said without emotion, then handed Falicia her business card.

"But he raped me!" Falicia insisted, with tears gushing from her eyes. "He violated me."

"They'll take care of you at the hospital." She walked away.

"What?" Ike barked. "Ain't no muthafucka finna fuck with my bitch and get away with it!" He stormed up to the police car. Velvet and Falicia hurried behind him, trying to calm him down.

"I just want you to get a good look at me," Ike told Gator. "Get a good look at me because you'll see me again." He glared at Gator, then walked back to the truck, telling Velvet, "Get my baby the fuck out of here."

At Emory, the examiner was so taken aback by the evidence, he said she most definitely had a case. He found the condom inside of her, her butt ring was ripped a little, and there were several scratches all over her vagina and thighs. Falicia called the detective several times and even left her number, but she never answered nor returned her calls.

She didn't want to believe the police wouldn't help her, but Ike was there just like he said. He had a difficult time accepting what had happened to her, and whether it was to make him feel like he was preventing something like that from happening again, or he thought it might make her a little more comfortable, he assigned Carlos as her bodyguard. What she enjoyed most about the arrangement was going out to nightclubs and going straight through the door because he knew the bouncers.

Whenever she was in the VIP section, or on the dance floor and Carlos was posted up, she often heard people saying, "Who is that? She must be a model or something." Along with the clothes and shoes, Carlos' presence only added to her persona. Falicia got wrapped up in a fantasy of being important and making a mark in the streets, gladly embracing the lie they were building.

At Body Tapp, she attempted to put the night with Gator out of her mind. She downed a shot of tequila at the bar, before dancing for a dude with a neatly cut fade and beard who couldn't keep his eyes off her.

"What's up, Sexy Black? With that tight-ass pussy," someone said in her ear.

Falicia stared in the mirror that outlined the wall behind the bar. It was Gator's ass, donning a smirk that gave her chills. She froze.

"Is something wrong?" the dude she was dancing for asked, glancing from Falicia to Gator.

Fear had her back at Gator's apartment, glued to the floor, gripping her chest. Gator pointing his pistol to her head flashed in her mind. He grinned harder, pressing his body against her. She bumped into Gator as she sped into the dressing room, calling the police, and then calling Ike. Dressing as fast as she could, her nerves were so bad, she had to sit on the toilet. When she came out, Ike and Carlos were dragging Gator toward the door.

"Don't let them take me outside!" Gator screamed, kicking and trying to get them to put him down. "Don't let them take me!"

"Hey! What is all this about?" the manager asked as they neared the door.

"Somebody help me!" Gator continued to scream.

A Treacherous Hustle

Falicia approached the club's manager. "DeWayne, he raped me three weeks ago. Now he's in here trying to taunt me," Falicia tried to explain, but it was so loud with all the screaming, he acted as if he didn't understand what she was saying. He hurried toward the officers who were headed in the door.

"Wow!" Ike said as he let dude go. "Baby, you called the police?" he asked Falicia, clearly irritated.

"I was scared," Falicia answered, right before they disappeared out the door.

Much to her dismay, just as the female detective dismissed her claim of being raped, DeWayne sent Gator back downstairs and told the police, "It's all a misunderstanding."

"Miss, is there a problem?" one of the officers asked.

"Yes there is." She began explaining.

Suddenly, they directed their attention toward DeWayne, who kept interrupting her. "No, there's no problem. She just got into it with a customer, that's all," he said.

Falicia was so upset she screamed. "There is a fucking problem, DeWayne! He violated me! Why don't you believe me? If it wasn't for me and your other dancers, you wouldn't even have any fucking customers!" She stormed out the door. *I'll never call the cops again for shit! No matter how many fucking times I really might need their ass.*

Ike pulled up beside her, and for a second she was too afraid to look, just in case it was Gator.

When they got home, he gave her a few shotguns of marijuana and rubbed her back until her tears stopped.

"Hey, Mama . . ." Ike sat next to her on the bed. "Do you still got dude's door keys?"

"Yeah." Falicia pointed at her purse.

"You ain't gonna have to worry about him anymore. Love you." He kissed her forehead and pulled out his cell phone. "Yo, Carlos. Meet me in the parking lot," Ike said as he walked out the door.

Ike didn't return until sunset and climbed in bed with Falicia, taking her in his arms. She didn't ask any questions, convinced the less she knew, the better.

Later in the morning, she awakened to Ike massaging her body. He would often rub her to sleep, and if time permitted, caressed her until she awakened. A sense of protection kicked in as she lay on her stomach thinking about how Gator wouldn't harm her anymore.

"Turn over," Ike said. Falicia did so, but was startled by something heavy around her neck.

She felt the chain around her neck, much thicker than most.

"What's this?" she asked, sitting straight up in bed. Ike beamed from one ear to the next.

"You like it?" he asked.

Falicia glanced down, staring at what she was able to see of a gold bolt lock.

"I got the key around my neck," he added. She gracefully slid out of bed and walked into the bathroom. A thick silver chain draped her neck with a gold and silver lock.

"I'll never take it off," she stated, trying to sound pleased. *Why do I have a fucking dog chain around my neck?*

Ike held up the charm and the key that hung side by side. "You'll forever be mine. I hold the key to your heart, to your soul, to everything." He walked up to her and stood directly behind her, beaming like a nigga who'd just put twenty karats around her neck. They stared in the mirror together.

"Baby, you already know you got those things. Is all this necessary?" She tried not to start an argument or seem ungrateful.

"You must not like it?" he questioned.

"I'm just saying, it's a bit much."

"Baby, we a bit much! This shit represent *us*. You and I are linked together! For life! It's us against the world! You the key to my future, my life . . . everything! This you and me, baby!"

Falicia grinned big. She was sold on the idea. Ike took her in his arms. They kissed passionately. Smiled at one another. This was her nigga, and she was his bitch—literally!

He pulled her into their room like a kid. "I got something else for you. Close your eyes and hold out your hand." His smile got brighter. She did as he asked. Without a doubt she knew what the cold steel was before she opened her eyes to a .38 revolver. "You bet' not let nan nigga take shit else from you again!" he instructed, looking serious as fuck.

"So you saying if a nigga try me, get his ass off me with this?" Falicia asked with a sinking feeling in her stomach.

"I'm saying, you better not let nan nigga take shit from you again!" Falicia stared at him. She hated when he wasn't direct. Talking in a roundabout way, leaving her to figure shit out on her own. But this was one matter she needed to be clear on.

"So if somebody try to rape me, handle his ass, right?" She hoped he wouldn't get upset because she made him repeat himself.

"If a nigga fuck with you period! I'ma beat yo' ass if you let a nigga take a motherfucking thing from you! You understand me? You *my bitch*! These motherfuckers need to understand it's hell to pay for fucking with mine!"

Falicia nodded, placing the .38 in her purse along with some bullets. Ike's stare evolved into a sinister grin. "You powerful now, baby. You ready to hit a lick now." His happiness was restored. Ike was beyond elated.

"I told you, baby," he said, taking her .38 out of her purse, smirk intact. "I'ma get you to the point that you love how warm blood feels running down your hand. I'ma get you to the point where you crave it!"

CHAPTER 25

Gifts weren't the only thing Ike gave Falicia when she returned from Miami. He started giving her penicillin and a One a Day vitamin every day, but it wasn't just her; it was all the girls and himself. "This is to keep us straight because y'all taking risks fucking for money, and y'all don't know if a nigga got something. I gotta make sure I'm straight too since we all been fucking each other." But what he didn't know and apparently Falicia and none of the other ladies did either, was by them taking an antibiotic daily had caused their immune system to depend on the antibiotic, thus weakening it from its natural ability to fight and resist infections and viruses. A common cold that should only last a week, lasted two weeks, and she didn't want Man getting anybody's germs.

Letty ended up getting Man to prevent him from having to go from place to place and to keep him well. Also, Falicia didn't feel her living arrangement was good enough for him. She may have been fooled by the idea of being loved, but she wasn't under false pretenses about the environment a baby should be raised in.

After dropping him off, she knew without a doubt she needed to get away from the 'A' for a minute, only this time she wouldn't be going to Florida with the purpose of relaxing and enjoying herself. Ike had given her strict orders to hit a nice lick. He was ready to leave all his 'hos behind so he, Man, and Falicia could start over. But before Falicia hit the road with Velvet and Shay, she had loose ends to tie.

Roy, a short, handsome, slim dude with a low haircut, who kind of favored TI the rapper, took an interest in her one night at Dancers Elite. Months earlier he wanted to trick off with her, but he didn't have a way home, except by cab. It was weird because all the dudes she had been with all had a vehicle where they would engage, but not this one. Ike drove them to Roy's apartment that wasn't far from where he and Falicia stayed in the Clairmont Lodge. She swiftly made her money and headed home.

The next day, Roy called and made plans to trick off with her again. He needed to handle some business first, then he wanted to see her, preferring if he could come to her.

"Do you do pills or coke?" he asked, handing Falicia back the blunt she smoked with him.

"No, but I do sell them."

"So, you can sell me some pills then?" he asked.

"Yeah."

He popped the three she sold him, but sixty minutes later, he wanted some powder. Falicia sold him an eight ball. Sitting back on the bed, she listened to him talk, watching every move he made. She didn't like the idea of dealing with niggas when they were high. "So, you got crack too?"

"Dude, you sure?" she questioned, tripped out by his drug use. Roy didn't strike her as the type.

"Yeah, I'm sure," he insisted.

Falicia sold Roy a fifty piece and watched in amazement as he smoked it. *Wow!* she thought, opening the patio door so it could air out. As far as she knew, she didn't fuck with niggas who smoked dope because it was the same drug that robbed her father, uncle, and step granddad of their lives. Plus, she hated the smell. It reminded her of her uncle when he bought dope from her ex-boyfriend. Finally in his zone, Roy was ready to fuck. Falicia watched him undress and stretch out on the bed, geeking.

"Come here," he instructed, rubbing himself. "Put this in your mouth." She stared down at his soft penis. No matter what she tried, he wouldn't get erect. He moaned as if he felt it, but his dick did nothing. Even as she jacked him, she found it unbelievable how Roy reacted to her touch but didn't respond. Her toughest challenge was his reaction, as if he'd climaxed, but she didn't see anything.

Afterward, he popped more pills until he was near comatose,

and she was afraid to send him home. She wasn't sure what he was talking about; he was muttering. She got another blunt. Apparently, the sudden movement spooked him. He sat up as well and looked at Falicia as if he didn't recognize her. *Shit! Now I'm spooked.*

"Roy . . . Roy . . ." Falicia spoke to him very even toned, not wanting to sound threatening. He stood up on the bed and faced her, mumbling something. She kept her feet planted on the floor and moved around so he couldn't attack her, if that's what he had in mind.

About twenty minutes of this weird behavior, she realized he was not being violent, nor did he feel she was either. Falicia kept her distance, but permitted him to just chill a while, until he could comprehend that she was calling him a cab and sending him home. She didn't understand it, but she felt sorry for him. She could have robbed him easily. He had a genuineness about him that made Falicia care about his well-being, and she barely knew him. She did, however, want him to go home and sleep that shit off.

The next day he called Falicia and asked what happened. She told him. "Nigga, I ain't ever gon' sell you all that shit again. Whatever that crazy shit was that had you geeking was disturbing, Roy. I thought we were gon' have to box. So you need to pick one drug of choice and stick to that. You scared the shit out of me."

"My bad," he replied. "You know I appreciate you, right?" he said, knowing that Falicia made her living by selling drugs.

Because she looked out for him, they became close. This encounter formed a bond between two new friends, and opened the door for Falicia to be honest with Roy and tell him the truth about Ike and Velvet. They had an understanding. Whenever he called, Roy had a purpose. He either wanted to spend some money getting laid, or purchase ecstasy pills. He was the one person she would drop everything for, or change her plans for. He was the only one that she was one hundred with, no secrets at all, including Ike's beatings.

"Here." He gave her money so she could come over and sleep.

As she was preparing to hit the road, Roy asked her to meet him at the bowling alley. After taking Roy his pills, Velvet and Falicia hit the road for her hometown, Jacksonville, where she revisited her old stomping grounds.

Once there, she visited her grandmother and took her to work almost every day. Nevertheless, she was working on the sneak tip behind the scenes. The night before Falicia left Jacksonville, she stopped by to see her grandmother Olivia one last time before heading back to Atlanta. She happened to show up while she was on the phone with her favorite aunt, Tasha.

"Guess who just walked in the door?" her grandmother Olivia said into the phone, staring at Falicia with a loving smile.

Falicia stood there, nervous but hopeful. Tasha hadn't spoken to her since she last visited Atlanta. It was Aunt Tasha's get-away trip from her man who was stressing her out, trying to fight her. Falicia had her come pick her up at the Lodge.

"I'm not feeling him," Tasha said, the second she met Ike.

"Mama, you know you can't be out all day wasting time with your aunt. You gotta go to work today. Time is money." He barely said hello to Tasha.

"Who is he talking to, Falicia? Who is Mama? He ain't yo' child," Aunt Tasha said.

"C'mon, lemme talk to you," Falicia told her.

Embarrassed, Falicia had Tasha drive her to Letty's house, so she would have a comfortable place to stay. After admitting she was a dancer, she talked Tasha into coming to work with her and Mylena. Aunt Tasha agreed to try dancing for one night. Falicia wasn't surprised, her aunt was a very beautiful woman, but also very blunt and not shy at all about airing her feelings.

At the club they were having fun watching the men lose their minds trying to get Aunt Tasha's red ass in front of them. Falicia's phone rang, and she took the call. After she hung up, she told her aunt, "I gotta go. I'll see you later." Ike received a call that someone needed dancers out of town.

"Wait! Why? Falicia, we just really got here," Aunt Tasha said, grabbing her arm.

"Just stay with Mylena. I'll be back," Falicia responded with a sad expression, but her movements were urgent as she tugged away and rushed out.

Ike swung by the club to pick her up and rushed her to the airport, leaving Aunt Tasha with Mylena. Both Tasha and Mylena were pissed off. Mylena already wasn't feeling Ike, but this made her concern about Falicia's relationship with him worsen.

Regardless of their opinions, Falicia couldn't convey to them why she was getting on a plane going somewhere she had never been, and why she seemed so passive now. What she couldn't tell either of them was that she felt she didn't have a choice, and it was hell to pay if she didn't comply. Falicia couldn't tell Aunt Tasha that the niece she used to know was long gone and was caught up in being whoever Ike's situation required her to be.

Unfortunately, while Tasha was waiting for Mylena to finish for the night, the club got raided, and she had to sneak out the back because she didn't have a license. Aunt Tasha was so upset that Mylena rode all the way back to Jacksonville with her. Aunt Tasha vowed to never come back to Atlanta again. And she hadn't been back, nor had she spoken to Falicia.

Please let Aunt Tasha be understanding about why I had to leave that night. Falicia prayed she could open up about what she had been living through at the hands of Ike. She wanted to explain to her that nothing she did during her visit was based on her decision. If anybody could tell her what to do, Aunt Tasha would. And for the first time Falicia considered dropping Velvet off with one of her homeboys and telling him to take her to greyhound bus station when they finished their business.

The instant Falicia said, "Hello, Aunt Tasha?" Tasha ripped a new hole in her ass. She finished blasting her with, "You ain't gon' ever be nothing." Then she hung up in her face.

Broken, Falicia called Ike. "That's why I always tell you, Sunshine, don't nobody love you like I do." She wiped her nose with the back of her hand. "So you just need to say fuck the world and just handle business so we can be together."

They hadn't hit a lick in Jacksonville as Ike instructed, but Falicia did run into a couple dudes she knew who wanted to trick off with Velvet, including Letty's long distance boyfriend, Marcus.

"Falicia, can I pay her in cocaine?" he had asked.

"Hell naw!" she snapped, offended.

Knowing that Marcus snorted powder made her wonder about her mother. Still she wasn't taking any chances with Letty's life. In the past, when Falicia and company would all be getting money together, she had to interrupt Velvet all the time because she would be fucking and not making money. Since they had been in Jacksonville, she had to flip out on her because she walked in the room to tell her they were leaving in five minutes, and Velvet was fucking this random dude raw!

"Bitch, is you serious? You all in here fuckin' this nigga like he yours! And his stupid ass dumb enough to put his dick up in a 'ho who sucks and fucks for a living. Get your motherfuckin' ass up right now!"

A couple hours later, Falicia wasn't surprised when Velvet was fucking someone else in her truck, and she didn't smell right. She wished Velvet was so much smarter than the way she behaved. She muttered three words that she knew wouldn't matter to Velvet one way or another: "Dumb ass bitch."

On the way back to the ATL, Ike's words ran circles in Falicia's mind. She nodded okay as if he'd just finished speaking about "fuck the world" and "nobody loves you like I do." Defeated, Falicia left the last of herself in Jacksonville. If Ike's love was all the love Falicia had, she knew she was ass out.

CHAPTER 26

Falicia accepted her life with Ike as her fate. She returned home to the erratic behavior he repeatedly displayed. As she was performing oral sex on him, Ike picked up the phone and called his baby mama and told her play by play everything that Falicia was doing to him. He'd even gone as far as comparing the two. Humiliated, Falicia walked away and ended up getting bashed in the back of her head with a telephone for talking back. This happened after her hair had been snatched out by the roots in the top. One comment from Velvet only made things worse, and he beat her up too, vowing to ruin her because Velvet had also caused him monetary losses.

"Mama, Velvet got a discharge the color of your dress in her panties," Shay informed Falicia as she washed her hands. She looked down at her neutral color dress and shoes.

"Let's go tell Daddy," Falicia said. She could see the concern on Shay's face. She and Velvet had been satisfying one another. Ike's godfather and his friend who also pimped women told him he needed to stop fucking his girls because it was making them envy each other. Instead, they told him to let them please each other. Now it did kill some of the animosity in the house, but Falicia would end up getting her ass beat because Ike was sexually frustrated. He would often be backed up, and it was her fault because he couldn't get a hold of her like he wanted to. When he wanted to. They told Ike about Velvet's hygiene issue.

"Well, you gon' have to take her to the clinic when we leave here," Ike replied. The girls dropped him off in Mechanicsville and took Velvet to Fulton County Health center across from Grady Hospital.

"Has any one of you had sexual contact with Ms. Harris?" the doctor in the Fulton County health center asked.

"Yes," Shay admitted, jumping up from her chair.

"Well, we are going to have to treat you," the doctor stated, then further explained that Velvet needed to be immediately transferred to Grady Hospital across the street for an emergency surgery. "She has contracted gonorrhea, and the infection has moved from her cervix and into her uterus, fallopian tubes, and ovaries. So she is going to have a hysterectomy."

It tripped Falicia the hell out! Falicia and Shay both stared at each other, mouths wide open.

"My ol' man has had contact with her." Confusion spread across the doctor's face. "It's a long story, but he has had sexual relations with her."

"Well then, I'm going to need him to come in," the doctor responded.

"Just write him a prescription," Falicia reasoned.

"I can't do that."

"Yes you can." Falicia had gotten used to people doing whatever she said.

"Ma'am, we have policies to follow."

"Oh, okay. Well then, I have had contact with her also. I need you to write me a prescription," she said, more concerned about Ike possibly being subjected to an STD. She frowned. *How in the hell could Velvet have contracted an STD when Ike got us all taking antibiotics?*

"Oh, and one more thing," Falicia called after the doctor. "I need a blood test."

Once Velvet was admitted to the hospital, Falicia relayed everything to Ike. "Don't concern yourself with her health anymore. Or none of the girls for that matter," he insisted.

He's hiding something. The thought settled into her spirit, but she didn't have time to focus on it. Shit was too stressful at the house. The girls were costing more than they were bringing in, let Ike tell it. The Florida trip was delayed because of Velvet's condition, and Falicia was doing what she could to keep the house as peaceful as possible. They had left Clairmont Lodge and were staying in an apartment in Velvet's name in Mechanicsville. It was most definitely in the hood, but it felt better than going to bed each night in a hotel.

When Velvet got home from the hospital, she had a bottle full of green pills that she refused to take. Falicia felt sorry for her; she was in her mid-twenties with no kids and had just lost her ability to bare children. The women tried to be sympathetic toward her, but it seemed everyone who lay in bed with her got sick in some kind of way. Sore throat, cough, or headache. So no one really wanted to be around her.

In the meantime, Falicia focused on keeping her home in order, which meant making money. She'd left the club with a weird-looking African wearing sweat pants and a T-shirt. Although he propositioned her for less than what she wanted, with the way everything was happening, she decided to take him up on his $350 offer. He gave up $275 dollars before they left the club, promising to give her the other seventy-five dollars when they finished, for the purpose of her not running off and leaving him.

Having cleared it with Ike, Falicia watched with suspicion as he drove to an industrial warehouse area and parked near the dock where delivery trucks parked to pick up their loads. The African led her to the side of the building with a very narrow space. *His ass must have been here before*, she concluded. Like some fiend, willing to do whatever, Falicia squatted in front of him and sucked his dick without an ounce of self-respect. Hoping to get him off. It didn't. She further degraded herself when she bent over and let him fuck her like some dog outside, amongst sticks and weeds.

Once he nutted, he zipped his pants and walked away. The faster she walked to keep up with him, the quicker he moved. So she sped up, almost running. When they reached his car, her door was locked.

Sereniti Hall

"I need you to open my door," she said as she looked across the car. He hastened to get in his car and immediately put the key in the ignition.

"Hey! Give me the rest of my money!" she yelled as she yanked on the door. "Nigga, give me my money!" He put the car in reverse. Falicia jumped on the hood, banging on the windshield. "Nigga, give me my money!"

The African backed his baby blue Nissan out of the docking area, throwing her off as he switched gears. Coming to a halt in slow motion, he then put his car in drive and charged toward Falicia at full speed. The nigga almost ran her over as she lay on the ground. Had she not rolled out of the way, he would have run her over. He'd missed her by only a few inches. His tires raced over her braids as he sped away. On the day when she should've been carrying her .38, she fell way short. She'd switched purses and left it at home.

"Sunshine, you don't leave with a motherfucker without him giving you all your money upfront," Ike insisted, taking her back to the club. She called him to come and get her and was still blowed by the incident. She stared out the window, her heart heavy.

"He said he was going to—"

"I don't give a fuck what he said!" Ike interrupted. "Now you would think I'm fucked up if I beat your ass for giving my pussy away for free."

"I didn't give nothing away."

"You might as well had!" he yelled.

Falicia closed her mouth, in no mood to fight with him. She quietly wiped away her tears. *Dude just tried to take my life, and all Ike is concerned about is how much I got out the deal.* When he pulled up to the club, she opened the door. "You want to just take off for the rest of the night and come chill with me?" he asked lovingly.

"Naw, I'ma get back to work." Falicia turned to get out.

Ike grabbed her arm and pulled her closer. "Mama, I love you," he said as he wiped where a tear had just fallen on her cheek.

"Yeah, I love you too." She got out once he released her arm. "By the way. I got something to do when I get off work. I'll call you." He watched her disappear into the club. *I'll be glad when we can get away and start over, so I can have my man back*, she thought, sucking up her tears. Pain now laid aside, she put on a mega-watt smile and walked to the entrance.

"How's it going?" she said to the doorman, on her way back into the club.

Getting money had become the only language she could speak that made sense to Ike and was interpreted as the only excuse she could use to be away from him without him bitching and/or fighting. Not going to see Man, or getting her hair done, or going shopping. This night she returned home after 5:00 a.m. By the time she cleaned the apartment, bathed Ike, and moisturized her skin, the sun was peeking across the horizon. Ike was clearly in the mood to fuck, but she was exhausted. He made an attempt to arouse her, but she couldn't get on his level. He sucked her pussy until she came, and then she fell asleep. He had made a few attempts to get her to engage, but she lacked the motivation to give herself to him. The love she once knew was turning into obligation; that same love had already been filled with fear.

After catching Ike fucking Velvet's infected ass because she was too tired, Falicia ended up having to run for her life so he wouldn't fuck her up for refusing to wash his dick. He had turned on the water in the tub to fill it, planning to dunk her head in it. She couldn't keep subjecting herself to this abusive, neurotic dysfunction anymore. Thankfully, she was able to get away and ran to Body Tapp for work, but she eventually left there and headed to The Lion's Den.

Of course, Ike showed up there looking for her, but he was big on public appearances, and she knew he wouldn't touch her. Falicia

Sereniti Hall

sat across from him as he stayed seated at a table. She folded her hands and didn't meet his eyes.

"Hey, Daddy. I think we just need to focus on getting this money. When we started all this we had a common purpose: to build something great so we wouldn't have to struggle. Somehow, we have gotten away from that." Plus she couldn't get the image of Velvet's flabby, naked ass body sitting in his lap, out of her mind. Velvet had lost weight too fast between stressing herself out and snorting cocaine. Her deflated skin was tell-tell signs of it. Disgusted by the sight of Ike fucking her raw, with white shit all over his dick from Velvet's discharge, forced Falicia to subtract herself from their threesome. Whatever diseases Velvet had, Falicia didn't want any of them.

"So what you saying?" Ike asked, as if he expected her to say the worst.

"I'm saying, I'm going to focus on this paper and not this relationship. I miss my son."

"Our son."

"Our son . . . and we just need to get shit together."

He stared at her, but what could he say? Falicia knew this nigga like the back of her hand, especially when it came to money. They finished each other's sentences, and all he had to do was look at her, and she'd know what he was thinking or wanted done. He wasn't about to debate her decision. And neither was she. Calmly, she left the table and went back to work to make their money. Her heart beat triple time as her secret crush caught her eye.

Usually, she wouldn't take an interest in someone as dark as Sweets, nor did she have the tendency to wonder about the next man, because regardless of what Ike did to her, she loved him. But Sweets! His chocolate ass did something to her! His jet-black dreads danced on his shoulders and were always neat. Whatever he wore, he made the outfit. Standing about five feet ten inches, and possibly 185 pounds full of muscle, with a pearly white smile that

A Treacherous Hustle

made her forget a possessive ass nigga was standing on the level above her observing her every move. This wasn't Sweets' first time in Body Tapp, but it was his first time acknowledging Falicia. He was known in the club as the go-to for buying the best weed in the city. Falicia and two other dancers were entertaining him and his date, who was making it rain.

Falicia didn't hesitate to drop it in his companion's lap, wishing it was Sweets that she was entertaining. She gave the woman her best, just in case the female dancing for him, slacked in the least, and he took a second to look over at her. When the song was over Sweets told Falicia, "Keep going."

Ike was waiting for her when she got off work. Out of the blue he handed her a number and told her to call and inquire about some weed. The second the dude answered the phone, Falicia knew it was Sweets. *Keep it playa. Show no emotion*, she thought, as Ike had her talk numbers with him for a possible business arrangement.

"So you know him?" Ike asked, once Falicia ended the call.

"Naw, other than the fact that he sells a lil weed," she answered nonchalantly.

"A lil weed?" Ike looked at her like she was crazy. "They say that nigga moving weight!"

"That ain't what they saying in the club. He's a runner is what I heard," she lied, hoping to discourage him. Sweets just wasn't a nigga she would want to hit.

"Well, you need to look into it because the nigga straight."

She rolled her eyes. "We'll see, but it's going to be hard when I'm not his type." *I ain't stuttin' this shit Ike talkin' 'bout. I'm glad Sweets don't come through The Tapp all the time.*

The days following, Falicia spent as much time away from home as possible. The club was open for business at twelve noon, so she got up at eleven, and was gone by eleven thirty. At first she was driving to and from work and would pick up some lunch from KFC or Papa John's pizza, but as Ike witnessed her constant focus on hustling, he'd ask if he could take her to lunch, and then drop her off at work. "No thank you," she said, knowing Ike was trying to weasel his way back in. Falicia was doing just fine with the way things were.

His next strategy was asking for the truck during the night, making her rely on being picked up or getting dropped off after a date of tricking off. Falicia began staying at the club until it closed. By eight each night, she would have already made her quota, and Ike had to bring her more pills majority of the time because she would have already sold what she came with. She knew without speaking it, that Ike was getting desperate. Also, she knew she needed to make some solid decisions about the future. At what point would she leave, if at all?

CHAPTER 27

When Velvet was well and ready to get back on her hustle, Falicia and the girls piled in her truck one Saturday night. Destination: the Crystal Palace. While en route, somebody came up with the bright idea that Falicia should snort a line of blow because she never got high. After much debate, Velvet held up some powder she had folded in a ten-dollar bill. That bitch was totally gone off that coke.

The last time Ike tackled Velvet like a quarterback, she swung at him, and he beat her ass like a man. By the time he stopped punching, Velvet called herself being done with him because he had busted a blood vessel in her eye again. "I got something for that 'ho," Ike said, vengeful. "Destroy her ass without redemption. All the money this bitch done cost me . . ." he told Falicia.

Some days later, he called Velvet over and told her he missed her. "I been fucked up about you leaving, to the point that I been snortin' that shit now." Ike convinced her to try it too since it was her fault that he was doing it. It became his new way of tolerating her ass.

Now, Velvet did whatever for the white powder. True enough, she was easier to get along with on the shit, but it was just sad to see someone so head strong crumble like that.

"Daddy, please let me be yo' 'ho," Velvet begged Ike while they were on the patio. Falicia ran up on them one night, intending to ask Ike about a re-up. *To go sell her body to make him money? Is this bitch crazy? I'm not positive what type of foolishness he's telling her ass, but I wish he wouldn't have ever asked that of me, and this bitch Velvet is begging to degrade herself.* She shook her head, bewildered.

With everyone looking and encouraging her to do it, Falicia scooped her nail in the dust, but instead of putting it straight to her nose and snorting it, she flicked her finger so whatever was in her nail would fall back out in the money. Then she put the empty nail to her nose and sniffed. Afterward, she made everyone get out and try to catch a date. Standing in front of her truck with the driver side door open, Falicia scrolled through her phone to see if she had anyone in particular to get some money from. She looked across the street.

Several Mexicans stood outside a small trailer home division, and a few females were trying to pick them up. "Cin dollars," one of the men yelled, meaning that he was willing to pay a hundred dollars. Further up the street, a little girl hung out on the corner with a wig on and some heels.

"I'll be right back," Falicia told Velvet. She jumped in her truck and pulled up on the little girl.

"Get in," she instructed her, barely lowering the window. She was frail-looking, and her body was still developing. She couldn't see who was in Falicia's Suburban, yet she climbed in and shut the door. Falicia locked it without a word as she pulled away from the stop sign and drove across the street to the parking lot directly across Blockbusters. Falicia's heart began to break because just like that, somebody could have taken this child anywhere!

"What you doing?" she asked, cutting the truck off.

"What?" She looked at Falicia, displaying much defiance. "If you ain't spending no money, you need to stop wasting my time," she popped off.

"How old are you?"

"Why? You ain't my man."

"You right, and the one you got ain't your man either."

"Lady, I don't even know you. If you ain't spending no money, let me out." She raised her voice.

"No, now you listen to me." Falicia raised her voice as well. The little girl sat back and folded her arms across her chest. "You wanna be out here like you grown, well then, I'm going to handle you like you grown, and when any bitch talking to me, they address me with respect. Now listen. Your man don't give a fuck about you. Deep down I know you know that shit."

"He loves me."

"Don't say shit while I'm talking!" Falicia snapped. Her eyes got big. "If your man loved you, he wouldn't have you out here selling your ass making him money."

"He take care of me." Falicia gave her a look like: I dare you to say one more word.

"You jumping in cars with strange people. I could do anything to you right now, and your man can't do shit about it. Them clothes you got on, that wig on your head, the food you eat, come from the money *you* make. You probably ran away from home because you feel like somebody trying to control your life and you can make your own decisions, or somebody has taken advantage of you." She looked as if Falicia was knocking on her door.

"Baby girl, I know you think your man is protecting you, and he promised to not allow anyone to harm you again, but being out here in these streets ain't protecting you. I know . . . I can hear you saying in your head 'You don't even know me, so how can you tell me anything?' And that's sad, but I'm going to leave you with this: I thought the same things you're thinking right now, until I got raped at gun point.

"Where would your man be if I put this pistol to your mouth?" She looked down at Falicia's hands like she expected her to pull it out. "Baby girl, go home. These streets ain't nobody's friend." Falicia unlocked the door. The little girl sat there.

"Is there somewhere I can take you?" She nodded no. "Is there anything I can do? Do you want my phone number in case you ever need it?" She nodded no. They sat quiet for a few seconds, as if her mind was contemplating Falicia's words. Then suddenly, barely above a whisper she said, "I got to go. Can't be gone too long. It's money to be made." And she crawled out of her truck.

Sereniti Hall

With hopes that she would at least heed her warning, Falicia parked her truck back in the same spot where she left Red chopping it up with some nigga. She cut the truck off and walked over to where she was, sitting on the back of a red pick-up truck, a F150.

"What's up, Red?" Falicia asked, but stared at dude.

"Oh, just catching up with an old friend," she answered honestly.

"Tell him bye."

Dude jumped out of his truck. "Who is you? Fuck you mean, tell him bye?" His eyes danced; he was high. Based on his temperament, Falicia assumed it was on blow.

"Clearly, you don't know, talking to me like that!" she barked back. "Red, let's go." She started to walk her way. He grabbed Red. "Nigga, let my bitch go!"

"She ain't going nowhere!" he yelled.

Falicia cut Red a look she knew not to question. "Trey, it's all good. I'ma go." She pulled her arm away from him.

"You don't have to leave because this bitch said you do."

"Yes, the fuck she does. Unless you talking about some money, you can get the fuck on! Red, put your dog in check before I do."

"Mama, no!" she pleaded. "It's not that serious."

"Mama? What the fuck is that?" he asked.

Taking her hand, Falicia led her away. Dude refused to let her go.

"Bitch, I said she ain't going nowhere—" Falicia pulled out her pistol. A few guys started running away from the scene.

"Now what? What you say about my bitch?" She pointed it at him, but didn't have any intentions on shooting him. Although she knew the street code was: don't pull a gun out unless you're going to use it. Plus, she wanted the girls to think it was the powder that had her out of control, so they would never ask her to get high again.

"So you think I'm scared?" Dude asked.

"I don't give a damn, personally. I just know I'm done talking."

Dude sped off. Eventually. Once he was out of view, she put the gun back in her Coach clutch. Her girls spent the next twenty minutes telling Falicia how irrational the powder had her. She just looked at their asses after she got in Red's shit. They were laughing it off when a dark purple PT Cruiser pulled up. Instinct told Falicia whoever was inside was looking at her. Slowly the window slid down. She wondered if she should get her piece or not. She stepped closer to her truck just in case.

"Hey, let me holla at you!" the male voice sounded familiar, but the car wasn't.

"What's up?" she asked Sweets, once she strutted over to his car and bent over into the window.

"Shit, looking at you in them jeans." Falicia tried not to smile too hard.

"Looking isn't going to satisfy your curiosity."

"So where your nigga?"

"I'm looking at him." He laughed some more, showing off them beautiful ass teeth.

"For real, where that nigga at? I saw him watching you." Falicia smiled a little, surprised he had pieced it together, but why was she? He was that nigga!

"At home still trying to figure out what to do with a bitch like me." He stared at her. Internally, she swore he picked up on her pain.

"You got a lil time on your hands? I got a lil change to blow. You can follow me." On the outside she appeared as if she was contemplating taking him up on his offer. On the inside, she was doing flips, the happy fool dance and singing.

"Naw, I got some people with me. But I can let them take my truck." Grateful for his tinted windows, she handed Velvet her keys. She hadn't let Ike touch her in a little over a month, anyway. Sick of the bullshit. So she deserved this night.

Sereniti Hall

Getting inside his car, he handed her $400 as he pulled off. "If you act right, I might give you something else." He smirked. Little did he know—she didn't care about the money when it came to him. Falicia had been watching his sexy ass for a minute. And was really about to have herself a good time with him. A moment she fantasized about. All she could think about was what it would be like to be the bitch he checked for, yearned to see, and waited for. Turning his ass out was all that was on her mind.

"Hmm, if I act right?"

"Yeah!" He grinned.

"If you act right, I might stop when you ask me to."

Falicia leaned over and freed his manhood. It was beautiful and black just like him. Curiosity filled his eyes. "Keep your eyes on the road," she teased, stroking him. Immediately he stiffened in her hand. Without thinking twice, she took him inside her mouth, positioned him in the back of her throat and didn't pity him in the least. Sucking his dick as fast as her neck would permit. Tension built.

"Damn!" Sweets said as he placed one hand on the back of her head. He jerked and convulsed while climaxing in her mouth. By the time they made it into the house that he said was used as a salon, she was soaking wet, ready for him to long-dick her. To put her in any position he wanted. The sun was rising by the time they stopped fucking.

Knowing she was about to get her ass beat, Falicia had him drop her off two blocks up, and she walked home, especially if Ike got wind that she was with him. Sweets gave her three more hundred dollars with a promise she would see him again. She rehearsed her lie in her head over and over. But the way Sweets made her feel like a woman and desired, even beautiful, seemed worth all the hell she was getting ready to pay. Somewhere in the midst of the beatings, she had lost sight of all that.

Needless to say, she got jumped on for coming home at close to eight that Sunday morning. But she knew Ike was just in his feelings because she had enough money to excuse her absence and for the length of time she was gone, but that was water under the bridge. She had gradually started warming up to her man as he transformed back into the dude she first fell for. Waking her up with new outfits and arranging her hair appointments.

Ike would take her out to lunch before he dropped her off at work, and it seemed they had once again reached that place where their love for each other was the fuel they lived off of. He couldn't get enough of her. He didn't care if someone was looking or not, when he got the urge to taste her—that is what he did. Whether it was to bend her over in the parking lot of her job. Ass up on her knees, or he might stand in the doorway fucking her. Giving her head in a fast food restaurant parking lot. Receiving head driving down the street, at a light, even if someone could see. In front of someone's house, as long as he could suck her pussy and slide off in her butt he was good, and she couldn't front: their sex game was one of a kind.

Her body only responded to him, though Sweets had the ability to take her to new heights. And before she left for Florida, they fucked the hell out of each other and enjoyed doing it. She entertained the idea of robbing him when they were together that second time because he had set his pistol with the silencer on it on the table and went to the bathroom. She couldn't. Falicia liked Sweets in the worst way.

To some degree she felt he was out of her league, with all the expensive jewelry, multiple cars, different homes, and tote bags of money. So to be spending all this time with him was a boost to her self-esteem! Prior to him entering her life, it had become hard to believe it when someone said she was beautiful. If she was, she often pondered, why Ike spent so much time trying to rearrange her face?

CHAPTER 28

Ike concluded it was time to hit the road, and Velvet was not open to the idea of leaving him for who knew how long. Once again, it was on for Daytona, and they would be pulling into town just in time for spring break. Shay and Falicia had already spent the day loading her truck with their belongings. Falicia was taking most of her stuff with her because Ike moved around so much, and she didn't want her valuables to come up missing. So she had her mink coat and almost every set of shoes she owned, loaded and ready to go.

Ike's plan was to wind down early and chill so he could spend time with all of them, and then send them to bed so they could have some time together. His idea was short-lived when he discovered Velvet hadn't followed his instructions. Perceived as disobedience, it resulted in a fight in which Ike beat Velvet down and left her in the Clairmont Lodge room alone. Shay, Ike, and Falicia went next door to Days Inn, where Carlos had taken over the spot where Monie, the chick who used to deal for Ike, set up shop. The one who was blowing up Ike's phone and trying to get back with him. Ike moved Carlos to another room so they could chill.

First thing the next morning they were bagging up the weed Falicia would be selling and loaded it in the truck. Ike called Velvet, demanding she bring her ass on. "I want y'all on the road before there's a lot of fucking traffic," he stressed. "So you need to bring it. Now, bitch!" It was nearing an hour when there was a knock on the door.

"Damn, the bitch finally showed up. I thought I was going to have to go put my hands on her again," Ike admitted as Shay jumped up to open the door. She glanced through the peephole and spun around, eyes wide, panic all over her face.

"It's the police!" she whispered.

Sereniti Hall

"Open up! I know you're in there," a man with a heavy country accent stated.

"Fuck!" Ike jumped up. "Stuff this!" he demanded. Falicia dumped the rest of the weed back into a Ziploc bag. He scanned the room to see if there were any more drugs left somewhere while Falicia rolled it up tight and shoved it up her vagina.

"Shayla Clark," a voice declared. "I have a warrant for your arrest! Open up, I already heard you talking." Shay stared at Falicia and Ike in horror.

"Bitch! Why didn't you tell me you had a warrant before I put this room in your name?" Ike checked her.

"I didn't know. I'm sorry." She looked like she wanted to cry.

"Does everything look normal?" he asked, before giving her permission to open the door.

As soon as Falicia saw his face, she recognized the cop as the same DeKalb County Sheriff that raided Ike's room once before.

"What do we have here?" he asked, walking in the door like a cowboy. He took one look at Shay. "I have a warrant for your arrest from East Point." He smirked. "Is that your truck out there?" He signaled with his hand, never taking his eyes off her.

"No sir, it's not," she responded.

"Then whose is it?" He stepped inside and spotted Ike. "That's your truck out there, boy?" Ike nodded no. "Hmm. You—" He directed his attention to Falicia, looking at her face, and then down at her legs. When she met him, she had micro braids, but knew the bastard recognized her with her gray contacts and braids down past her butt. Because when he raided Ike's room, he pocketed her nude pictures.

"Sorry to tell you it's, it's . . . not," she assured him, trying to maintain her poise. When he looked away, she cut her eyes at Ike, then at a sandwich bag on the floor near the foot of the bed with some weed in it.

"How did we miss that? It has to be Carlos'," Ike mouthed.

Placed in cuffs, the trio was sent to jail, following the sheriff knocking over shit and ranting about the key to her SUV. Some junkies walked by. "Let Carlos know what's going down," Ike managed to tell them.

Minutes later, Falicia and Ike were being removed from the same police car and escorted inside the county jail for booking. "Don't worry about this, Sunshine. Carlos gon' have us out in no time," Ike assured her.

Though she didn't let it show, she was petrified of jail. Shit, there was a lot of stuff she was scared about, but just didn't let on. Going to Florida to hit a lick was one. Fearing something may happen, and she'd never see Man again was another.

At the jail, the deputy informed her that she would have to get the metal chain and lock cut off her neck.

"No you not! My nigga bonding me out anyways."

"Where's the key?" one female correction officer asked.

"Around his neck!" Falicia bragged, as if it was something to be proud of.

The woman shook her head at Falicia's insanity, her willingness to nut up on anyone talking about removing a chain of bondage from her neck. Where she wore it proudly and felt it was absolutely normal for her to have it. By the time they fingerprinted her, Ike had posted her bail. And gave her the keys to the F150 they rented.

"If for some reason I'm not home by tomorrow, just go ahead and hit the road. I called Carlos and told him to go to the room, get the keys out my jacket pocket, and get the truck before it gets towed. Catch up with him, and then go lay low off Campbellton until you hear from me. Velvet already knows what's up."

It didn't take long to process Falicia out. She wondered, *Why does he want me to get out so fast? Is it because he loves me and knows his queen doesn't deserve to be in such an environment? Or is it something he doesn't want me to discover, possibly my ability to think on my own? Or is he missing out on money by me being locked up?* She also wondered if he was concerned that she would have a change of heart concerning the life they were living because it put them at risk for a place like jail every day. Or did he merely feel it was his obligation to get his wife out as he confessed the first time she got arrested?

Falicia had been to jail before when she stole her client's Lexus. First, she hit the fool up for the two g's he'd left in his glove compartment while he went to buy early movie tickets. Then he came looking for her at Body Tapp, eager to spend more time with her. Therefore, he set himself up and later dropped the charges when the police retrieved his vehicle.

Ike did promise her after the arrest that it was his obligation to keep her out of jail, but his actions still weren't sitting right with her. Neither was her inability to reach Carlos.

"Daddy, I understand what you saying," Falicia argued. "But I'm telling you something ain't right."

Long story short, Carlos had been tricking off with a female who smoked dope. At some point, she got Carlos to smoke with her. Whether it was her idea or his, their asses stole a lot of Ike's clothes and shoes and just about all of Falicia's shit, including her truck. Falicia wanted to cry, overcome with rage and frustration, just knowing her shit was gone. But shit. The whole crew was looking to her to be strong and figure out their next move.

Instead of pining over what they had no control over, the women jumped in the F150 and fled their issues in Atlanta to create some income, further south, where they could possibly bounce back from Carlos' hit. All in his feelings because the same shit they did to eat was done to them, Ike stayed behind. But sent Falicia away with an extra-large order involving Velvet.

"Get rid of the bitch! I don't want to see her ass ever again."

The level of stress was so high, Falicia could have done away with all their asses. Trying to rest because she wasn't able to sleep, fighting her own battles. In turmoil about the mission she was sent to fulfill, the two bitches started arguing about some dumb shit. "I don't give a fuck!" Falicia snapped when both girls tried to tell their side. So Velvet called Ike, whining about Shay.

Until their mission was completed, he ordered Falicia, "Beat that bitch ass!"

Falicia passed the order on to Shay. In the midst of them tussling on the bed, Velvet got the best of Shay's big ass, and they ended up on top of Falicia. She lost her gray contact. Ike was screaming in her ear, "Mama, I told you to beat her ass." Pulling her pistol out of her purse, she shot up into the ceiling. Everybody got quiet!

"You stupid bitches! I told y'all to shut the fuck up!" Falicia shouted as she brushed past Velvet. She went into the bathroom so she could cry and release the frustration that she had no way to otherwise release. She emerged from the bathroom and looked at both girls. "Get y'all shit so we can get the hell out of here before the police come knocking on the door. Got me shooting up in here and shit. Hurry the fuck up!" Without a word, Velvet and Shay gathered their things and hurried right out.

They were on the interstate when Ike called. "Have you gotten rid of the bitch yet?" It didn't sound like a question, but more of a demand.

"Naw, I don't think it's a good idea," she responded, attempting to deter his request. Falicia didn't have the mental space for more drama.

"Fuck that! Handle that!" He hung up. Falicia glanced at Shay, riding shotgun on the passenger side, all into her feelings.

"Y'all teamed up against me," Velvet accused.

Falicia didn't waste time explaining her position. "You can believe whatever you want to as far I'm concerned! As long as you get this money." She pulled over on the road. Velvet got out to stretch. "Go back there and redeem yourself," Falicia insisted.

"How, Mama?" Shay asked, looking hopeful.

"Your Daddy wants to get rid of the bitch. Open the door and throw her ass out."

"What?" She looked just as surprised as Falicia first did.

"I know it's fucked up, ain't it?" She nodded in agreement as Velvet got back in. Falicia may not have loved the bitch, but she didn't wish harm on Velvet either. She couldn't wrap her mind around it, but Ike had a purpose for everything. Shay took her shoes off and started toward the back of the truck. Velvet caught her with a right before she could get back there good.

They began fighting like their life depended on it. Falicia glanced in the rearview from time to time. At one point she thought Shay was actually going to flip the bitch out when the door flew open, but Velvet wrapped her legs around Shay and was holding her own. It wasn't until Falicia saw one of her ankle boots fall out and get run over by the vehicle behind them that she told them to stop. She already had practically lost all her shit, and now the little bit she had left was scattering all over the damn highway.

"Close the motherfucking door!" Falicia yelled. "Chill the fuck out!"

"Yeah, y'all ain't fucking with me," Velvet said as she released Shay's hair. "Ike want to sic his bitches on me. I ain't the one!" she said, huffing and puffing.

"Bitch, who you talking to?" Falicia yelled as Shay closed the door. "You need to be mindful of who you talking to because I haven't got in that ass!" She mugged Velvet through the rearview mirror. "Direct that shit to where it belongs, dumb ass bitch. In love with a nigga who don't give a fuck about you!"

"Whatever, Falicia!" she fired back.

"Naw, bitch. It's Mama to you."

"Fuck you. Fuck all y'all!"

"Keep motherfucking running your mouth, and we'll see where you end up. I done tongue wrestled with you long enough." Velvet smacked her teeth, and then started trying to fix her hair. Falicia was fuming! *Talking to me like that, I should pull over and pistol whoop her ass.*

She didn't hear another thing out of either one of them on their drive into Jacksonville where she dropped Velvet's ass off at the Greyhound station. If she didn't have any money on her, Falicia knew she would fuck and suck for it. After she and Shay stopped at a pharmacy to find some hair glue to fix her extensions, Shay got in the driver's seat and drove them back to Daytona. They tricked off with several dudes, but Falicia didn't see a lick in the making.

As the weekend ended, she had this bright idea to get Ike's name on her neck. He had asked her to do it months ago, but she wasn't willing because shit was so rocky with them. Uncertain if they would make it until eternity, yet she wanted to put his first and last name on her permanently, like she was branded. Shay got his first name on her neck. Looking at it in the mirror. Falicia was convinced this would make him feel a little better. In the event she didn't hit a lick, at least she had finally expressed her devotion to him. Some days they went hungry trying to keep gas in the truck and find some nigga with money. At least she would have something to show for the trip.

After being gone for two weeks, fear drove them back to Atlanta. Falicia pulled what was left of her luggage out the backseat of the truck. Her cell rang from an unfamiliar number. It was a doctor calling from Fulton County health center.

"We have some test results for you, and I'm calling to find out when you can come in so we can discuss them?" the man said politely.

"Well. Actually, I'm headed to Daytona for vacation," she lied. "You can just read me the results right now. I can give you my social security number or whatever you need to verify this is me."

"Sorry, ma'am, we are not permitted to disclose such matters that way. You can take down my info, and whenever you get to where you are going, you can stop by any local clinic, get them to contact us, and we will fax them the results." Her face froze with concern.

"Is it that serious? Why can't it just wait until I get back?"

"Ma'am, we don't prefer that you wait. It is serious, but you will be fine."

"Sunshine," Ike sang as he approached the car. "Who you talking to, looking crazy like that?" He snatched away the phone.

"Who the fuck is this?" he asked as she headed up the stairs to their room, freaked the fuck out. *What could I possibly have that he couldn't tell me over the phone?*

Ike found her in the bathroom, staring at herself in the mirror so worried she was nauseous. "Mama, you don't have to worry about that no more," Ike stated, trying to hand her back her phone. She wouldn't take it, more concerned about her results. He stood behind her resting his chin on her shoulder, looking at her in the mirror.

"Mama, what's the matter?" She was as stiff as a board. "What's up?"

"It's just . . . I don't understand right now. Everything is crazy, like it's too much going on." She swallowed, ridding herself of the knot in her throat.

He nodded. "Let me ask you something. Why in the fuck you let this 'ho put my name on her neck and you come back empty-handed?" He caressed her stomach, gradually inching up to her breasts, and then her shoulders.

"It just didn't go like you said," Falicia said, barely over a whisper. Tears had already begun to well in her eyes. Their eyes met in the mirror. Ike wrapped his hand around her throat. She closed her eyes, anxious to get oxygen.

"Open your eyes," he said. She obliged. Ike didn't look right. She closed them quickly. "Open your damn eyes!" he demanded again.

Oh my God! Ike's face didn't look the same. His eyes were sunk into his head and slanted with dark rings around them. His ears pointed at the top like a leprechaun. His nose and mouth seemed to all go together. Falicia squeezed her eyes shut. She hadn't smoked a blunt, but she had to be tripping. He tightened his grip.

"I said open your eyes." His face was still dark and disfigured. Tears fell down her face. He was creeping the shit out of her. "The next time I tell you to do something and you don't . . ."

I can't breathe. She tore at his hands. Her hearing muffled; her life force was slipping away as her heart pounded rapidly. *Maybe dying ain't so bad after all.* Her body jerked as she reached for his hands, the counter, anything. His lips moved. Whatever he said, she couldn't comprehend it. Man flashed through her mind. Letty would give him a better life. *Hope he knows that I love him . . .*

The room went black.

CHAPTER 29

"Mama!" he yelled. "Wake the fuck up!"

Falicia awakened to Ike slapping the shit out of her. Gagging from a lack of oxygen, she looked around, wondering how she ended up in bed.

"Bitch, you tried to leave me?" Ike was pacing back and forth. Falicia couldn't talk. Her throat felt raw. "You tried to leave me! How?" She wasn't absolutely sure what had happened, but she did recall him choking her. "Keep fucking playing with me, Falicia!" He stormed out the room. "Get your ass ready for work!" he ordered. The front door shut. No other words were necessary. She dressed quickly and headed to work.

Large eyes, ebony hued skin, and the receding hair line made the guy odd looking enough. He always came into the club with an air of eeriness following him like a thick fog. The man stared at Falicia long enough to make her uncomfortable. She never could meet his soul-piercing dark eyes for long.

"You should let me read your hand," he said, sitting in his favorite spot at the first table by the bar. His black trench coat was sprawled across the chair.

"How many times do I have to tell you that it's not okay to go to people's jobs and try to get their money?" Falicia asked. "That's like going to Burger King and asking the person working at the register to buy you a meal."

"Just let me read your hand," he insisted. "You don't even have to pay me. I just feel so strongly about this."

"If I let you, will you leave me alone?" He had been bugging Falicia for months. Always wearing an empty expression.

"Okay, I will . . . Just have a seat." He immediately grabbed her hand and held it for a second, shuffled his cards, and started flipping his deck. The third card he flipped over was the Reaper, the symbol of death. The next card was another Reaper. He closed his eyes. Falicia cut her eyes at him. *Nigga, you full of shit. Glad this will be over soon.* The dude's head twitched. His eyes opened, wide and frantic.

"You got death all around you," he replied, his speech slow and precise.

Falicia tried to pull her hand from his grip. His hold became stronger; his eyes were now dazed. "You're in a situation that's not you. You're pretending to be something you're not, and if you don't get out before it's too late, it's going to blow up in your face." He sat quietly staring at her as if he could see it all playing out before his eyes. Then his neck twitched, and he blinked until his face finally relaxed. "Death surrounds you," he stated, like someone who was spooked. He jumped up, grabbed his coat, and nearly sprinted to the exit, looking back at her in despair.

The reading stayed with Falicia like a rotting tooth. She was unable to dismiss what he said. True, Falicia had heart and believed if something happened to Ike, it was law to ride for him, check any nigga or bitch in the street about hers. But she didn't want to take anybody's life! Robbing niggas was one thing, as long as no one got hurt, but Ike was beginning to be on some other shit. Falicia was almost convinced that the reading only confirmed that she was going to get killed, either by Ike, who'd almost succeeded in choking her to death. Then he slapped the shit out of her to bring her back to the present. Or by the streets.

"Shot of tequila, please," she ordered. Then downed several more shots. Yet the tequila wasn't doing it for her.

"Let me get a double shot of 151," one of the dancer's said to the bartender.

"What's 151?" Falicia asked.

"Girl, it's that truth. Straight up kerosene! If you trying to get fucked up, this that shit!"

"It'll burn the hairs on your chest," the dude she danced for commented.

A Treacherous Hustle

The smell alone burned Falicia's nose. Still, she took a deep breath and threw it back. It set fire to every organ it came in contact with.

"Shit!" she screamed. Everyone laughed. By the end of the dance, she was a tipsy bitch! She ordered another one.

"Mama, wake up! Get up!" Falicia looked around. She was curled up on the sofa in the Lion's Den. "Get up," Ike ordered. "We got some business to take care of." He helped her to her feet.

"What time is it?" she asked, trying to wake up.

"It's one, baby! Get yourself together. We got shit to do."

"Daddy, I'm fucked up."

"Too fucked up," he commented, escorting her to the dressing room for her stuff. Dressed and ready to go home and sleep off her high, Falicia climbed in the back of the F150.

"Hey, Mama." Shay sat behind the steering wheel. Ike got in the passenger seat.

"Pull over here to this Waffle House," Ike said and bought Falicia a sandwich when she wasn't even hungry. He rolled down the window as Shay headed out of the parking lot, so the fresh air would sober her up. All the early a.m. air did was make her shiver.

"So check the move." Ike turned to face her after they'd been on the road for at least an hour, and Falicia was showing signs of sobering up. "You remember Rick? The nigga from the bottom that I introduced you to."

Ike had brought Rick by the club one night for her to feel him out, curious to know if Rick was another trick, or somebody worth doing business with. Falicia tried everything in her power to seduce him. Though he was generous with his tips, he was faithful to his wife and simply enjoying the perks of having plenty of money without disrespecting his household. She respected that. Ike didn't. Because he didn't honor his own.

"He called me because he needed someone to handle this lick. The dude is a political powerhouse in a small town. And his wife is his secretary. She told Rick about a drop that's supposed to happen in the a.m. It's supposed to be both money and dope. As soon as the transaction takes place, you'll run up in there.

"You probably gone to have to hit that nigga in the head with your pistol to get him to take you serious, but after that, he should open the safe. Wife gonna make sure the bags and shit get to the front door. Then you instruct her to lay on the ground with her hands behind her head."

Falicia thought about the task at hand, frowned. It sounded too good to be true. *Is this nigga really going to take two 'hos seriously? But why isn't Ike coming and doing this shit with me?*

"Get off on the next exit, so we can get some gas," he instructed, and waited until Shay had gotten out the car. "So check it, right. I want you to get rid of her clingy ass. Shoot her with your pistol, and shoot him with her gun. Make it look like a robbery gone bad. Wipe your pistol off and put it in his hands."

Falicia stopped breathing for a quick second. "So you want me to kill them both?"

"Yeah. I'm tired of Shay's ass."

"Daddy, then send her home. You don't kill her."

"Naw, she know too much. Got to put one in her."

Falicia stirred her straw around in her cup of water, eyes staring out the window. *What's gonna happen to me when Ike gets tired of my ass?* First Velvet, and even though he hadn't physically taken her life, putting her on cocaine had already robbed her of so much. For one, her ability to bare children. And now Shay. She was only twenty-one years old.

Shay opened the door and got back in the truck, dropping the receipt for their gas in the console between the seats. Her presence brought Falicia some relief. Now she didn't have to continue this stupid ass conversation. She eyed Ike, sitting on the passenger side, talking to Shay like it was all good. Who the hell was this man that she called herself loving? Falicia lay on the seat with her back to him, as if she was still in her liquor. He had just blowed her with his bullshit! She cuddled to the best of her ability and held herself tight. Thinking of the reading, her life, Shay's life. A tear escaped her eye, wetting the leather seat. *Jesus, I don't know you. I don't know if You really exist. When I was a girl, I tried to get saved, but I didn't last long. But I don't know who else to talk to. So I'm asking that you do something. Don't let this happen. I don't want to do this! I don't want to take anyone's life.* Falicia prayed the same thing for hours as Shay, Ike, and she headed to Rick's house. Once there, they picked up the weapons he provided and headed to the location, driving behind Rick and his wife.

Please, God . . . I don't want to do this. Please, listen to me. I don't want to do this, she kept praying. They followed Rick for a half hour before he abruptly pulled into a gas station. Ike got out and stepped to the side with Rick. Ike's movements while talking to Rick were aggressive. His face became distorted as he stormed back to the truck and snatched the door open.

"Mama, give me your gun." Falicia handed it to him.

"This busta ass nigga don't want to do it. Said his wife backing out. For whatever reason, she didn't know there was guns involved! Who the fuck commits a robbery with no gun?" He slammed the door and gave Rick back the pistols. Falicia could have screamed, but cried instead. God had listened to her cry and answered her prayers.

"Rick, you gone pay for this!" Ike threatened. "I missed money coming down here! Pussy ass nigga!" He got back in the truck.

Ike made good on his threat and stole Rick's brand new Tahoe. He took the rims off, sold them in the street, and took the truck to the chop shop. Rick left several messages on Falicia's phone telling Ike he was tripping and to hit him back up. But Ike didn't give a damn. So they had to post up in the Suburban Lodge, out of sight. Being that he knew where they stayed and where Falicia worked.

"Mama," Ike said, "I met this girl named Peaches."

Sereniti Hall

"Okay," Falicia said with attitude.

"She stay beneath us with her mother, brother, sister, and her newborn son. She got a two-year-old daughter too. Peaches is short, brown-skinned, thick with a big ass and golds in her mouth. She not that pretty, but she ain't ugly. With all that ass she carrying, she can definitely bring us some money, but . . . she don't like men. Only women. I told her all about you."

So he had been in her head about me? Falicia thought.

The next day Falicia was still in bed when Peaches knocked on the door, came straight in, and got in bed with her. Falicia shot Ike a look. He nodded. Impressed by her boldness, instinct quickly told her Peaches was most definitely going to bring in some money.

All day Peaches hung out with Falicia, expressing that she was down for whatever. Falicia put some clothes on her and took her out with Velvet and Shay for the night. As expected, niggas were trying to mate, but she didn't want them. So they peaked interest with a little girl-on-girl teasing, then Falicia would handle their client. It lasted only a few days. Peaches needed money like everyone else.

Although she sent Shay home with the intentions of being done, with Ike's permission of course, Shay came back after a few weeks. By now, Peaches was Falicia's distraction, different from the rest of the 'hos she dealt with and easy to confide in. Eventually, Falicia shared the depth of her feelings about Ike and his cruelty. Peaches had become the only bitch Falicia would turn a trick with and put her mouth on. She was Falicia's bitch now, and for whatever reason, this made Velvet mad.

Someone convinced Falicia and Ike there was money to be made out of town. Enough so that it would be a major come up. It was Peaches' first trip out of town with her and Ike. She was ready to get that out of town money.

A Treacherous Hustle

"This your time, Mama!" Ike said as he and Falicia lay in bed together the previous night.

"What you mean?" Falicia asked.

"You got her away from everybody. It's your time to start molding her. She seem like she love you, and now you gotta make her fear you." Falicia's forehead wrinkled. He sat up. "Right after you fuck her and y'all laying there, just get up and beat her ass. So she'll think you crazy."

"Daddy, what? Just beat her ass for no reason?"

"Hell yeah! I did it to you. You don't get it. Same shit . . . it's all about controlling the mind. Look at these 'hos!" Falicia was in a zone beyond stunned. This man had actually laid out the blueprint as to how he fucked up her mental. This was some sick ass shit.

Hitting Peaches wasn't something she was willing to do. Instead, she talked to her. Told her how Ike preferred for her to be very firm with the girls, but she wouldn't do Peaches that way. Then she fucked her until she was ready to go to sleep. They connected. Falicia loved Peaches the same way she was in love with her nigga. But Peaches became her baby. She was the only one she ever took with her to go see Man.

Velvet seemed to always be laying in the cut, waiting to go tell Ike some shit that Falicia and Peaches were doing. Clearly, there was division, and as the old saying goes: "A house divided cannot stand." Especially when it's occupied by jealous, back-stabbing females.

CHAPTER 30

"I gotta get my damn test results!" Falicia said as she lay in bed worried. She had gotten up extra early with the intention of going to the clinic. She and Ike had already discussed this the previous night.

"Mama, I need you to do a lot of shit for me today," Ike said as he sat up and snatched a blunt off the nightstand. Falicia bit her lip, trying to refrain herself. She was annoyed by him getting up and actually talking about all the shit he needed her to do before she went to work.

"Daddy, I'll do what I can when I leave the doctor's appointment, but I can't make any promises."

"What the fuck you mean? Time is money."

"I have to go to the clinic. You know that."

"Girl, so I'm supposed to miss money because you sitting your ass somewhere wasting time?"

Falicia tried the same thing again at a different time, but it was the same 'wasting time' bullshit! With her mind made up, she was going even if she had to make up a lie about it. Her cell phone rang.

"Hello?" she answered.

"What's up, girl?"

"Nothing. What's up, Roy?"

"Y'all coming to hang out or what?"

"Yeah, we'll be there."

"A'ight. I'll see you later."

"A'ight."

Once again, by the time she finished running errands for Ike, it was time for them to get ready for the yacht party on Lake Lanier. According to her calculations, she had just enough time to whizz to the health center and not be late to the festivities. Ike was only willing to let them go if it was guaranteed to benefit them aka 'him' financially.

Sereniti Hall

Roy assured Ike, "Man, you know somebody gonna be down for the cause. But it's an all-white affair." So Peaches and Falicia hit the mall and got cute real quick.

Lady Enyce did the honors of accenting their bodies. Ike donned Sean John. It was a pleasant experience to see how people who were financially established, relaxed and enjoyed themselves, but it didn't profit them much. Falicia had met some of Roy's sisters, and she still couldn't believe just how beautiful they were. It blew her mind that they popped pills. Roy pulled Falicia aside.

"This is Dre," he said, making quick introductions. He whispered in her ear, "This the dude you need to buy your cocaine from."

"Okay." Falicia and Dre shook hands.

Although the scene was different from how they did things, that night wasn't very profitable, and that presented a problem for them and Ike. To make up for the lost money the party didn't bring in, they dropped Ike off and got in Velvet's dad's Blazer and cruised the streets. It had been a long day, and Falicia was exhausted, but none of that meant a thing to Ike. Especially the simple fact that she had been up for two days trying to make up the slack of the other girls. Ike was one hateful individual when there wasn't enough money coming in. Therefore, it was best to stay out of his way, even when Falicia wanted to go home and sleep.

"Y'all bitches betta not bring y'all asses home tonight, if all of y'all don't make my fuckin' quota," he stated, before closing the door.

Exhaustion took over Falicia's body. She stopped at a light and rolled the window down, hoping the night air would keep her awake. Peaches was knocked out sleep in the passenger seat. Turning off Marietta, Falicia headed to Northside Drive. Suddenly Peaches yelled, "Mama!" She yanked the steering wheel left. The Blazer missed the light pole by inches as the manufactured rim scraped against the pole. Falicia had fallen asleep and "something" just woke Peaches up! She assumed it was that same "something" that yanked the steering wheel left. Falicia needed rest, and this would be one night that Ike would have to be all right.

Peaches and Falicia had their days. She was attracting some self-made niggas, and they were yoking their asses, and then there were days they barely saw anything moving. Falicia had a chance to see how real niggas moved and not the bullshit she was being exposed to with Ike and his bum ass friends.

Cruising the streets, they lucked up on some dudes who were from Ohio and had been hanging out at Magic City. They went back to their hotel. They left the guys' room with close to $2,700. Fifteen hundred was for sex and the rest was what Falicia took out of dude's pocket while he got his dick sucked. She tucked the stolen cash in her hairnet under her wig. Shit got real crazy when dude realized his money was gone. But she played her role with finesses and ordered her girls to get naked.

Everybody looked at her like she wasn't speaking English. "Cush wants his motherfucking money. So, get naked right now, everybody." His friends looked sideways as two of them pulled off their shirts.

After she removed all of her clothes as well, Falicia showed him what he had given her and counted it out in front of him. Then her girls stripped. Falicia picked up her money from the bed. "Y'all enjoy the rest of your night. Call me," she said on their way out the door.

At five in the morning, they headed back home in a rental, a champagne colored Chrysler. Falicia fell asleep, dead tired. So did Peaches. Velvet got in her feelings, bitching because she had to stay awake and drive, forgetting Falicia was the reason she made money on the streets. The bitch was so wrapped up in her feelings, fussing on the phone to Ike, that she wasn't paying attention to how fast she was going. The police pulled her over on I-85 right before Cleveland Avenue.

"Mama, wake up. The police is behind me. Wake up!"

"Where they at?" Falicia asked, jumping up and reaching for her purse. "Keep going so I can get rid of this shit. I ain't tryna get locked up. Just keep going," she instructed her.

"Mama, it's too late."

"What?" Falicia looked back as the police was pulling behind them. "Bitch, why your stupid ass didn't wake me up before you pulled over? You know I'm dirty!" Falicia was about to smack her dumb ass, but the officer was approaching the car. Velvet handed her the phone.

"This dumb, emotional ass bitch done got pulled over," she spat in Ike's ear. "And she waited until she stopped to wake me up! All this shit I got on me." Falicia prayed this would be a simple traffic ticket, and they could move on.

Velvet took the rental receipt out of the glove compartment and handed it to the police. He opened the paper. Marijuana seeds and residue was folded up in the paper. Ike had a really bad habit of breaking up weed and rolling a blunt on receipts.

"I'm going to need back up," the Caucasian man said after he realized what was on the paper.

"Bitch, we going to jail," Falicia said to no one in particular. "Damn, Daddy! You keep fucking with this stupid ass broad! I got powder, pills, and a gun on me! Fuck!" Velvet just looked discombobulated. Falicia wanted to kick Velvet's fucking face in. "Dumb ass 'ho!" she snapped.

The officer asked if she would pop the trunk. Velvet did, thinking nothing was inside. But Ike's baby mother had a book bag with some weed in it inside the trunk. Falicia woke Peaches up. As she saw another officer arrive, she reached down in her purse as discreetly as possible and felt around in her small pocket that zipped up for her stash of cocaine and pills. She balled it up in her hand and waited. She kept Ike on the phone trying to keep him afloat to everything that was going on.

A Treacherous Hustle

The first officer stood slightly in front of the car. She could see him through the windshield. Another officer arrived. A black cop. He walked around to Falicia's side of the vehicle with his gun drawn. Then he opened the door.

"Ma'am, I am about to search you. Do you have any sharp objects or weapons I need to know about?"

"Yes, sir. I have a pistol in my purse." His face told her how this was going down. He got on the radio and called for more back up.

"Is it loaded?"

"Yes, sir."

"Do you have a license for it?"

"No, sir." He leaned in and grabbed her purse and set it on top of the car.

"Please get out of the vehicle, ma'am."

Falicia stepped all the way to the edge of the expressway. Down below was a train track. Discreetly, she eased her hands behind her, and she dropped the dope over the expressway. *I hope nobody is down there to tell the police something had just fallen from the interstate.* She looked down. No movement. Falicia was arrested for the firearm, and Velvet was arrested for the weed in the trunk. Peaches wasn't going at all, but she needed someone to come pick her up. She couldn't drive, and instead of towing the car, if someone with a license could be there within the allotted time, they could keep the vehicle. Ike told Falicia to give Peaches the money they had just made. It was hard giving another bitch her money, even her bitch. Falicia was the first to post bail and quick to get herself a new gun.

Headed their way, Ike was stopped for speeding as well. Found not to have a license, he was arrested on the scene. With no funds to post his excessive bail for his repeated offenses, Falicia and Shay conspired to get enough money to get him out. They met a cute ass lil red nigga outside Crystal Palace and went to his spot. He ended up being a college boy living off his parents' luxurious gifts. The all

Sereniti Hall

white Benz with the caramel leather-covered seats, the six karat earrings, and the fancy clothes were all his rewards for his aspiring football scholarship, he boasted.

As Peaches and Falicia tricked off with his ass, she took his favorite earrings and replaced them with her fake ones. He obsessed over them and had set them directly across the bed on top of his DVD player. Falicia sent Peaches out first, telling her and Shay to go get in the truck and prepare to dip. She told him she was about to go get one of the other girls to come join them and ran down the hall, thinking they were leaving, but Velvet was still fucking. Falicia tapped on the door and peeped in.

"May I?" she asked the roommate. He grinned. Falicia rubbed Velvet's breast and kissed her neck like she wanted to join them. "Bitch, I just stole this man's shit, and you still in here fucking when I told you five minutes ago to get in the truck. I'm about to leave your stupid ass here. Or you can explain to your daddy why in the fuck we all got held hostage in this bitch?" Then she walked out. Once she reached the front door, she ran up to the car. The girls were in the truck already.

"You ready, Mama?" Shay asked, ready to back out.

"Naw, Velvet's dumb ass still in there fucking."

"Mama, you should just beat her ass."

"I do want you to turn this truck around though so we can just dip. I'll be back."

Dude ended up chasing them down the street in his boxers, but they got away with the earrings. Only earning six-hundred dollars for them. Falicia still needed nine more to get Ike out.

The following morning, she arrived at Body Tapp before the doors opened. Twelve hours in, and she was still coming up short. As it neared midnight, she was convinced if anything was going to happen, it would have happened by now.

By 3:00 a.m., Joe waved at her as she descended the stairs. She headed his way.

"What's up?"

"You got straight? You got something?" he inquired.

"Yeah, you want your regular?" He nodded yes. She went to the dressing room, got her purse, and got him a hundred dollars' worth of cocaine.

"So what's going on with you?" she asked, taking a seat beside him. Desperate to get at least five hundred dollars out of him.

"Nothing. Needed to get this and head on home." Joe had always been real chill, slow to speak, laid back, never excited. Falicia often wondered if it was the drugs or his personality.

"You want some company? I'm ready to go, and I'm still coming up short. I need to put a down payment on this apartment I'm trying to get."

"Shit, I would love for you to come with me, but I only got $700 left that I set aside to pay my rent." She stared at the bald, bright-skinned, man. Falicia needed to know if he was being honest about the $700 because she could just fuck him to sleep and get that. Then, she would have enough to get Ike out of jail.

"Why you looking at me like that?" Joe asked. She didn't even realize she was still staring at him, but through him.

"I'm just trying to figure out why you don't want to put that dick up in me. Especially, when I just admitted I needed you."

"Uh umm, don't take it like that." He reached in his pocket, pulled out his wallet, and took out the bills. "See, it's just seven."

She grinned with her mind on taking it. "Well, I guess you'll have to make up for it later because I want them lips wrapped around my pussy tonight."

Bitter always came after the sweet.

"Sunshine, baby," Ike chimed in, barely above a whisper.

"Daddy!" Falicia cooed into her cell phone. Excitement always filled her at the sound of his voice.

Sereniti Hall

"Where are you? And whose phone are you using?" She matched his tone.

"Check the move." He ignored her questions.

"Ike."

"Take care of that lil bit over there. Then meet me in the parking lot at Body Tapp." As always, his tone was serious and direct when he gave orders. A cold silence lingered between them as Falicia tried to collect her confused thoughts. *How did he get out of jail so fast?*

"Just handle that, and let's go, baby. It'll be perfect. We'll leave the Honda in the parking lot. Last time anybody saw you, you left the club with a trick. And very few know that I made bond. I'm just ready, Sunshine. Ready to get away from these 'hos and start over." It was everything Falicia wanted—to get back to life when it was only the two of them, well the three of them—Ike, her son Man, and Falicia, but one thing stood in their way.

"Daddy, I can just leave now and come straight to you." She smiled, envisioning them driving away from all the drama in the ATL and into a new state and a new life.

"Naw, ma, get that money first," he instructed.

She looked around the dining room of the man she intended to rob. The initial plan was to get enough money to bail Ike out of jail, who just so happened to be out already. "Well, now that you already out—"

"Just off the nigga and come on!" Ike said in a gruff voice.

The smile left her face as Falicia searched her brain for anything to change his mind. "He has a stick shift, Daddy. And I can't drive a stick."

"Then call me when you done. We'll come pick you up."

"He only got like $700. Maybe you should just try to get that and run." After Joe had purchased cocaine from her, he told her he only had $700 left for rent. He hadn't lied. She had gone in his wallet and counted seven 100 dollar bills, but hadn't taken any of it.

Not yet. She heard him approaching, and quickly placed it back on the coffee table.

"You heard what I said."

Shit! Falicia's mind raced with apprehension. Her stomach churned. "But . . . there's one more problem." She glanced down the hall for any signs of Joe.

"What," Ike didn't seem moved in the least bit.

"Just before you called, he rolled me a joint and I was reaching inside my purse for a lighter and my pistol went off. I didn't even feel the trigger. I could've been shot, but the bullet went into the baseboard. And that shit got Joe shook. He was pacing and on edge and everything. It blowed me too. Maybe it's a sign."

"Sunshine, it's a sign to go ahead and handle your business! Crazy shit *always* happens right before you're about to take care of some real shit." Ike didn't understand.

"But, Daddy. He was practically walking on egg shells. He asked me what the hell I was doing with a gun. His hand was shaking when he picked up my purse to put the safety on the pistol."

"What you tell that trick?"

"That I'm a female dancer and I sell dope. I would be stupid to be out here in these streets without one. Joe just shook his head and told me to be careful. I could tell he was spooked because he was still trembling. He told me I made his nerves bad. So he just went in the other room to snort some coke to calm down. I'm just waiting for him to finish."

"A'ight. Perfect. Go 'head and do that lil bit. Then come to daddy. If you need me to come get you, just call me. Then start walking." Ike ended the call. If it was possible, he would have heard Falicia swallow her fear.

As she waited for Joe to return, not even five minutes later, her phone rang again.

"Hello?" Falicia answered, sounding flustered.

"Uh, Unique, you ready?" Joe asked, calling Falicia by the

moniker he believed was her government name. His sudden presence startled her. She turned to find him standing there glassy-eyed, with his thin, hairy chest on display.

"Yeah," Falicia replied, then pressed the end button on her phone and flashed him a nervous smile. *How can I get this trick's money without any blood spill?* Joe let her lead him down the hall to his bedroom. "Oh wait! Let me go get my purse. I'ma put my phone in it so we won't have any interruptions." She rushed back to the living room and grabbed her purse off the table, dropping her phone inside. The pressure from Ike was getting to her. Briefly, she stared at the pistol. *There's no fuckin' way I can kill this man.* Fear of death, jail, and her own safety also threatened her mentally. She returned to the room. Her phone vibrated. Joe's smile dissolved quickly when she snatched it out of her purse.

"Yes!" was all Falicia offered when she answered.

"What the fuck!" Ike screeched into the receiver. She peered over at Joe, paranoia setting in his eyes as he watched her every move.

"Now is not a good time," she replied.

"I don't give a fuck! Do you know I'm sitting out here in this parking lot waiting on you?" His voice boomed.

"I'm going to have to call you back." Falicia hung up and turned to meet Joe's cautious stare.

"Sorry about that," she said.

Joe glanced at her purse, looking more uncomfortable as he sat on the bed and removed his pants. She placed her purse on the nightstand and got in bed next to him. Again her phone vibrated. "Don't worry, Joe. I'm not answering it. No more interruptions," she said, hoping to put his weary mind at ease.

That night was filled with several ignored calls from Ike to Falicia that even proceeded into morning. By 6:00 a.m., Ike's demand changed from "take care of the nigga" to just "bring your ass home." He didn't want to hear any explanations about why

Falicia didn't come through with the plan. Ike just wanted his bitch—Falicia—in his possession. In that instant, she knew this wouldn't turn out good.

Joe showered and got dressed for work. Soon he and Falicia were in his Volvo driving down a congested I-285 toward her apartment. The sky was cloudless. She wouldn't be studying the shapes of each cloud and making them into what she wanted. No magic carpet, or her own private jet to get the hell away from what she knew was coming when she got home. The uncomfortable rumbling in her stomach confirmed her fears.

Damn! She rubbed both arms, staring ahead. The sun beat against her skin, despite the cool air that seeped through the vents. Although Falicia wasn't trapped, she couldn't shake the suffocating feeling that anxiety brought on. She glanced at Joe, who kept his hands on the steering wheel at ten and two, staring ahead. She couldn't read what he was thinking, but last night he clung to his wallet like desperately needed oxygen. Then again, Joe was just a coke-sniffing trick, driving her back home. So his thoughts really didn't matter. Money did. It's the only thing that ever mattered.

Joe hit brakes suddenly. She noticed the traffic jam they were in and welcomed the delay. Once traffic moved enough for him to make his exit, he seemed to pick up speed. Blocks later, she instructed Joe to, "Make a left right here," as he entered Mechanicsville.

Her heart pounded and her palms moistened. Falicia's mind raced with thoughts of stinging, vicious slaps and powerful, solid body shots that always landed. And blood. *He's about to beat my ass! I know it!* Once the car stopped in front of the walkway that led up to the entrance, she opened the door to Joe's silver Volvo.

"If I never see you again," she said calmly to the man whom she'd been exotic entertainment for, and to whom she'd been selling cocaine for months. "Know that God was with you."

"What?" Joe asked as he rubbed his shiny baldhead. His

eyebrows bent as his puzzled eyes met the side of her expressionless face.

"I was supposed to kill you last night, Joe, and the fact that I didn't may have cost me my life." Tears threatened to fall, but she knew crying wouldn't do any good.

"What!" His eyes widened as if a ghost sat beside him. "Unique, please get outta my car."

Falicia grabbed her purse, her heart pumping fiercely with the same dread she was certain Joe now felt. As she stood and slammed the car door, she winced. Feeling Ike's fist smash against her cheekbone before a single blow ever landed against her face.

CHAPTER 31

The closer she got to the door, Falicia's heart gradually sank to her feet. Ike was waiting for her at the entrance. She could barely look at him, but she knew better. He didn't say a word, his expression was unreadable. He seemed calmer than normal when someone was about to feel his wrath. They walked to the elevator in silence. Once they stepped on, he pressed the button to go to the twelfth floor.

"Let me get your purse," he said and removed her gun.

Her heart raced as she watched to see what he was doing with it. *Is he about to shoot me?* He checked the safety and put the pistol in his back. Then he looked back inside her purse and took her money, counted it real quick, and put it in his pocket. He held the purse out to her.

"Let's go," was his next instruction as he stepped off the elevator and headed to their apartment. Her stomach tightened as they walked into an empty apartment. All of their clothes, shoes, bed linen, and toiletries were gone!

"Take your clothes off." His tone was flat and direct. She wasn't sure what he was up to, but she knew right now wouldn't be the time to make him repeat himself.

"Come here," was his next command. He eyed her naked body as if the sight was pleasing. She walked over to where he was standing in the bedroom. "Daddy," she spoke, barely over a whisper. "I'm sorry," she added with sincerity as he walked to the closet and grabbed a roll of silver duct tape.

"You will be." Ike held her wrists together and began taping them.

"Daddy, I need you to understand why I couldn't do it."

"You didn't do it because you don't love me."

"I do love you. I just couldn't . . . my gun went off . . . he was watching me."

Sereniti Hall

"If you loved me, he would be gone. Get your motherfuckin' ass in that closet and shut up!" He pushed her in the direction of the closet.

"Daddy, please! I just couldn't do it. Please, I just couldn't, but I love you. Daddy, I love you. Please, don't do this!"

Bam!

He slapped her.

"Shut the fuck up! I sat out in that parking lot all morning waiting on you!" He was up in her face, as if challenging her to a fight. "You chose that trick over me. Period! All you had to do was off that nigga and you didn't. I fucking love you! And this is what you do to me!" He yanked her arms over her head and started taping them to the post that the clothes once hung on. "I love you, and this is what you do to us." He continued to rant.

"Please, just look at me. Baby, you know that I love you. I-I-I was just scared." Her heart raced as tears fell from her face. *Why does it have to come to this?* He reached up on the same shelf he had gotten the tape from and grabbed some clipper guards that came with this clipper set. He dropped them on the floor.

"Stand on these and don't you move. I better *not* catch you off 'em."

The sharp plastic didn't seem that bad at first, but the longer she stood on them, the more uncomfortable it became. Once Ike had her secured in the closet, he grew more irate, convinced that she loved her trick.

"You don't want no life with me. You fucking with my feelings. You really do love that trick more than me, huh?" He splashed rubbing alcohol on her. "Bitch, you scared? You scared! Huh?" he yelled as he thoroughly drenched her in it. "Well, I guess I better make sure you fear nothing!" He lit a match and tossed it at her.

Whoosh!

Flames instantly covered her body. Falicia screamed and tried to free herself from the tape. The closer the flames got to her upper body parts, the more she could feel the heat engulfing the hair on her vagina. She pissed herself.

"God help me! Help me, please!" she screamed and jerked as the heat rose past her stomach. The post broke. She patted out the fire. The smell of her scorched pubic and stomach hairs rushed up her nostrils. Apparently, the flames that were on her backside died as the alcohol dissolved. Ike watched, his dick rock hard. Bent over in pain, Falicia wept because the man she so willingly sacrificed herself for had just found pleasure in her terror.

"I better not *ever* hear nothing else about somebody raping you again after that," he commented. Her strength departed, and she hit the floor. Seconds later, a noise that sounded like electricity popping made her sit up. Ike had cut the lamp cord, plugged it in the wall, and pulled the exposed cords apart and was making them touch, causing sparks. She rolled out of his range quickly.

"What the fuck you gon' do next time I tell you what to do?" he asked, fully prepared to electrocute her if Falicia answered wrong.

"Why . . . why are you doing this?"

"What the fuck you gon' do . . . Bring yo' ass here!" He grabbed her arm, dragging her back across the room by the cord. "I'm going to ask you again? What the fuck you gon' do when I tell you to do something?" He caused sparks again and tried to touch her, but she crawled away. "Bitch, you better answer me!" he demanded. "What you gon' do?"

With tears clouding her vision, Falicia answered, "Do it . . ."

When Ike decided Falicia had been disciplined enough, they got in the truck and went straight over to Campbellton Road. Ike parked in front of his boy's house and cut the ignition off.

"I don't know, Mama . . . It seems shit just ain't working out. It's like when I stop praying, shit just . . . I don't know . . . Maybe we need to just go our separate ways. Because we seem to make more money apart than when we are together, you know?" Ike seemed to be in a state of perplexity as he babbled on, never finishing a thought. "Shit just crazy. Like, all I do know right now is that I love you. Do you love me?" He looked over at Falicia as if his heart was breaking in pieces. Who the fuck could answer that question after being set on fire then nearly electrocuted?

Fresh tears strolled down her eyes. "That's all I ever tried to do was love you. Show you that I love you."

"I think we need to go separate our ways. Don't you?"

Fear of what he'd do to her next gripped her heart and wouldn't let go. She was in survival mode. "No, I don't want to leave you. I want to spend my life with you, but I don't want you fighting me and doubting my love. It has always been us against the world," she cried as she tried to reassure her man that nothing had changed in her heart. Just somewhere along the way, he changed. Before all the abuse, he was a wonderful man, and he had his ways of making her feel special.

Falicia reached over to touch him, maybe then he would be reminded that they were in this together. The contact with his skin gave her chills. She eased back slowly, not wanting to be obvious and just took a good look at Ike. *What am I begging to hold on to?* she asked herself. The man sitting across from her had Ike's voice, but his face was not that of the man who promised to take care of her. Falicia tuned in to what he was actually saying. Ike spoke a lot of truth, but she was too smart to hang herself. Carefully, she listened, quietly waiting for her chance.

"I think I'm gonna just put you in a hotel room, and you can go from there," he said.

She couldn't even begin to explain how this ease, this feeling of hope, like someone in recovery after a major procedure sounded. This knowing feeling that turmoil wouldn't last always engulfed her heart. "Daddy, I think you should just set me up in a hotel room and toss me an ounce. Just give me a month, baby. I'll flip the dope and stack my bread. We can hook back up in a month," she lied. "You of all people know I know how to get this money. Then we can go wherever you want." The second Ike dropped her off, she would be MIA!

"So you think I should put you up?" Her heart was about to explode. Was she really about to get out of this hell hole?

"I think it would benefit us financially—"

Bam!

Ike punched the shit out of Falicia. "Bitch, you owe me your life! What the fuck you mean? You think you gon' leave me?"

Bam!

He punched her in her ribs. "I'll take your motherfucking life before you leave me!" He slammed into her body with several more powerful shots.

"Daddy!" she screamed, trying to get him to stop, but her words were no match for his anger. Falicia started swinging and kicking him back, terrified for her life and somehow she managed to open the passenger door. A kick landed in his chest and knocked him against the door. She crawled upside down out of the truck, landing on her back. Jumping to her feet, she raced into the house to the back room they stayed in. Several of Ike's friends and his girls reclined on the sofas inside, shocked by the intrusion, oblivious to what she had endured all morning.

Shay's presence startled her as she ran behind Falicia.

"Mama, are you all right?" she asked, trying to wipe away Falicia's tears. Before she could answer, Ike burst through the door.

"Get your motherfucking ass out!" he instructed.

"Daddy, what's wrong with Mama?" she asked, genuinely concerned, still trying to wipe away her tears.

Bam!

Ike jumped across the bed and punched Shay in the back of her head, knocking her to the bed. Falicia stood against the wall in utter shock. He then pounced on top of Shay and choked her out until she passed out, gradually sliding off the bed and onto the floor. When it appeared her life was leaving her body, Falicia took off running, but without missing a beat, he reached up for her and yanked her to the bed.

"Bitch, you owe me yo' life!" He hovered over her. "So you wanna leave me? That's what you want to do?" he yelled in her face.

"I never said I wanted to leave you, Ike."

"*Ike*? Bitch, what you mean *Ike*? My name is Daddy! I'ma show you! I'ma show you who you fucking with, since you don't know!" He grabbed her leg and began to bend it upright. "We gon' see how in the hell you gon' get away with broken fucking legs!"

"Jesus! Jesus!" Falicia screamed, and kept repeating His name, knowing her bone would snap any minute. Ike stopped.

"Quit making all this noise. We got company," he said, getting up and walking out of the room. Falicia rolled over and shook Shay until she responded.

I can't believe this . . . I can't . . .

"Get up, baby!" She helped her off the floor. "You okay?" she questioned, eyes watering because she thought Shay was dead.

"Yeah," she whispered. Falicia liked Shay. She was the only female in the house that didn't act like she was a threat to her and did whatever she said without an attitude or hostility.

Falicia rambled through her clothes and found something to wear. She grabbed this lavender halter top and short wraparound skirt, with deep red roses all over and a pair of red wedge heels. She went into the bathroom to get cleaned up, washed away any piss and alcohol that may have been on her skin, and the remains of the burnt hair on her vagina, but she couldn't wash away the inner wounds that Ike carved in her inner most being. The reality that he had regarded her in the worst way hit her. Yet, she still gave room to question whether he truly loved her!

She managed to get dressed and was sitting down to pee when Ike invited himself in. Falicia was more likely to fall off the toilet before he assumed he was sticking his dick in her mouth. She hurried to the sink to wash her hands.

"Excuse me," she said, without looking up at him.

"You just gon' act like you don't know I came in here for you?" He stood in front of the door, bogarting it.

"Ike, please. I'm tired of fighting. I don't want to do this anymore."

"You don't want to do *what* anymore?" He closed up the space between them.

"I don't want to fight anymore. My body hurts." Tears slid down her face. "I can't think straight. I just want a minute to myself . . . to just be alone . . . wrap my mind around everything that has unfolded today, so I can focus on getting this money later tonight." Ike looked down at her, his face balled up, muscle in his jaw tight. He looked as if he was preparing to swing. She watched his body language carefully, just in case he was on the bullshit. As if she hadn't said a word about wanting to be alone, he grabbed her breasts and pulled her closer. He used both hands and caressed her booty, grinding his erection into her. *I know this man don't think I want to have sex with him after all the shit he has done to me.* He pulled his shirt off and was about to pull his dick out.

"Ike." It slipped from her mouth before she realized it. "Daddy, please. I just need a minute to get my head together." She looked down at his hands, now balled up in fists. Somehow, she knew what was next. Falicia moved her head just in time, and his fist went through the mirror.

"Bitch!" he yelled as the glass cut his knuckles. She pushed past him to get out of that corner and centered herself in the middle of the floor by the toilet and tub.

"You gon' pay for this," he threatened as he leaned over the tub, plugging it up and cutting the water on. She realized he wasn't washing his hands, but was trying to fill up the tub to dunk her in it. She ducked around him and unplugged the tub. He bent down and did it again. Falicia reached around him and unplugged it. They wrestled. He grabbed her neck as the tub began to fill. She squeezed his cut-up hand until he let her go. Pushing past him, she bent over and unplugged the tub again. But before she could stand, he connected his fingers together and cuffed her body, forcing her to stay doubled over as if she were touching her toes. He shoved his dick in her anus.

"Ike stop! Please stop! You're hurting me!" she screamed, but he didn't listen. He gripped her tighter and ripped her ass apart as he forced his way into her. Once he finally pulled out, her legs gave way, and she fell to the floor in a fetal position. Crying.

"Ssss, you done split my dick!" he said, and then the door opened. "Hurry up and come out of here. We got company." He walked out. For a moment she lay there crying, feeling ashamed, filthy, and confused. Slowly, Falicia stood to her feet and broke down when she saw how much blood was between her legs.

How could he do this to me? Falicia asked repeatedly as she wiped herself over and over, trying to make the blood stop. Her tears were unending. The pain was unbelievable, but the ache in her chest was much heavier than what her body was experiencing.

Ike walked back into the bathroom. "I thought I told you to hurry up and come out of here!" More punches and more blood followed.

All the people who were in the living room just looked down or away as Falicia attempted to look at them. She walked by without saying a word and went into the room and found a box of panty liners and put on a pair of thongs. It was the only kind of panties she had, and she needed something to catch the blood. *I gotta get the hell out of here.*

CHAPTER 32

"I'll be back," Falicia told Ike on her way out the door. She decided not to take a change of clothes so she wouldn't give off the wrong impression.

"Mama!" he called after her. She turned to face him, heart racing. "Where the fuck you going?"

"To make some money." She tried to sound as reassuring as she could. "I'll be back."

"Yeah!" he replied. "Y'all hear that?" he asked everyone in the room. His homeboys looked confused. "The rest of y'all 'hos go get dressed and go make some money too! Get the fuck out of here. Always wanna sit up under a nigga. Sick of bitches . . . go sell some pussy!"

Falicia turned on her heels so she could get a head start, not wanting anybody following her on her mission to find her mother's new house. Letty had to move out of the previous one because once Falicia left, she couldn't afford it alone.

"Mama!" Ike called after her again. She glanced back. "Be back before midnight." His intense gaze made her eyes well up. Their connection was broken. She didn't know if the gaze was an expression of love, or just a threat. Looking straight ahead, Falicia walked out the door. She could hear him yelling, "I love you!" as she closed the door behind her.

A sprinkle or two fell from the sky as she headed to the bus station, anxious to see her son and mother. She needed a dose of something that wouldn't make her feel so demoralized as Ike had done to her, almost in the company of their guest. They heard her screams and cries, knowing he had been doing something awful to her, but none of them had the guts to intervene. On the other hand, there were times when neither had she. Still, she needed an escape plan. She walked around Letty's neighborhood for hours, and was almost snatched up by a dude wearing a hood and was stopped by a pimp who wanted to make her a part of his "harem." Little did he know that she already had a foot in the grave and wasn't looking to put the other one in there anytime soon.

By dark, Falicia spotted Letty's car. She sighed with relief as she hurried to her front door. Mastering the courage, she knocked on the door, hearing laughter coming from inside. Letty stopped laughing.

"Who is it?"

"It's me, Ma!" Falicia tried not to be so emotional, although just hearing her mother's voice comforted her. Falicia didn't know how to address Letty's surprise at seeing her, other than to insist, "Ike is out of town and the house got raided. I jumped out the window, and I didn't know where else to go." Falicia was dying to tell her the mother the truth, but something about the way Letty looked at her, as well as her male company sitting there and staring, made her uncomfortable. Ashamed. And embarrassed that she had been allowing this man to beat her ass.

"Well, you can't stay here," Letty replied. Falicia wished for death the moment the words left her mouth. The little hope she had left, abandoned her body. It was only a matter of time anyway before Ike was going to kill her. "I mean, you can stay the night, but my landlord ain't gon' let you stay too long."

She smiled. "Where's my baby?" Falicia asked.

"He sleep, and I want you to leave him that way."

Falicia hurried in the direction her mother pointed, squatted next to his bed, and silently cried. Shattered, she knew she wouldn't get to see him grow up and become a man.

"Get up!" Ike shook Falicia from her sleep. "Roy on the phone. Getcha ass up." She stretched and reached out for the phone. Peaches lay snuggled underneath her.

"What's up?" she answered.

"Hey! I know you still sleep, but I need you," Roy said. He knew he only had to ask once and it was done. She rubbed Peaches' back and booty so she could wake up. She stretched and grinned at her mama.

"Get up. We got somewhere to go," Falicia told Peaches.

Upon arrival, Roy asked Falicia to take him to the bank up the street. They were in the drive-thru when her cell phone rang. She didn't answer the first call, but it didn't take long for a second call to come through.

"Sunshine, where y'all at?"

"Taking Roy to run an errand." She didn't want Ike to know what was really going on.

"Sir, will that be $1,500?" the bank teller asked.

"Who was that?" Ike asked.

"We at the bank," she replied.

"How much he getting out? Five hundred dollars?" Ike inquired.

"No."

"Eight hundred dollars?"

"No."

"A thousand?" he guessed.

"More."

"Fifteen hundred?"

"Yeah."

"Oh bet! Get all that."

"Huh?"

"Yeah. Bring all that home witcha'," Ike said, hyped and betting on payday.

She eyed Roy in her rearview mirror, counting what the teller gave him, while still holding the phone to her ear. "He got something to do," she mumbled. "I doubt I can get him to spend it all, but you know he don't mind shopping with a nigga."

"Oh, I don't give a fuck about his plans. Get that money. This was meant to be. We been struggling, and our struggling days are about to be over. Handle that business and bring your ass home. Where Peaches at? Hand her the phone so I can tell her what's up. I love you."

Falicia gave Peaches the phone. She looked over at her as a blank stare traded places with the smile on her face. Peaches hung up.

"I know, right?" Falicia told her.

"Go on up there to that chicken place up the road, so y'all can put something on y'all stomach. Then y'all won't have no excuses to not sip on something with a nigga," Roy insisted, before her or Peaches said another word.

Falicia barely touched her food as she sat across from Roy. Her heart softened as she listened to him make future plans to buy a Cadillac Escalade before the year was out, and the vision he had for his photography business. It was fucked up that Ike called a hit on his head. Roy of all people. She let out a deep sigh, but she needed to gather her thoughts and regain her composure. The reality was that Roy wouldn't get a chance to do any of those things he planned, unless she could think of a way out, get Ike some cash, and keep herself and Roy alive.

"What's wrong with you?" he asked as he was finishing his meal. "What that nigga done said now? You been different ever since he called you. I wish you would just stop fucking around with him."

"You of all people know I've tried. It just seems impossible. Every time I leave, he finds me, and where am I gon' go?" she replied, preparing to get up before she broke down in tears. Peaches sat quietly. "Overall, I wish I would have never moved up here." Falicia's admission dulled the mood.

"Let's get out of here," Roy said, after releasing a sigh. They all climbed back in the truck. Roy insisted they have some drinks when they got back to his apartment. No sooner than Falicia finished her first drink, Ike called.

"What's up, Mama?"

"Having some drinks right now. Nothing."

"I want all fifteen hundred. Handle that. And *don't* bring yo' ass home without it!" He reminded her of how serious he was about her carrying out his demands. Every time her phone rang, it only added to the stress she already felt. Although her body was there with Roy and Peaches, her mind was a hundred miles and running far, far away. She tried to wrap her mind around Ike's demand as Roy poured her a glass of 1800, in hopes of loosening her up.

Shortly thereafter, Roy received a call and ended it with good news. "My best friend Dre is on his way over. You met him briefly at the yacht party," Roy said. Falicia didn't respond.

"Huh?" she finally said, oblivious to Roy's words.

"He was saying you met Dre at the yacht party," Peaches explained.

Roy had been trying to properly introduce them for some time, and now would be as good a time as any. He wanted Falicia to turn a trick with Dre and make him her main supplier. "The dude you use, put too much cut on his cocaine," Roy said.

Now Falicia had actually tuned in and smiled for the first time. His news sounded great to her ears and provided hope that Ike would fall back. "A'ight. That's cool!" She sat back and happily dialed Ike's number. Dre provided some of the best coke in the city. So now she'd have a new hookup.

"Daddy!" she sang into the phone. It was apparent that her spirits were lifted.

"What, Sunshine? You handled that?" He sounded happy.

"No. Actually, I was calling to inform you that I'm not going to be able to do that."

"Why not?" Ike seemed confused.

"Well, Roy's best friend is on his way over here. So I can't do it.

Sereniti Hall

I'm just gon' chill and just see how much they gone spend." It felt good knowing she was off the bull.

"You talking about Dre? The nigga we met at the yacht party?"

"Yeah, that's him. So call me if you need me." Falicia was preparing to get off the phone.

"Sheit! That's even better! Two for one. Take Roy in the room, handle business, and when dude get there, handle him as soon as he comes in the door."

"Daddy, I don't think that's a good idea. I think . . ."

"Did I ask you what you think? Handle that business and bring your ass home! Give Peaches the phone."

She stared at Falicia as she handed Falicia back her phone. "You don't wanna do it, do you?" she asked.

"No, of course not." Falicia could have sunk to the floor and cried like a baby, but true feelings didn't have a place in this life. She joined her friend in his room.

"What are you doing?" she asked Roy as he sat on the edge of his bed.

"You should be asking me what are *you* about to do," he said.

"If you want my mouth on you, just say that." She tried to lighten the mood up.

"That." He smiled. Roy was so handsome, so he wasn't hard to please, but she couldn't get lost in the pleasure of satisfying him. The weight of her obligation to Ike was more than shoulders could bear. She did as Roy asked and gave him some head, and then lay in bed next to him. Listening to him talk, she felt torn, overwhelmed, and hurt. He didn't notice because of the way her head was positioned, but she began to cry. Why Roy of all people? They weren't the best of friends, but they had gotten close, albeit under superficial circumstances. But none of that mattered.

Peaches walked in the room. Falicia used her presence as an excuse to step out. When she returned, she slid her pistol under the pillow. Roy was entertaining Peaches. She held the gun, trying to psych herself out enough to actually do it. Something wisped across her hand. A cute and furry cat, tapping her hand and the pistol. An obvious sign not to do it. To think twice. She put the pistol back under the pillow to put back in her purse later.

Dre arrived not long after that. Falicia and Roy left Peaches with Dre as they headed to the mall so Roy could buy these earrings for his girlfriend. He and his sisters and close friends planned to celebrate her birthday the following weekend. Roy seemed so excited and truly seemed to adore his girl. Falicia's mind raced with how to handle this without anyone getting hurt. She called Peaches while Roy ran back inside to get his wallet.

"Hey, Mama. What's up?" Peaches answered.

"Hey. I'ma figure something out with Roy, and when I get back, we'll figure shit out with Dre."

"I don't wanna sleep with this nigga, Mama," Peaches whispered.

"I know that, baby. I don't wanna do the shit that I was told to do either. But this the kind of business we're in." Falicia ended the call, thinking of ways to get her hands on Roy's money. Everything but simply asking him to just give it to her.

They parked at Lennox Mall, and Falicia pushed the button to roll up the windows. The window literally came completely out, and Roy was left holding it. *Another sign.* Falicia couldn't hurt him. Eventually, they handled his business and returned to his crib to find Peaches and Dre lying in bed together. Falicia's cell rang. The phone calls from Ike were beginning to come more frequently.

"Mama, you ain't handle that business yet?" he asked.

"Daddy, I can't."

"What the fuck you mean, Falicia?" She sat on the floor in front of the stereo, adjusting the volume so no one could hear them.

"Daddy, please."

"I don't want to hear that shit! Straight up. We over here in this bitch struggling! I'm over this bullshit we so-called got with these 'hos. I'm ready to bounce, period! Handle that shit and get here." He ended the call.

Falicia sat in front of the stereo. Roy sat on a milk crate next to Peaches, who was seated at the coffee table. Dre sat on the sofa behind them.

Indecisive, she pulled the pistol out and stared at it for a long minute. So long she didn't notice Dre setting his attention on her.

"Girl, what you doing with that gun?" he asked.

"Nothing." He'd startled her. "It ain't loaded," she lied. He walked on into the kitchen, did something and came back out. Roy went out onto the patio with the grill, but came back inside. Falicia closed her eyes and tried to imagine what the night would bring. What it might be like for her if she survived this, once she went home again without carrying out Ike's orders. *What else might he possibly do to me?* Taking a deep breath, she looked over at Roy. *I think I can take it. I've already survived all the other shit he's done, so . . ."*

Her cell phone rang. "Hello." She wished it was anyone but who it was.

"You still at Roy's apartment?" Ike sounded pissed.

"Yes," Falicia answered as her stomach turned.

"Bitch, I'm on my way."

"For what? What you mean you're on the way?"

"I'm coming, and if I get there and you haven't handle that!" he screamed into the phone. "They gone find your ass stinking in one of these hotels."

"Ike, you trippin'. You don't understand . . ."

"Fuck that! I'm sick of you playing with my feelings! You don't love me. You owe me your life. I tell you what . . . I'ma tie your ass up somewhere and make you watch while I torture your mother before I kill her."

Maybe this is what she had been feeling lately. Like she'd run out of options. She'd heard that when it's your time you'll know it, and maybe this was hers. Roy boasted of his future, when she couldn't even imagine one. This was it. Had to be. Maybe this was the straw that would break the camel's back. This just might be what caused Ike to end it all.

"Ike, Ike . . . Why would you say that?" she asked, then realized that he ended their call. Twice more she called, and he answered.

"What's up?" he said.

"Daddy, please."

"Falicia, I'm not playing with you anymore."

"Okay . . . okay! Wait. Just wait. Please . . ." she cried. "Just don't hang up. Don't hang up." *I can't let him hurt my family.* She set her phone on top of the back rest of the sofa, staring at it to make sure he hadn't hung up. The light was still lit and the seconds were blinking.

With a face full of tears, Falicia cocked her gun, putting a bullet in the chamber. *I don't have a choice.* Weeping, she raised it and pointed at Dre. Even now, she searched for the courage to do it. He must have heard her crying, or felt something because he looked back, with his phone still up to his ear.

"Aww, hell naw! It ain't going down like that," he said as he made an attempt to stand up. Falicia pulled the trigger.

Roy screamed as he ran across the room and dropped in front of his love seat, snatching the pillow from it. He sat on the floor with his knees and the pillow up to his chest, rocking back and forth.

"Roy, I'm sorry. I'm sorry, Roy . . . I'm not gone hurt you. Calm down. I'm not gone hurt you." He continued crying and rocking. "Roy, I'm not gone hurt you," Falicia stated again, trying to comfort him. Suddenly, white film bubbled from his mouth, and he fell backward. "Oh shit . . . Roy! Roy!" she whispered. He looked as if he had stopped breathing. *Did he overdose?* she wondered as she looked over at Peaches.

"Get the money," she instructed her, looking at Dre slumped over the arm of the sofa.

Oh my God! What have I done? Falicia asked within. She called Ike, her hands vibrating from both fear and shock.

"Hello?" Her voice trembled.

"Good girl!" Ike admonished. "Now wipe down everything and take everything you touched. Then come home."

"Okay."

"I love you, baby," Ike cooed.

By the time they pulled into the high-rise, Falicia knew that had been the worst mistake she had ever made. Ike greeted her with open arms. Nothing felt the same. The way everyone looked. How he felt holding her. Even the light in the apartment seemed dim. Ike rolled her a blunt on his way out the door and said he was about to go by their weed man and get some more. Falicia paced the floor trying to process everything. Mainly Roy. She'd shot him and didn't recall ever pointing the gun at him, or even the direction he ran in, zig-zagging back and forth in front of the patio glass door.

Oh my God. What have I done?

CHAPTER 33

Just as ill-gotten gains are said to never last, Ike proved the theory true. He called Falicia saying the young dude they normally shopped with for weed couldn't be found. Falicia then told Peaches, who'd told Ike about some dudes she grew up with that sold weed not far from where he was. He headed that way after she called them, so they would be expecting him. A few minutes passed and Ike called back.

"Mama, I think I'm about to leave. Something just don't feel right. It shouldn't take this long to do a deal." Suddenly, a female screamed in the background! Falicia rose to her feet and went in the kitchen so she could hear what was going on.

"Here go the money right here! Hear go the money right here!" Ike yelled. A bunch of commotion followed. After a couple minutes someone said, "It's done!" And the phone disconnected.

"Oh my God! What just happened?" Falicia panicked as sweat beaded up on her forehead. Ike left in the Blazer, but he had the keys for the other vehicle on him. Falicia called one of his babies' mothers and asked her to take her through the area to see if Ike had been hurt, but he was nowhere to be found.

"Ain't nobody going to sleep until I get my money back," Ike burst through the door ranting, his velour outfit covered in red mud. Every dollar Falicia took in the robbery was gone.

"Get your asses up," he ordered. "I want you and Peaches to walk past them dudes' house and murk everything movin'!" Played at his own game, he couldn't stomach it.

"We can't do that," Falicia insisted. "They'll kill us for sure."

Later, Ike and Shy eventually found the guys and did a drive by, shooting at everyone standing outside.

Grabbing everything they thought they touched, they stuffed it in a leather bag and exited the high rise. The sun was positioning

Sereniti Hall

itself to set and it started sprinkling. "They say every time it rains somebody dies," Peaches stated, breaking the fearful silence.

"Girl, what just happened?" Falicia asked.

"I don't know." A long silence fell between them. "What are we gonna do now, Mama?" Peaches asked, shaking her head.

Peachtree Street was the location Ike decided they would find their next John Doe down in Buckhead. As expected, it was thick out there for a Saturday night. Once they parked, Ike and Shy stayed in the vehicle. "I'll do the next one. You took too long the last time," Peaches said, once they got out the Blazer.

"We ain't doing that, Peaches. Let's just find a nigga to trick off with and go home." Falicia meant that shit and headed down the street. The nightclubs were stacked right next to one another. She was in a trance. Shit was happening too fast. She hadn't even had time to absorb the God-forsaken acts she committed earlier, and now here was she was with Ike on some other bullshit.

"Ay, miss lady!" A tall, brown-skinned dude called after Peaches as he headed from his vehicle. The heavyset guy was cute and rocked a low haircut. It didn't take him and Peaches long to decide that they would hook up. Although Ike hadn't seen the guy, he felt it was the move and dropped them off in the parking lot of Club 112.

Meech, the dude Peaches was about to see, pulled up with his homeboy. They passed a joint around. Falicia sat back just thinking, trying to figure out how her love for Ike had turned into this fear. Meech dropped his friend off, and Peaches got in the front seat. *We'll just rob him then go home. Simple as that.*

He didn't live that far away from Falicia's new favorite strip club, Strokers. Meech pulled out an air mattress that they all reclined on. With her mind only on robbing him, Falicia watched TV lying right beside him as Peaches rode him. At some point after they were done, he ended up on his sofa. He wanted more because they had smoked a lil purp with him. Pretending she was going to join in, Falicia got off the mattress, walked over to Peaches, and whispered in her ear, "Give him slow head. When he go to sleep, we rob him and get the fuck outta here. I'm ready to go."

As he was dozing off, snoring slightly, Falicia pulled out her pistol and cocked it. He woke with a start, pissing on himself. "He pissed in my mouth!" Peaches yelled, spitting his pee out and running to the bathroom. Falicia jumped to her feet, aiming the gun at him. She stood on his left, between the sofa and his love seat.

"Listen, I'm not gon' hurt you, but I do need you to cooperate with me. All I'm going to do is take your car, but first tell me where the money is."

"I don't have any money," he replied. She looked him over. A blue snake skin watch wrapped his wrist, and the face was drenched in diamonds. A set of diamond earrings, a platinum necklace that looked like silver bones, and where the tendon would be between each bone, was a diamond with heavy diamond-clustered medallions, and a bracelet to match. "I barber for a living. I'm not out here in these streets, though it may look like it. What you want, my jewelry?"

"Where the money at?" she asked again, not buying it.

"I got it!" Peaches yelled from in the back. "I found his stash!"

"I thought you didn't have any?" He dropped his head. Falicia didn't know if he was praying or thinking, but she gave him his moment of silence. "Now, when we leave with your car, you are not to try to find us, call the police, or tell anybody about this night, you feel me?"

"Please, don't take my car," he pleaded. "Please," he begged as if his life depended on it.

"I'm talking about sparing your life and you concerned about a car!"

Peaches came from the back wearing a leather Gucci fishing hat. She held her purse on her arm and a pillowcase full of shit in her hand, and her pistol in the other hand.

"What the fuck is all that stuff?" she fussed.

"Stuff I wanted." Peaches replied. Falicia rolled her eyes. She'd later find out it was electronic gadgets.

"Tell me where some tape or rope is, so I can tie you up." Falicia directed her attention back to him.

"Please don't do this," he said again, seeing Peaches wearing his Gucci hat and carrying a pillowcase full of his valuables. "What you want, my jewelry?" He began taking it off, throwing it on the floor. Peaches ran to pick it up.

"Give me them earrings," she demanded.

"These, they ain't even real!" He snatched them out of his ears and tossed them on the floor. "Here's my ring. It's all I got left. That's all of it. For real." He took it off and tossed it. It fell on the floor by the loveseat.

Peaches reached down to pick up the ring. Meech saw an opportunity and took it, tussling with her to get the pistol that fell when she bent over for the ring. She should have never had all that shit in her hands in the first place. Racing to the other side of the room to help, Falicia wanted to slap the shit out of Peaches for putting them in this position.

Truly, Falicia had no intentions of harming him. But she stood in shock as the over six-foot-tall man tussled with the five-feet-tall Peaches for her pistol. Falicia ran to the opposite side of the living room so she wouldn't get shot in the midst of them wrestling. They began to stand upright. Meech had the upper hand. The only grip Peaches had on her gun was the barrel.

"Drop the gun, dude!" Falicia screamed. Things went in slow motion as she watched Peaches' hands lose the grip on her gun. Falicia raised her gun and started firing. Stuck in time. Uncertain when the bullets stopped flying, or how long she had stood there with the gun still in the air. Finally she stared at Meech's lifeless body, as his blood spilled all over the carpet.

"Oh my God! What have I done again?" Falicia backed away from him some. She took her focus off Meech and looked at

Peaches. "What the fuck you doing? I'm ready to go." Peaches ran across the room with a bloody pillowcase and into the kitchen, searching in drawers and cabinets, looking for something to put her stolen items in. Falicia picked up the air mattress and covered him up.

"Bitch, I'm ready to go! You been doing dumb shit all night!"

"I'm coming! Chill out, Mama."

Falicia grabbed the car keys off the counter, and they raced out the door. She couldn't get the car to start! Her nerves were so bad. She took a deep breath and tried it again. They took off and were just about to get on the expressway.

"Hey! Did you get your clip from under the sofa?" Peaches asked.

"My clip? Why in the fuck is it under the sofa?" Falicia replied.

"I put it there. For you . . ." She looked at her as if she had lost her mind.

"Well, bitch, you gon' have to go back in there and get it."

Falicia turned around and went back to his complex. The sun was up, and she looked around to see if anyone was paying them any attention. It didn't seem that anyone was, but she was still scared as hell. Peaches probably didn't even understand just how much.

When they got home, Falicia didn't want to be bothered. She got in the tub and cried. Peaches told Ike what happened as she stood in the kitchen washing that man's blood off the shit she stole. She didn't know what tomorrow would bring, but killing someone else was not up for discussion. Once she got out the tub, Ike told her to get dressed. They were going someplace else to lay low. So they got a room at Days Inn off Northside Drive.

The next few days only got more and more frightening. One of Falicia's clients, a cop, told her they were riding around in undercover cars looking for her with five by seven pictures of her and Peaches. Rocky, Roy's sister had taken the police to

Goosebumps and had gotten them to give the police Falicia's license. She couldn't go anywhere. As Falicia made a quick stop at Body Tapp, she was told they had come for her there too. They'd missed her by seconds. Another dude she was cool with told her that she was considered armed and dangerous! Shit got real.

"Uh-un. Don't make no sudden moves, Fantasia. Or I'll have to shoot you," the bouncer said, standing on the side of Dancers Elite. Falicia was sitting in a parked car.

"Really? Ted, this me!" Falicia told the heavyset, baldheaded sheriff who moonlighted as a bouncer.

"I know . . ." He looked around to see if anyone was watching them. "And I always thought you were a sweet girl, but the house mom said you carry a pistol in your purse, and that girl Rocky telling everybody you killed her brother. She said if she catch you first, they won't have to do an investigation. The best thing for you to do is lay low. Go somewhere and chill. It ain't safe out here for you." He said what he said and stepped back from the car, as if they never had a conversation.

Falicia was scared as fuck! To say the least. One night she went to Club 112 and tried to get in with her pistol in her purse and was immediately turned around. As soon as Peaches, Velvet, and Falicia got back inside the car, she saw Rocky and her man walk by. She wore shades and was hugging herself. The sight made Falicia want to cry. She didn't have to see her eyes to know the type of agony she was causing Rocky and her family. It was real fucked up that she was the one subjecting them to it.

Needing a place to lay her head, Falicia tried to go to the room, but Ike told her she was being paranoid and needed to relax. Shortly after, he discovered they couldn't make as much money the way they used to, so something had to give. Peaches had an idea! She used to be a manager at Mrs. Winner's and knew what time they made the drop. It should be an easy lick. No one would get hurt. Just make them give up the money, and they would be out.

CHAPTER 34

"Boo-Boo, call me," Letty said, and then attempted to hang up her landline phone without success. This was the first message Falicia got once she checked her phone.

Letty's cell phone rang and she answered.

"Hello?" Letty said.

"Hello. May I speak with Ms. Ford?" a female voice asked.

"This is she. And you are?"

"I'm Leslie Brookins calling you from Bailing and Bonds, in regard to your daughter, Falicia Blakely."

"What about her? Is she in trouble?" Falicia picked up the pain in her mother's voice.

"Ma'am, have you seen her? It's important that we get in contact with her."

"Is she in trouble?" Letty was relentless.

"Ma'am, if you've been in contact with her, please inform us."

"Listen. No, I haven't heard from her! Now tell me, is she in some type of danger or trouble? Damn, just tell me . . . you would want to know if it was your baby, your only child . . ." Letty was getting emotional.

"Ms. Ford, she may be in some trouble, that's why it's important that she gets in contact with us."

Falicia hung up her phone, disturbed! *What have I done?* That question kept ricocheting through her mind. After this incident, she got extremely paranoid, looking out of windows, expecting the police to appear any second.

Desperate for money, they went through the drive thru and peeped out how many employees were inside. They calculated that it shouldn't take any more than five minutes to rob the joint. And they did it with stocking caps over their faces and wigs on. They went in and forced everybody into the cooler and made the manager open the safe. They felt that it was quick and easy. Falicia was happy that it was a clean robbery. Nobody got shot, and there was no blood shed. Velvet was the getaway driver. But one thing they didn't anticipate—Peaches' old employees recognized the voice, height, and shape of their former manager and the woman on the drive thru register was the wife of one of Ike's homeboys. Not only did she know it was them, she recognized the .38 revolver Peaches pointed in her face. It seemed things had gone so smoothly in the previous robbery, that Ike wanted them to try their hand again and they did.

By the time the third robbery was approaching, Ike had pulled Falicia off to the side. "This is it, baby!" he said. She saw the same look in his eyes that she saw the morning after he'd place the dog collar around her neck. "This is our last lick, and then we outta here. We can have our new life together." He grabbed her face and kissed her lips. It was everything Falicia had been waiting for since the beginning, but she had a nagging concern. Her son. What type of woman would she be to take her baby out of a safe environment and on the road with her as a fugitive? But if she didn't, she might never see him again. And not just him, but her mother as well. Had she sacrificed her entire life for this? Is this what the rest of her life would consist of?

"Sunshine." Ike pulled her from her thoughts as she got dressed for this final robbery. "When you get back, I'ma take care of everything. I'll burn dude's car. I already arranged for you to get your dreadlocks, and we out this bitch. Straight to Texas. My brother drives trucks up there. Everything is gone be all right," he professed.

"Are you sure?" she asked.

"I promise it is, and I won't let them take you from me, either." She wasn't sure that she understood what he was telling her.

"I'll take your life before I stand by and let them motherfuckers take you from me," he said with all seriousness. *Wow!* Falicia was speechless as she sat next to him. *Nothing about him killing me instead of me going to jail sounds comforting to me.* In fact, it did the very opposite. There was no way she could possibly subject her son to this madness.

A couple of hours later, Falicia, Velvet, and Peaches pulled up to the Mrs. Winner's on Piedmont Drive.

"It's old people and children in there right now. I'm not going in until they leave," Falicia stated what it was. The sun had barely pierced the sky. "They must've been on their way to Sunday School," Falicia told Peaches and Velvet, referring to the elderly Caucasian couple and several children.

Time passed and they sat and waited out the elderly and the children. Other children approached. Falicia gave Velvet and Peaches the eye like: don't try me. She wasn't about to leave those kids with the vision of someone pointing a pistol at them or another individual. Ike called wondering why they hadn't made it back yet. Another couple hours had passed. They grew tired of just sitting there. They decided to go inside, grab something to eat and peep out the setup and camera system. Five minutes later, and a young black woman who could have possibly been the manager, walked over to their table.

"Excuse me. Is that your blue vehicle parked outside?"

"Yes," Velvet answered.

"Can you please move it because the delivery truck can't get in?"

Velvet dashed out to move the car and came right back in. They finished their food.

"Let's do this shit and get it over with!" Peaches felt they needed to go ahead and hit this lick.

Falicia looked out the window to see if anyone else was approaching with children. She spotted a purple PT Cruiser up the street at the top of the hill, and a police car sitting next to it.

"The police up the street!" Falicia blurted. Velvet and Peaches both looked in the direction Falicia was staring at.

Sereniti Hall

"We need to handle this and go." Peaches didn't hide her frustration. Falicia looked at Peaches and back out the window, not really thinking much of the cop talking to someone. She was burnt out. "I just want to be done with all this!" Peaches jumped up.

"Fuck it!" she said, pulling her stocking cap over her face, as if they hadn't just been sitting there. What was the point of hiding their identity now? She pulled her pistol out and was heading straight for the Employee Only door when the police came from all directions. They had the building surrounded.

"Shit! There goes the police!" Falicia yelled. Peaches and Velvet took a peek and saw all the cars. Falicia noticed a K9 car and started to run in the opposite direction toward the door on the opposite side of the restaurant. She was willing to take her chances running from the police. But somebody grabbed her arm, and she turned around. They ran into the restroom, each going into their own stall. Falicia didn't know what kind of refuge the restroom would provide, but to a certain degree, there wasn't any time to think. They did manage to get the weapons off them, not that it would help lessen the charges. She hadn't thought of anything in a minute. The police told them the place was surrounded and they needed to come out with their hands in the air. Velvet called Ike crying, and she passed the phone to Falicia.

"Daddy, I'm about to go to jail," she spoke softly. "I knew this was it."

"What happened? What you mean? Where you at? You ain't coming home?" His questions spilled out one after the other. It really wasn't much to say as the police encouraged them to surrender. "Mama, I love you! Don't be scared. I love you!"

"I love you too," she replied. "I've always loved you."

By the time Falicia went to court for her preliminary hearing, she had been denied bond and processed. She couldn't care less about the chain being cut from her neck now. It actually felt as if she was being freed from the obligation that came with it. For the first time in almost two years she wasn't Mama, that bitch, or Lil Ike. She was this young, dumb ass little girl who had just blown away her possibility of ever making Ike be held accountable for all the low down, evil shit he had done to her. Scared as hell, Falicia had no one to turn to.

On August 25, 2002, the exact same day she moved to Atlanta back in 1999, Falicia had been arrested for the murders of Roy, Dre, and Meech. It was the first day that she had ever sat in one place for so long in her life. By the time she was escorted to the interrogation room, her codefendant Peaches, had already turned state, wrote out a lengthy detailed letter of her version of events and talked about licks she only heard that Falicia had committed. She was singing about shit she knew nothing about!

Later on, Falicia was told how they had been identified. When Velvet ran outside to move the vehicle, she'd left her cell phone on top of the car. The young manager ran over to stop her from pulling off.

"Ma'am!" She ran up to the car. Velvet jumped, obviously frightened by the sudden presence. "I'm sorry. I didn't mean to startle you. I just wanted to catch you before you pulled off. You left your phone on top of the car." She handed Velvet her phone. Later, the woman told police it was something about the way Velvet responded that shook her to the core. She thought about the gender and type of car that was reported for the sequences of robberies. That's when she contacted the police. Velvet went to Fulton County jail for the Mrs. Winner's robberies. Peaches and Falicia were picked up by DeKalb County.

As Falicia sat listening to the detective tell her how pissed they were for having to search for her for two weeks and all the evidence they had against her, it felt unreal. As if her mind couldn't comprehend just how serious this was. And in her ignorance, she

Sereniti Hall

lied about what had happened. Falicia said they were snorting powder and she flipped, to take the heat off Ike. She planned to stick to that lie, feeling the need to protect her man. Plus, she didn't want to be considered a snitch.

During processing, she was given a bag with a small tooth brush, state toothpaste, hotel soap, some deodorant and a mat with a wool blanket and sheets. The place alone was scary as hell! Thank God everyone was already locked down in their cells for the night, so she didn't have to face anyone. She was put into pod 100, in a one-man cell. Twenty-two hour lock down would be the schedule Falicia's life would abide by for months. One hour in the morning to bathe, watch TV, or use the phone, and the same for that evening.

Her mother came for a visit the first day she was permitted. They popped the door, and Falicia stuck her head out.

"You got visitation," the correctional officer (CO) said into the intercom. Falicia closed her door and exited the pod. There were a series of steps that led to this area with several booths side by side. She walked up the stairs and spotted her mother and son on the opposite side of the glass window. Man stood in the window playing with the glass. The sight of him made her smile. Joy leaped in her heart. Falicia sat down and grabbed the phone.

"Hey, Boo-Boo."

"Hey, Momma." She waited for her to ask what happened, to fuss at her for messing up, to judge her.

"I love you," Letty said. Falicia looked into her eyes; she meant it. "I love you, no matter what!" Falicia broke down. Right when she was at her lowest place, when she had done the God-forbidden acts and was still trying to protect this man, this amazing woman only wanted her to know that she loved her. Letty hadn't so much as asked if Falicia had done the things she was accused of doing. It didn't matter to her. Falicia was her baby and nothing could have come between that.

CHAPTER 35

On September 4, 2002, Falicia spent her nineteenth birthday in a cold cell all by herself. It wasn't the ideal birthday, but she was grateful to have seen it, and so was her mother.

"Mama, how did you know I was here?" Falicia asked, surprised once she gathered her composure.

"I saw you on the news." Falicia knew they had put a gag over their faces and withheld their names, saying it was for their own protection when they went to their preliminary hearing. "I saw your eyes. And I said to myself, 'That's my baby!'" her mother said.

Falicia's mother was there every weekend. She didn't miss a beat. Nothing was too important that she couldn't go see her only child. Not only did Falicia's mother come to visit, but Falicia also put one of Ike's baby mothers on her visitation list. She came to visit, and she dropped a hundred bucks on the account for commissary. Also, she was the connection to Ike. Falicia would call home a few times and get her to call Ike on three-way, despite how she felt about him.

"So Sunshine, I can't wait to see you. I'll be waiting on you," he said one day when Falicia called. He was talking in code. They had already planned an escape, and he was ready to execute it. Falicia would go to Grady hospital, and he would handle things from there. It was a certain location where inmates entered and exited the hospital, and he was going to break her out of there by any means necessary. He'd be waiting with a change of clothes for her.

On September 16, around ten that night, Falicia sat on the edge of her bed in only her panties, bra, and T-shirt. Contemplating if she really wanted to carry out their plans. She thought about her son and her mother and the fact that she might never get to see them again. It was a fucked-up situation. However, on the other hand, Ike needed her. He was having a hard time coping with life without her. Falicia started plucking at this cavity in her mouth trying to make it bleed as it often did. She needed to spit some blood out, giving off the impression that her mouth was bleeding. She spat on the toilet, thinking it might look like she had been hovering over the toilet bleeding. She lay on the floor and closed her eyes. *Just keep your eyes closed! Whatever you do don't open them, so that they'll think something is wrong.* She replayed what Ike had instructed her to do in her head.

Falicia could hear the officer panicking, yelling for the other officer in the booth to pop open her cell door as she did rounds and discovered Falicia passed out on the floor.

"Oh, baby. Are you okay?" she said, rushing into the cell.

Playing possum, Falicia neither moved nor opened her eyes. She was immediately taken downstairs to the infirmary. They took her vitals, and Falicia heard them report her numbers as healthy, but she still refused to open her eyes. She couldn't give up now; she had to get out of there. Ike was waiting on the other side. Falicia lay on the stretcher naked as the cold temperature filled the room. Reality had set in once again. She wasn't going anywhere. Defeated, Falicia opened her eyes; she felt like a fool. She thought she and Ike had it all figured out, but they neglected to think about the vitals, the one thing that played a major factor in being ill. The doctor's nurses and guards knew now that she was full of shit and trying to pull a fast one.

"I'll do it tomorrow," she told herself, knowing deep down inside she didn't want to, but Ike . . .

The next day Falicia was lying in bed and her door opened. A thick, black sister in a CO uniform, and with plenty of attitude entered.

"You think you slick!" She stood next to the stainless steel sink and toilet.

"I think I'm slick about what?" Falicia sat upright on her bunk, pretending to have abdominal pain.

"I know all about your plans . . . you think you gon' get away?"

"What? Ma'am, what the heck are you talking about? I'm thinking you coming in here to see if I need some help, and you in here on the bullshit."

"So you're not trying to get to Grady hospital where a family member will be meeting you there with a change of clothes?"

"What's your name?" Falicia asked the officer as if she had some authority. "I respect that you got a job to tend to, but I don't appreciate you coming in here accusing me of some shit. Now, unless you're willing to get me some medical attention, I would like you to leave please," she stated in a matter of fact tone. Falicia's mouth and body were having two different sets of feeling. She was talking big shit, but she was scared as hell.

"Just mark my words . . . it ain't gone be pretty! They might get you out, but it's going to be a blood bath." She removed her hand off her hip, rolled her eyes, strutted out and slammed the door.

Falicia wore a serious look, but she was wigging out! *How in the hell did she know my plans, when Ike and I hadn't even discussed details on the phone?* Falicia was tripping and now needed somebody to talk to. As soon as it was time for her to come out and her door opened, she headed to the phone, and the old lady that stayed next door called out to her.

"Baby girl, why was that CO in your room?" the elder woman asked, sitting on something so she could have a straight view out of her flap.

"It's crazy . . ." Falicia wasn't sure she wanted to share her business. She hadn't said anything other than hello since she'd been there. *Shit, what is it going to hurt?* At this point it didn't matter, because she damn sure wasn't about to follow through. She squatted down so nobody could hear her and explained how her man had this grand scheme, and she got caught.

"We really hadn't said much of it over the phone. Then, early the next morning this woman comes in and tells me the details of

Sereniti Hall

my plan. Like who the fuck she been talking to?" Falicia took a deep breath. "This may sound crazy, but I feel like . . ." She struggled to say it. "Like a prophet or some divine being told her, or somebody. *Nobody* should have known those details like that." Falicia was freaking out.

"Chile, let me tell you something." She scooted closer to the door. "God is real. He does exist, and He has the power to do such a thang!" She reminded Falicia of her grandmother Lula, her paternal grandmother. "My advice to you is that you stay off that phone and get yourself together."

"What do you mean?" Falicia was confused.

"Look at you."

"I don't think I understand."

"Shh . . . Stop talking and listen." Falicia gave the older woman that she felt was wise, her undivided attention. "You done tried it your way and look where it got you." She let her remark linger for a second. "Why don't you give God a try and see where He'll take you?" She didn't say another word. Falicia sat there considering what she meant. She had tried this thing called life, and it only brought her heartache and confusion.

"Don't disturb her . . . just leave it on her flap," the CO instructed the inmate who was assisting her with passing out everyone's trays. Today made the third day Falicia had been on her knees crying, asking God for the faith to believe she was forgiven. As if someone had flipped on the light bulb in her head, her eyes were opened now, and finally she saw all the evil she had done, the lives that she took, the pain that she caused. She believed that God had forgiven her, but forgiving herself was the real challenge. Her neighbor gave her a Bible and told her to start reading it, beginning with the Gospels, and at first it didn't make sense to her. Why were they telling the same story over and over? But as she kept reading, even though she didn't get it—it finally started making sense. There were men who had walked with Jesus, giving us the recollection of their encounter with the Messiah. She also learned that God is the Creator, Maker, Heavenly Father, and Jesus is His Son that He sent into the world to redeem everyone from their sins. He is the Messiah also known as the Christ, the Savior of the world. Falicia thought they were one and the same.

That same night, Falicia received a letter from her grandmother telling her that God had already forgiven her, therefore, she needed to forgive herself. *To not forgive yourself is like telling God: I know the agony Christ endured on the cross, the bloodshed, the beatings, and the separation from your presence to reconcile me back to you, but none of that was good enough for me. It just wasn't enough.* Falicia cried because she hadn't spoken to her grandmother in a while. She hadn't spoken to anyone about her struggle to forgive herself. God loved Falicia enough to impress it upon her grandmother's heart to encourage her. It was comforting. Falicia learned that was called confirmation.

Falicia had been having a few attorney visits with Mrs. Claudia, but she didn't trust her. She always made her feel as if she was working for the state, and though Falicia was lying about why she committed the crime, she wasn't about to confess anything to her. Finally, she was beginning to see Ike for who he really was, or at least she was now allowing herself to see who he really was. They made arrangements for him to meet up with her mother and give her a lump sum of money, but he never showed up.

Thanks to Peaches, her codefendant, detectives from all over the United States were coming to see Falicia about any unsolved crimes that were related to hers. One of the last interrogations she had was with some detectives from Florida. She was a little disturbed by the allegations they were making, and requested for her attorney to be present. They couldn't get Mrs. Claudia to come, so they sent Ken Driggs, someone who had worked Death Penalty cases for years. He would have come into the picture earlier, but he was out in the field. But this time he showed up on her behalf. After he introduced himself, the moment he opened his mouth she knew he was God sent.

"Here's the deal. You don't say anything! You are already in a lot of trouble. You don't need anymore. No confessions, statements, remarks, fingerprints . . . nothing! Just listen." They were a little pissed that she had nothing to say, and despite her attorney telling them they couldn't have her fingerprints, they took them anyway and had her taken to medical, put on the table as if she was receiving an exam, and took pictures of her vagina, looking for piercings.

Ken began visiting her weekly, and one day he just flat out told her, "Listen, I know you aren't telling me the truth. You're hiding something. You got a son who needs you. I think it's time you start telling the truth."

Getting to the place where she needed to be honest wasn't easy. She eventually got moved into pod 200, into Peaches' cell. Shortly after, Peaches got moved into her cell, because she and the company she was keeping were being labeled as a disturbance. God positioned Falicia to see with her own eyes. Peaches had written all over the walls: *Peaches and Ike. I'll be home soon. I love Ike.*

People didn't have to tell Falicia what Peaches was saying. She recognized what she was dealing with, but she still loved her, just as she did Ike. Understanding had finally entered her mind—just because you love someone doesn't mean you must be in their lives or tolerate them. Just love them from a distance, pray for them, and leave them to God!

God had blessed Falicia with some good bunkmates. She felt they brought on a lot of her healing through countless hours of talking to them about what she had endured as she reformed her mind and sought God for her purpose. One day she was served with some papers telling her that they were seeking the Death Penalty for the murders. She signed for the document, and then openly declared, "I'm not worrying about this, God. You know why I did what I did. I trust you with my life." And that was the mindset she had from that day forward. She spent her days seeking out who she could encourage and helped them see their need to change their lives before returning to the streets and doing the same things that led them to the county jail in the first place.

Her next challenge was a result of a discovery of a knot that had popped up above her navel. She had been going back and forth to Fulton County to court for the Mrs. Winner's robberies and threw herself into exercising when she felt a lot of stress. She went to the doctor, but the knot couldn't be diagnosed. So there was nothing the doctor could do.

"Oh well, do you need to test my blood or something? I already signed for that co-pay. You need to do something for my five dollars."

About two weeks later, a male officer came and escorted Falicia to the medical floor. He was flirting, trying to get her to talk about her life as a stripper. She had been down almost a year, and the room she was being seen in looked unfamiliar. As she looked around the room, she began to feel indifferent. The picture of various infections covered the wall. The officer stood outside the door, giving her the slick eye.

A pretty, bright-skinned, African American nurse with a short cut sat down next to her.

"Ms. Blakely, how are you doing?" She was polite.

"I'm fine, and you, ma'am?" Falicia replied.

"Great, thanks for asking."

"Of course."

"So . . . I called you because you had some blood work done a few weeks ago."

"Yeah, I remember," Falicia said, but she had forgotten.

"Well, I'm sorry to inform you that you are HIV positive."

Sereniti Hall

Did I hear this broad right? Is she talking to me? Falicia looked up at the officer. The look on his face told her that she had heard her correctly.

"Excuse me?" The words managed to form and emit from Falicia's lips. "I don't understand how . . ." She blinked her eyes as if she was thrown off. "Do you know who I am?" Falicia interrupted.

"I don't think I understand the question."

"I wear shoes that cost more than everything you got on, including your hair and nails," Falicia retorted. *There is no way I can be infected.*

"That may be true, but you are still infected."

Falicia couldn't believe it. She didn't understand why God saw fit for her to have yet something else to endure, but she was going to trust Him.

"Do you know where you could have contracted this from?" she asked as they were wrapping the visit up.

"Yes, I know exactly where I could have gotten it from." She thought about the arguments she and Ike had gotten into when she tried to go to the clinic. Falicia remembered the time this dancer named Jodie that she sold powder to, told her the health department had come to the club looking for her.

"Fantasia, when I met you, you were so innocent, staying to yourself and getting your money. Now you leaving the club with strange men. Do you realize how serious it is when them folks come looking for you?" she asked Falicia as they stood in the bathroom exchanging drugs for money. "Baby girl, you better slow down and get away from that nigga you with." Falicia was so disturbed she couldn't even work anymore that night.

She thought about the times they were having sex and Ike was about to climax, but then it would just go away. Or when he woke up from a deep sleep in a cold sweat, or when his appetite was fluctuating, and all the times she nursed him back to health because he had the flu.

"Would you like me to call him and inform him?"

"No, I will, but I do have a co-defendant who has possibly been exposed to it. You should check on her."

"Give me her name."

The next month or two was the hardest time in the county for Falicia. She was too ashamed for anyone to know. She would walk around all day smiling and be genuinely concerned for others, but when the lights were out and her roommate Lira fell asleep, she'd lay there weeping from the depths of her own soul. Ken was the first person she told, and he bought her some material so she could read up on it. She educated herself, and then she felt the need to tell her mother during a visit.

"Momma, I got to tell you something. Ike done left me with something else to deal with." She looked dead in her mother's eyes through the glass that separated them. Her mother shook her head as if she already knew.

"What, Boo-Boo? You not pregnant?"

"No, I'm not. I would have had the baby by now if I was."

"What is it? You got AIDS?"

"No, I don't have AIDS, but I am HIV positive." She covered her mouth, and elephant tears fell from her eyes.

"Oh my God! My baby! My baby!" She wept. "God, she's just a baby," Letty kept saying. Her son turned to look at her as he sat in her lap. He attempted to make her stop crying.

"Okay, okay, Mama . . ." He patted her cheeks. Falicia cried also.

"Momma, it's gon' be all right. The way we have advanced in medicine these days, I still can live a long, healthy life. I been taking my medicine, and the doctors have already seen improvement."

Letty cried a river. After she gained her composure, she looked at her only child. "I love you," she confessed. "We'll get through this together. I love you."

"I love you too!" Falicia responded, knowing she needed to speak to Ike ASAP.

Sereniti Hall

Ike had finally done it. Falicia was over his mind games. She had her home girl call him on three-way.

"Ike." It had been months since she reached out to him, and she had taken his baby's mother off her visitation list.

"What's up, baby?" He always answered his phone in a way that gave women the impression that they were the only female calling him.

"You know who you talking to?" she asked, knowing he didn't.

"Wait a minute, say something again."

"Do you know whom you're talking to?" There was a quick silence.

"Sunshine!" he yelled. "Oh my God, baby! It feels so motherfucking good to hear from you! Like . . . Damn, this shit just made my day!" he continued. "What's up? How you doing?"

"I called you because I had some tests done and found out some things. I'm calling because you need to go to the doctor."

"Oh no! I'm out here at this gay pride thing, and they got booths set up everywhere. I just got tested. I'm good." She knew he was lying.

"What the hell are you talking about? You can't get the results in a few minutes!" She flipped and asked God to forgive her for cursing. Her friend hung up the phone in his face.

"Oooh, I can't stand him!" Shanie said.

Falicia kept silent, trying to put her feelings in their proper perspective. Why had she expected him to man up? He never had manned up before, and she wouldn't find out until four years later that he had known all along. Just like it took fourteen years for her to learn that Letty never spoke to Ike on the phone that one day when Falicia was ready to leave him and go back home. Falicia had asked Letty about the phone call because she had been holding a grudge against her mother for the longest over that. Letty plainly told her, "It never happened." Straight faced. Another ploy used by Ike to further separate mother and daughter. Falicia truly thought her mother had told Ike that she couldn't come back home because she already seemed happy enough with Ike. Letty also hadn't hung up in Ike's face as he reported. *Fourteen years later!*

"Falicia, is there something you want to talk to me about?" Shanie asked, pulling her from her thoughts.

"Naw, Shanie. I love you though. I gotta go." Falicia ended their call. It wasn't that she didn't want to tell her, she just feared how she—well—how *people* would treat her as a result of being infected. But shortly after, she got to a point where she felt it didn't matter what people thought; it wasn't the end of the world. It was too damn hard living day in and day out worrying if someone had found out her secret. She was done being in bondage mentally. If people wanted her to be their whispering subject, then so be it. If someone treated her different because she was HIV positive, then so be it. It just meant that she didn't need that person in her life. She built up the courage to talk about it instead of keeping it hidden. Lira, her bunkmate was the first to find out among inmates. The women in the pod would crowd the TV on days she went to court, thirsty to know what the latest updates were. Falicia would go sit in the center of them, just to take the power away from them for constantly making her feel horrible about something God had forgiven her for. People couldn't say anything. She had already been open to the people that mattered. No secrets. Now she believed in living transparent from day to day, no matter how ugly her truth was. As a result, God began to deliver her from the opinion of others. She felt as if she was getting a fresh start, the new Falicia Blakely. Without Ike.

CHAPTER 36

Going to court served as the hardest obstacle she had faced yet. She was no longer Falicia, she was a teenaged triple murderer. She was everything anybody put in black and white. She was the youngest female in the State of Georgia to possibly face the Death Penalty. Falicia asked to apologize to the families when her court hearings began, but was told to wait until the day of sentencing.

Quietly, she sat as she listened to the District Attorney, Tom Clegg, prove his case against her. She listened as some of the family members poured their hearts out about the loss of their loved ones. She respected every single word they said. They felt they were justified. She had taken something that she didn't give, and that was life, all for the wrong reasons. Falicia wished she had made better decisions, better choices. She wished she were back running track and going to high school, preparing a proper future for herself and Man.

"And she didn't even have the decency to apologize. Clearly showing she isn't remorseful, but a cold-blooded killer!" Meech's mother said to the court. She teared up, looking to the attorneys.

"You know that's not true," Falicia murmured to her attorney.

"It's okay, as long as you know," he replied.

The judge asked Falicia to approach the bench. She complied.

"Judge Seegler, Your Honor, I have been wanting to address everyone, but I was told I had to wait until my sentencing day," she began. "I wanted to give God the glory and the thanks for . . ." Tears ran down her cheeks. "I want to give God the glory and thank Him that you all are giving me this opportunity to personally apologize to you all. I'm so sorry that my poor judgment and lack of wisdom are the reasons your loved ones are deceased.

"To the family of Mr. Twitty and Mr. Christmas, I can only pray that—" Ms. Twitty sobbed. "At some point in this life you will forgive me and heal from this awful misfortune that I have caused your whole family.

"To the family of Mr. Goodwin, I don't even know where to begin. I can't take back what I have done, and this will be something . . ." She tried to choke back her sobs. "That we will both have to live with for the rest of our lives. I'm sorry I allowed a mere man to put the type of sin in my heart that resulted in me taking the life of an individual. Honestly, Mr. Goodwin was more than just a man to me. We had grown to be friends, and God only knows that I miss him, and I am overwhelmed with sorrow because of my stupidity. Even though I have spoken these words, the fact still remains that they're gone, and the words 'I apologize' doesn't change a thing. But I do want you to know that I mean it from the bottom of my heart."

For Falicia, it felt as if the presence of God had just swept through the room. There wasn't a dry eye present. Judge Seegler took a second to gather his composure.

"It's an unfortunate situation . . ." he said. "First of all, Ms. Blakely, what has been described to me—what your life has been—is almost incomprehensible . . ." He cried a little. "I also believe it's true. It's a terrible existence, and you've . . . you've lived a horrible life, with all kinds of circumstances." Judge Seegler paused briefly before speaking again.

"But I also know that you've taken from three men . . . something—the most valuable thing they could possibly have—their lives. If you don't have your life, you have nothing. And I cannot forget that." He gathered himself. "Do, therefore know, that I am going to go . . . I am going to go along with the State's recommendations on their request for sentencing.

"And I therefore do sentence you, on each of the malice murder counts, to life imprisonment, without parole. On Counts 1, 2, and 3. They are to run consecutive with each other. On the armed robbery, each one of the armed robbery cases, I sentence you to twenty years to serve. But they will run concurrent. With the theft by taking, I do sentence you to ten years to serve. They will also run concurrent. After all that's been said today, I believe nothing more can be said. You may have a seat, ma'am."

As Falicia returned to her seat, she looked to her mother. Letty was crying, but was she was holding up for Falicia, her one and only child. "I love you," her mother told her. She made it back to her seat and turned around and closed her eyes.

Three consecutive life sentences, she rehearsed Judge Seegler's words in her head. *Well, Lord, maybe now they'll all have some peace,* she prayed. *Thank you for giving me the chance to apologize. Strengthen my mother.* Her attorneys arranged for her to have a few minutes with her family. Her uncle Tracy cried the hardest. As she sat and looked at her grandmother, mother, and uncle covered with a face full of tears, she couldn't think about her own pain. All she could think to do was encourage them.

"Listen, dry your tears. This is not the end of the world. God got me. He's been watching over me this long. He's not going to come up short now. At least I still got a life to live." She bowed her head and prayed for them. *Lord, please don't see fit for me to die under these circumstances.* She blew her family a kiss as they stood to leave. She thought about the pain she had caused the victims' mothers. As much as she wished she had the possibility of parole, she respected the decision that was made concerning her freedom, and she prayed that Ike wasn't doing to another young girl as he had done to her.

Once everyone was out of sight, Falicia's knees buckled and she dropped to the floor. *Lord, please give me and my mother the strength to endure the path that I have set for us to walk.* She felt that they would make it, they would get through, but only by the grace of God.

An open letter . . .

To the families and friends of Mr. Goodwin, Mr. Christmas, and Mr. Twitty,

First and foremost, I want to apologize again from the depths of my being for the life of unending pain, heartache, despair, loneliness, confusion, turmoil, hate, and God alone knows what else I am causing you. I am so sorry for the times you've wanted to merely pick up the phone and call your loved one but couldn't. For the times you wished your father could hold you and tell you it was going to be all right but couldn't. I'm so sorry that the mere mention of my name has the ability to ruin your entire day. There is not a day that goes by that I don't think about what I've done and how you must be affected. Many nights I've asked God why He didn't just allow my life to be taken, instead of your loved ones. I'm sorry that I didn't make wiser decisions that may have positioned me to have a better outcome, other than the one that I had.

Please know that by all means, I am not trying to point the finger or cast blame on anyone else for what I subjected you to. As a woman, I take full responsibility for my actions, despite the circumstances I endured that led up to the day I caused your lives to be altered forever. You may never truly understand the power of fear and what state your mind can be in when you're subjected to certain things day in and day out. And I respect that! I just hope that you can find the courage to go forward and make the most of the rest of your life, even in the face of what I'm forcing you to live through.

I am so sorry that I took something I didn't give . . . Life. Your fathers, brothers, sons, uncles, husbands, boyfriends and friends' lives. I am deeply sorry for all the pain and turmoil you must be feeling as a result of this movie and book that is coming out. I am sorry for all the feelings that this is forcing you to live through all over again. I am sorry that you may not ever forgive me, but I don't blame you, because my apologies won't bring them back.

In closing, I apologize if you feel that my addressing you is inappropriate. I have no ill intention. I just wanted you to hear from me that I recognize what I've done, and I'm sorry.

Wholeheartedly,
Falicia B.

Author's Bio

Sereniti Hall wears many hats, author, publisher, wife, mother, and friend. Named to the Library Journal's top ten list for Street Literature for her first novel *Feenin'* (published by Wahida Clark Publishing), Sereniti continues to flourish. Since then she has released three more titles, *Still Feenin'*, *Endless Tears* (nonfiction), and *Traces of My Blood*.

Today, Sereniti serves as president of 7 Figure Publications. Her mission is to create a trusted brand and deliver great content.

Currently, she is working on her next project and resides with her husband and three daughters in Augusta, Georgia.

E-mail: serenitihall@yahoo.com
Facebook: Sereniti Hall
Twitter: @Serenitihall
Instagram @serenitihall
Website: www.serenitihall.com

www.ingramcontent.com/pod-product-compliance
Lightning Source LLC
Chambersburg PA
CBHW032038090426
42744CB00004B/56